GLOBAL OUTLAWS

CALIFORNIA SERIES IN PUBLIC ANTHROPOLOGY

The California Series in Public Anthropology emphasizes the anthropologist's role as an engaged intellectual. It continues anthropology's commitment to being an ethnographic witness, to describing, in human terms, how life is lived beyond the borders of many readers' experiences. But it also adds a commitment, through ethnography, to reframing the terms of public debate — transforming received, accepted understandings of social issues with new insights, new framings.

Series Editor: Robert Borofsky (Hawaii Pacific University)

Contributing Editors: Philippe Bourgois (UC San Francisco), Paul Farmer (Partners in Health), Rayna Rapp (New York University), and Nancy Scheper-Hughes (UC Berkeley)

University of California Press Editor: Naomi Schneider

GLOBAL OUTLAWS

CRIME, MONEY, AND POWER IN THE CONTEMPORARY WORLD

CAROLYN NORDSTROM

UNIVERSITY OF CALIFORNIA PRESS
BERKELEY LOS ANGELES LONDON

University of California Press, one of the most distinguished university presses in the United States, enriches lives around the world by advancing scholarship in the humanities, social sciences, and natural sciences. Its activities are supported by the UC Press Foundation and by philanthropic contributions from individuals and institutions. For more information, visit www.ucpress.edu.

University of California Press
Berkeley and Los Angeles, California

University of California Press, Ltd.
London, England

Library of Congress Cataloging-in-Publication Data
Nordstrom, Carolyn, 1953–.
    Global outlaws : crime, money, and power in the contemporary world / Carolyn Nordstrom.
        p.   cm. — (California series in public anthropology ; 16)
    Includes bibliographical references and index.
    ISBN-13: 978–0-520–25095–6 (cloth : alk. paper)
    ISBN-10: 0–520–25095–8 (cloth : alk. paper)
    ISBN-13: 978–0-520–25096–3 (pbk. : alk. paper)
    ISBN-10: 0–520–25096–6 (pbk. : alk. paper)
        1. Transnational crime.   2. Organized crime.   3. Smuggling.
4. International economic relations.   I. Title.
HV6252.N67   2007
364.1'35 — dc22   2006017929

Manufactured in the United States of America

15   14   13   12   11   10   09
10   9   8   7   6   5   4   3

This book is printed on Natures Book, which contains 50% post-consumer waste and meets the minimum requirements of ANSI/NISO Z39.48–1992 (R 1997) (*Permanence of Paper*).

To the War Orphan

"Some definitions"? which Chapter?

CONTENTS

Jay →

GLOBAL OUTLAWS

HIGH-STAKES GAMES. TRUCK STOP, AFRICA.

ACKNOWLEDGMENTS

Acknowledgments in a book about outlaws are not easy. The more someone has helped, the greater the likelihood they would prefer their name not appear in print. Yet my debt of gratitude to such people is large: researchers know how much it means when someone takes time out of their busy day to talk to us — how much more is the gift when they do so knowing what they say could put them in jail, or worse? Perhaps I should thank my field — anthropology — as well, for being sufficiently ethical and insufficiently powerful to put people at their ease.

There are people and organizations I can name — and I do so with a true depth of gratitude. The John Simon Guggenheim Memorial Foundation provided the fellowship for this book — both to conduct the global research and to write a new kind of ethnography that can convey the roiling complex global realities of the twenty-first century. The John D. and Catherine T. MacArthur Foundation provided the fellowship for the research conducted in warzones for this study. My debt to these two institutions is considerable: they took the chance on a lone anthropologist promising to do ethnography on invisible (illegal) realities and placeless hyper-placed global flows.

The University of Notre Dame provided me with generous leave time and valuable support. My department, especially, kept the home fires burning, and I doubt I would have survived without the administrative support of Diane Pribbernow and Suzette Vandewalle. My students are always ready to extend a helping hand: discussing ideas, offering research support, bringing chocolate and a story. The University of Notre Dame campus in London was a home away from home as I traveled between continents. The University of Witwatersrand, South Africa, and the Uppsala Program for Holocaust and Genocide Studies at Uppsala University, Sweden — made possible by Dr. Ivana Maček — hosted me during this research.

Research and writing, it is often said, is a lonely business. I have found remarkable systems of camaraderie providing both community and knowledge. My most sincere thanks go to Debra Lebeau for her invaluable research help and road trips in Africa; Vanja Padelin for teaching me about the world of shipping; Marissa Moorman and Leandro Lopez for adopting me in Angola, and the McKennas' Cottages for the same in South Africa; Monique Skidmore for sharing research adventures on the Burma/China border, and Dinah Shelton for those in the South Pacific; Jeff Sluka for his great feedback on my writing; and Carole Swayne and Stephanie Lawson in England and Tony Robben in the Netherlands for (continually) taking in a road-weary anthropologist. I am beholden to a number of organizations, primarily in Angola and Southern Africa, whose kindness allowed me to travel to remote and frontline locales: in Africa I flew with the World Food Programme; shared food, information, and much needed companionship with people working with the United Nations, Concern, Médicins Sans Frontières, Christian Children's Fund, Development Workshop, Save the Children, and Care. In Angola, the United States Embassy, the Bureau of Public Information, the Universidade Agustinho Neto and the Universidade Católica de Angola, and the Methodist Guest House were most welcoming. Many people and organizations spoke off the record in Angola: I trust they will read their anonymous words in this book and recognize my deep appreciation.

This warm gratitude extends globally: I was surprised at the graciousness of the port and harbor officials worldwide. Perhaps this is part of the mystique and graciousness of the sea. Equally, security organizations offered untold hours of affable conversations, coffee, and tours — I am indebted to the United Kingdom Custom and Excise, Scotland Yard, the Scorpions (South Africa), United States Customs and Border Protection, the U.S. Coast Guard, and the Netherlands police. Some I was able to name in the book's quotes; others asked to remain unknown. Those I can thank by name, and who generously gave of their time, include Augusto Alfredo, Professor Justiño Pinto de Andrade, Professor Vicente Pinto de Andrade, Bill Anthony, David Arian, Manny Aschemeyer, Captain Bremner, David Carapiet, Eric Caris, George Cummings, Filip de Boeck, Christian Dietrich, Richard Flynn, Peter Gastrow, Sheila Gonzales, Charmian Gooch, Charles Goredema, Lisa Grande,

Alan Hall, David Hesketh, Tony Hodges, Tom Hougee, Dr. Richard Jaehnke, Howard Marks, Colin McClelland, Eunice Nacio, Godfrey Needham, Peter Neffenger, Karl Otto, Justin Pearce, Johan Peleman, Greg Rawlings, Mario Adauta de Sousa, Robert Thornton, Marcel van Dijk, Willem Viljoen, Eshetu Wondemagegnehu, Art Wong, Alex Yearsly. This book would not have been possible without their help.

My hometown of Burlington, Iowa, proved most supportive. Amid the hard traveling for this research, my mother's home on the banks of the Mississippi River is a peaceful oasis. Many pages were written in the appropriately named Digger's Rest and Mister Moto's coffee houses; and my thanks to Bob Saar for his writing advice. The cover photo was made possible, in the middle of the Mississippi River, by photographer Ken Moehn, the Hazell family, and Phill Manke (and Sheriff Wheeler's rifle).

And, as always, this book would not exist were it not for my editors, Naomi Schneider and Rob Borofsky, William Rodarmor, Marilyn Schwartz, and Sue Carter — they have unfailingly supported my belief that a book is not a product, but an experience.

WAR-DISPLACED CHILDREN FIND THE WORLD. ANGOLA.

PREFACE

> The Roque [a vast unregulated international market in Angola] was
> born in a conversation between two businesspeople expelled from the
> city. Two miserable marginalized people who after many setbacks, met
> one another outside the city, not far from the ocean, at a clandestine
> locale to sell and earn what they could so that they could help maintain
> their families. So began everything . . .[1]

HENDRIK NETO (2001)

Who are the criminals of the twenty-first century? The businesspeople
who lie on a customs form to reduce their taxes so they can send pharmaceuticals more cheaply to the needy? The customs agents who let these
shipments through because "everyone benefits"? The people who understand how this system works and slip explosives into the pharmaceuticals
speeding unchecked across borders? The robber barons who make a profit
on all this regardless of who lives or dies? In order to answer this question, I spent three of the first five years of this fledgling century exploring on foot the pathways of global crime. It is an anthropological journey that began with survival and profiteering in the center of Angola
when that country was still suffering a severe war; it then wound across
the smuggling routes of several continents to the wharfs of Rotterdam
and the Port of Los Angeles. In the flux that defines the world of the illegal, beginnings are often endings and vice versa — vice being the opera-
tive word here — so I begin this book with one of the later entries in my
fieldnotes:

As I sit watching the 446 cargo ships enter and leave the mega-port of Rotterdam a day, I know I am watching somewhere between 200 and 446 ships breaking the law in some way. By most estimates I have received in these five years, it is more along the lines of 446. In the world today, this is called crime. Most of these ships are well respected, most carry commodities from well-respected corporations. Some are world leaders. While this is formally called crime, it usually is not called anything at all. Or perhaps it is just called business. Something far different is generally singled out as crime. As I sit watching the ships, I open newspapers and magazines. Young men holding automatic weapons, holding up civilians, holding society hostage, carry the label Crime. The men pictured are marginals: they are the proverbial rabid dogs biting at the heels of civil society. Their bite is dangerous, they can infect a society when they sink their teeth into it. There is a cure, but it is a painful one.

For every hundred stories on illegal narcotics, I may find one on illegal pharmaceuticals. Maybe. This despite the fact that the World Health Organization estimates that fake drugs make up at least 10 percent of global pharmaceutical commerce. While anyone with access to media has seen pictures of illegal narcotic overdoses, few, if any, have seen pictures of deaths from counterfeit pharmaceuticals. Yet, as the [Capetown] *Weekend Argus* writes: "From bogus anti-malarial therapies to useless oral contraceptives, vaccines made of tap water or snake anti-venom containing no active ingredients, the world is awash with fake treatments. . . . The accumulated evidence suggests that mortality and morbidity arising from this murderous trade are considerable, especially in developing countries."[2] Drug dealers are unshaved men in jeans selling crack, not corporate businesspeople in pressed suits selling substandard cancer medications.

When government leaders, "upstanding citizens," and business moguls are indicted for criminal activities, the stories almost always carry the impression that this criminality is the exception to the rule of orderly societies. That one bad apple can exist in a barrel of good apples—but when that bad apple is removed, the rest are untainted. Reporting seldom explores the question of whether the barrel is in part defined by the intersections of bad and good apples, and that indeed, all apples play the game of crossing lines of legality in some way or another at some point or another in their lives. The question cannot be asked: for crime is by definition marginal. Its mere existence places it outside regular society. Or so we are led to believe. But why?

Trillions of dollars move around the world outside of legal channels. These dollars flow through millions of hands, thousands of institutions, and hundreds of borders. They ruin the lives of some and create vast empires of profit for others.

The sum total of all extra-legal activities represents a significant part of the world's economy and politics. The power that leaders in extra-state empires wield can rival that of state leaders, and the revenues generated can far surpass the gross domestic product of smaller nations.[3]

Yet we don't know how these vast sums affect global markets, economic health, and political power. No statistical formula exists to assess the impact of laundered monies on a nation's financial stability; of nonstate power regimes on state authority; of globalizing smuggling and criminal systems on security. In truth, we know little about the actual life of the extra-legal: who is doing what, how, and why?

This lack of knowledge can prove dangerous; the research in this book suggests that extra-legal networks constitute a series of power grids that shape the fundamental econo-political dynamics of the world today.

In the midst of these vast global flows, a young war orphan street child in a remote area of Africa sells smuggled Marlboro cigarettes, one by one from a rumpled packet, on the dusty bomb-cratered streets he calls home. His story is as central to these multi-trillion-dollar transactions as are drug and arms cartels and international money-laundering enterprises. This book delves into these uncharted fortunes and introduces the people who are made and broken by these invisible confederations.

I am interested in the intersections of crime, finance, and power in activities that produce something of value: monetary, social, and cultural capital, power, patronage, survival. The unbalanced individual who kills a spouse in rage does not figure in this accounting. I deal very little with the isolated street robbers who kill their victims. Public media focus on such aggressive individuals under the sensational banner of "crime," yet this interpersonal violence constitutes a small percentage of the universe of criminal actions. Smuggling cigarettes brings in far greater profits and economic repercussions. Robbing an entire country or controlling a transnational profiteering empire is the gold standard of crime.

While this book explores the major commodities that shape the illegal and the informal, from blood diamonds and arms through drugs and exotica to staples of life such as food and oil, it begins with the homeless boy selling a single tattered cigarette for a very specific reason. And while it is common to focus on high-profile and "sexy" illegalities like arms and narcotics, illicit fortunes as large, and often larger, are quietly reaped from common commodities. Worldwide dynamics ultimately rest on a compendium of individual exchanges: a single cigarette sold from a bedraggled pack, a multi-billion-dollar deal in cyberspace. The war orphan and his cigarettes, multiplied across all the millions like him throughout the globe, are not merely linked to global flows of unregulated goods; they are essential.

This kind of research is easier said than done: how do we research the illegal? Or perhaps more accurately, the "il/legal": a term I employ to designate the intersections of legality and illegality.[4] Answers aren't easy to find. They are obscured in the shadows; hidden by the power of profit, blurred by shifting borders of il/legality. But they are not impossible. Ethnographic fieldwork offers a powerful approach: every action across the spectrums of il/legality is enacted by a person, a person who moves according to a complex set of values and worldviews.

The trick is how to get the stories, and how to report them responsibly.

Writing about the extra-legal isn't necessarily any easier than researching it. It might seem that returning home after several years of traveling the haunts of those who work outside the law would signal the end of the most demanding work. But in truth, writing about these studies is equally fraught with risks: this is an ethnography that takes the reader into the thick of the illegal to meet the smugglers, victims, power elites, and profiteers who populate the economic "warzones." Juggling my responsibilities to those among whom I have worked, to my own morals, to the larger ethical universe that sweeps across the world in which we live our lives, and to my academic discipline is not a simple process. No text, no academic guide, provides straightforward maps for navigating these whirlpools and eddies of professionalism. Ultimately, I must author my texts with a moral as well as an intellectual compass: the safety of those among whom I work, my own safety, and responsibility to my discipline as a whole depend on this. New scholars will follow me to the field, and their access and safety will in part be shaped by the actions of those of us who have gone before. As with my previous books, I have carefully thought through what names and places — what identifying features — I should give for each example and quotation presented here. This book seeks to develop the means to convey firsthand ethnographic data, the methodologies by which it is gathered, and the larger theoretical issues these link to, while at times remaining sufficiently decontextualized to protect the integrity of the research and those with whom I worked.[5] The reputation of the discipline of anthropology rests on crafting scholarship in such a way that our students, and their students to come, will be welcomed to the field by people who have not been hurt by academics and story seekers who, however well intentioned, are determined to illuminate whatever comes across their gaze, with no heed for the consequences.

This book is meant to be experiential as well as academic, to take people to the frontlines of the il/legal.[6] Hopefully readers will find, for a moment, that they have left their comfortable chair and reading envi-

ronment to stand on the dusty African savannah and squint into the
bright sun next to the trucker, dying of AIDS, who is trading diamonds
and a handshake for a Mercedes truck and the cargo to fill it for an "unregistered" run in the next country; to stand on the dusty plains of moral
imbroglios and deep ethical dilemmas and squint into the bright light of
parched theory to make sense of the world; to feel the impossible contradictions the Coast Guard captain at the Port of Los Angeles feels trying to protect one of the world's largest ports and his country with a couple hundred personnel and a limited budget; and to see, as both the
trucker and the captain do, in a global moment, the connections between
all these realities.

. . .

The chapters are set up to catch the powerful confluence of the extra-legal
and twenty-first-century globalization and advanced technology and to
show how the tendrils of the uncharted reach across multinational
empires and into everyday lives. The book unfolds in an expanding funnel model: each chapter is devoted to a site along a continuum from the
decidedly local to the vast transnational interrelationships defining the
global market.

The first chapter opens with the young Angolan boy I call Okidi, who
is situated simultaneously at the center and the end point of a massive,
global set of extra-legal empires. This logic startles twentieth-century
habits of thinking based on linear relationships of space and time. But as
the hyper-contemporary relationships depicted in this book show, dis-
tances of time and space and simple linear exchanges have become illusions. Today, distance is a red herring: it is as easy to ship commodities
between continents as between towns. Markets are everywhere concur-
rently center and periphery. And the relevance of the moral state is being
redefined: the cigarettes the boy holds in his hand have traversed many
industrial, national, continental, legal, and ethical borders. A very human
and very transnational drama is enacted as he sells a single smoke for
enough pennies to keep body and soul together.

The chapters then progress as follows.

Locally, in Angola:

– the shop owner who fronts the cigarettes to Okidi, and the ways
   he buys mundane goods for his community (food, cigarettes, electronics) with illicit resources (diamonds, weapons)

- the Gov'nor and the military, who can come to "own" a country, and how these fit into transglobal ideals of "robber barons" exploiting the intersections of the extra/legal to create empires
- average people, even the most marginalized, who can set up powerful informal economies that, while illegal, sustain development for entire countries — such as the enterprising women land-mine victims who survive starvation by constructing informal international markets

Moving internationally:

- the border posts, where truckers and global supermarkets meet; and a glimpse of the ins and outs of money laundering
- the African ports, where economics become intercontinental and the illegal becomes globalized

Out to intercontinental trade and the impossibility of security:

- one of the world's largest ports, Rotterdam: what is smuggled, how this is done, by whom, and why
- the ironies of "illegal drugs": narcotics and smuggled pharmaceuticals, with perspectives ranging from street-level markets to the World Health Organization

To the larger ethical and cultural universe of criminals and law enforcement:

- the cultures of criminals, explored in interviews with a former drug smuggler, and the cultures of the law enforcement officials who try to stop them, such as the detectives at Scotland Yard

Bringing this "home":

- a voyage on a transatlantic freighter as "human cargo"; and a trip through the Ports of Los Angeles and Long Beach (meeting the major players, from port officials and the Coast Guard, through longshoremen, to shipping agents engaged in illicit practices) to show the myths, the illusions, and the realities of security and the illegal in all arenas of transport and trade

The ultimate goal of this journey is to craft an understanding of the world of the extra-legal in total — not just the arms and drugs, not just the trafficking and criminal organizations — but the universe of thought and action that falls beyond the scope of the legal. To illuminate the dragons, so to speak. Old maps used dragons to depict the unknown parts of the world. At least they knew where the dragons were. As Art Wong of the Los Angeles Port Authority said to me:

> No one knows the world of smuggling and the illegal: there are dragons here, like in the sailing days of the middle ages, and no one comes to look over the edge of the world, to understand what is really going on.

The chapters are organized to delve into the values, ethics, and morals surrounding the il/legal and to illuminate the contradictions, paradoxes, and competing complexities surrounding them. These intersections capture the heartbeat of humanity — the place where we truly live our lives. Not according to neat linear theories, but as roiling, multifaceted, ontological compositions. The foundations of societies — those that produce not only the laws of a nation but also the worldviews that underlie them — are forged in these debates.

Does she explain anything, or simply describe?

NATIONAL

CHOOSE LIFE—HOMELESS BOY SELLING CIGARETTES. AFRICA.

CHAPTER 1

THE WAR ORPHAN

I remember him well.

He was a quiet child, with the impish charm of a boy not yet nine. The fine layer of street dust that covered his body couldn't disguise his good looks or the bright intelligence in his eyes. He moved through the shell-cratered streets, along bombed-out buildings and around United Nations peacekeeping trucks like he owned them, in some small way. This was, after all, his home — a small Angolan town I am calling "Muleque." Like anyone living in a dangerous place, one filled with predators and unseen pitfalls, he maintained a ceaseless vigilance, even in play. Somehow, he radiated a charisma that made him seem fashionable in a tattered pair of shorts with more holes than material, and a ragged T-shirt that might once have said "Coca-Cola," a hand-me-down from humanitarian aid workers. I remember thinking, in that curious juxtaposition of remote warzone and twenty-first-century techno-culture, that he looked like he could have graced an MTV music video. On a deeper level, the boy had a gentleness about him. But he was a street fighter too. He had to be a fighter, gentle or otherwise, he explained, to survive. I call him "Okidi" here, a name that means "truth" in a local language.

It was the dawn of the twenty-first century, and, though no one knew it at the time, the final years of the war in Angola. Okidi had lost everything several years back in a blinding moment during a long offensive that tore his town and his family apart. His parents had been killed, his home destroyed, and his life irrevocably changed by the fighting in which he and his loved ones had no stake beyond survival.

He was four years old then.

Okidi had created a new family, a group of war orphans like himself.

Families of this kind are never in short supply. War, starvation and deprivation, illnesses and lack of health care, coupled with the vagaries of violence, produce a steady stream of homeless children. He and his group lived by their wits, and they were all brilliant children.

The others just didn't make it.

The day I met Okidi, I was sitting on a wall in his hometown, watching him and his friends trying to sell old coins to a band of UN· "Blue Helmets," the common name for the UN peacekeepers. Their interactions were intricate. The children knew they had to negotiate the fine line between hungry child and trustworthy vendor. The Blue Helmets struggled with their attraction to the unusual coins and their fear — so common to adults — of "feral children" and what they mistrust as the scam of innocence. I began to appreciate the children's sophistication in trying to understand human nature and the nature of business in a world where these are cast as adult pursuits. In trying to understand war and the will to survive, it was the children, not the peacekeepers, who caught my eye.

The children were playing "grown-up work," as children do all over the world. The peacekeepers were well kept by the UN. Beer and food delicacies were flown in from their home country to keep them happy; they had access to good pharmaceuticals, which are worth their weight in gold in these war-torn places; they had gasoline, arms, clothing, and foreign currency. To Okidi, these Blue Helmets were diamond mines on the hoof. The children knew that handouts didn't come easily from grown-ups. Food, medicine, currency, freedom from hunger and fear were bought or bribed or traded or bartered. They were uncertain whether their unusual coins would make them rich, but they knew that if these coins brought in even a tiny fraction of what was available to the Blue Helmets, they would serve the children well. At their age, "rich" meant a full stomach and a safe place to sleep.

As adults, these orphans would learn how to play the game fully. Instead of trading old coins for food, in the years to come they might negotiate international currencies for arms deals, bumper crops for medicines and industrial equipment, diamonds for power. They had already learned a key point: wealth springs from sources you least expect.

They had learned what journalist Maggie O'Kane witnessed in Sarajevo in the early 1990s: peace is a contentious reality. The peacekeepers who risk their lives for others, who leave home and hearth to stand in the middle of a firefight they have no mandate to control, who represent some of the best values in the world's collective community — these peacekeepers also run "hot" markets at times. The international composition of the UN provides for a truly international marketplace in the most remote of locales.

The UN soldiers are making themselves and the Sarajevo mafia rich. The locals are the middlemen for a trade in cigarettes, alcohol, food, prostitution and heroin, worth millions of pounds. (O'Kane 1993: 1)

Having concluded their business with the Blue Helmets, Okidi and the other children came over to me, and the boy simply held out his hand to show me his treasure: old coins of the fallen colonial regime. He wasn't trying to sell me the coins. He had noticed my interest in his dealings with the soldiers and was now sharing his story. He had a look only children can fully achieve: deadly serious and yet delighted. His was a hungry band, but they had discovered valuable assets by which they could better survive.

> "Beautiful," I said to the boy.
> *He nodded seriously in agreement.*
> *The children all gathered around me, talking all at once:* Yes, they are beautiful; look how they shine in the sun. These are very valuable, you know. And they are ours, *they were clear to point out—they had not stolen them from anyone.*
> "Where do they come from?" I asked.
> Come, we'll show you.

The boy took my hand and led me through town. In his world, discoveries and treasures are shared in camaraderie and not spoken of in abstract words.

We walked to the center of Muleque, an eerie place that was at once a ghost town and a provincial hub of commerce and politics. The battles that took Okidi's family had bombed every building in the downtown into ruins. Shell and mortar blasts and countless bullets left gaping holes in whatever walls were remaining. Roofs had been blown off, and upper floors collapsed onto lower ones. Everything of value had long since been looted, and the rain dripping through open ceilings watered weeds growing on rubble-strewn floors.

A handful of enterprising government officials had found a few habitable rooms in the less-destroyed buildings and had set up rickety wooden desks from which to attempt to work in a town whose entire infrastructure had been destroyed and land-mined. Their job was daunting: energy and water systems, roadways and communication lines, agricultural and resource sites all lay in ruins. With trade severely compromised by war, many didn't even have pencils and paper. The men and women didn't look up as the children walked over to the demolished Central Bank and pulled me through a mortar hole in the wall and into the building.

Once inside, the children wound a complicated path around craters and mountains of debris. I belatedly hoped that they were winding around unexploded ordnance and land mines. Well-trodden paths smoothed by months and perhaps years of little feet seemed to indicate that the children knew what they were doing.

Suddenly they stopped in a back room and dropped to their haunches to dig in the dirt. About a foot down, they grasped a handful of coins. I had never seen coins like these: they must have been colonial currency discontinued at the national independence over twenty-five years before. I couldn't estimate their value, but those coins were indeed buried treasure. During the bombing raids, bags of money — either forgotten in the dusty vaults and the mists of political change or hoarded with an eye to a profitable future — had probably been hit by shells, which then broke through the floor and carried the coins into the earth below.

The children pulled me down and taught me how to dig for the coins. I marveled at the difference between childhood and the onset of "maturity": few adults would invite a virtual stranger to share their only source of wealth. The children pressed handfuls of their valuable currency onto me. I returned the coins, saying that they were the fruits of *their* labor and their chance to eat the next day. But I kept one, a tangible reminder of a day that digs deep into the utility of humanity.

Then a change came over the group. They sat back and grew serious. The animated talk and laughter gave way to a more considered silence. One of the girls went to the corner and picked up a bucket filled with grain and set it on her head. She returned to take my hand and say goodbye. The boy withdrew a packet of Marlboros three-quarters full, as if he were taking something important but somewhat dangerous from a safe.

> "What is it?" I asked.
> We have to go to work now.
> "What do you do?"
> The girl is hauling grain to sell; I sell these cigarettes in the market areas. Some, they look for work helping in the fields, carrying things in the markets, helping people however they can. Others look for "opportunities" — you know, grabbing a handful of rice from a bag that falls and breaks open, finding something left and forgotten, a good merchant who hands them something at the end of the day.

The boy and I began walking down the road toward the marketplace. The playfulness he had exhibited while digging for coins was replaced with wariness as he watched the movements of the people about him. One teenage male, with all the hallmarks of a bully, shouted aggressively at him as he passed by. The boy mumbled to me, in a tone both fearful and defiant:

> He's somebody else who works the streets.
> "Are you scared of this man? What does he do?"

Scared? We have to be. He's bigger. He can beat me up, take whatever
I have, what money I've made, my cigarettes.
"How do you make it?"
We little ones have to be smart. Smarter. We are careful. We help each
other.
"Are all the older ones like this?"
No. Just the worst. This is what war has brought us.

We both pondered his statement in silence, walking easily beside each
other now. I asked him where he got his cigarettes. He made a gesture:
Wait, you'll see. A little farther down the road, he pointed out a store:

This is where I get my cigarettes.
"Do you have to buy them?"
He shook his head no:
The man gives me a packet, and when I have sold all the cigarettes, I
return to give him his share of the money, and get more.

The ethics of economics; the morals of survival. It seemed a harsh clash
of realities. On the one hand a businessperson makes money from a desperate orphan living on the streets. On the other, the boy was able to survive; without this man and his "investment," the child might not make it
at all.

And in all this, a child selling foreign cigarettes on bomb-cratered roads
far from the world's economic centers links into global extra-legal
economies that reap trillions of dollars annually.

We paused to look at the shop before parting ways. It belonged to a businessman I'll call "Kadonga" — a word in Portuguese-speaking Africa
meaning goods that move outside the law. In a town largely bereft of
energy sources, communication and trade systems, or vehicles and industry — a town where the minister of health admitted that more than 60 percent of the population lived on the brink of starvation — Kadonga's shop
offered gleaming new television sets, VCRs, and other luxury items that
peeked out from darkened back rooms in a building as bomb ravaged and
bullet pocked as the rest. An expensive Mercedes truck was parked out
front. In a remote location ravaged by war and bereft of basic survival
goods, cosmopolitan dreams from the world's urban centers called out to
shoeless, shirtless passersby.
But some people had the means to buy these luxury items. These people didn't deal in kwanza, the local currency (which isn't traded on the
international market). They had access to

- the country's valuable resources that converted to hard currency;
- the international markets with glittering cosmopolitan dreams;
- the trade routes that would bring these goods across war-troubled lands; and
- the means to ensure that officials worldwide would turn a blind eye to less-than-legal transfers.

A vast network stretched from this town out through the country's gem and mineral mines and along its precious timber and valuable agricultural resources, through troops and civilians, profiteers and thieves, and then across international borders to link into large exchange systems that operate both legally and illegally, running all the way to far-flung criminal organizations, multinational corporations, and superpower urban commodity centers.

A good part of this complex global network becomes visible in the journey of a pack of cigarettes from their source, through an intricate set of international exchanges and negotiations, and into the hands of a poor war orphan on the frontlines of a conflict from which he will see little profit. Some 50 percent of all cigarettes in the world are smuggled. Whether these travel legally or illicitly, they do not travel alone.

The cigarettes may make the journey alongside dangerously illegal products, unregistered arms, and illegal drugs, or they may travel with the merely illicit — pirated technology, for example. Popular media would have it that drugs travel a "drug route," arms an "arms route," and computers a more cosmopolitan "high-tech corridor." In fact, shipping routes are markets, and thus they are matters of opportunity. The number of markets and routes to these marketplaces is not unlimited. Once routes are operating with confidence, all manner of goods can pass along them. A shipping container can "contain" arms, cigarettes, and the latest pirated DVDs, along with a host of other commodities ranging from the seriously illegal to the merely mundane. In fact, such transits work more smoothly than they would if all routes were separate: arms buyers find an easy market for cigarettes, videos, and information technology (or Mach 3 razors, 4 × 4 all-terrain vehicles, or pornography).

But most likely, the cigarettes will travel at least part of their journey with unregistered (and therefore illegal) commodities that are overlooked because of their very normality: food, clothing, books, industrial parts, software, toiletries, car parts, electronics. They might cross a border in the shirt pocket of a person who walks this route daily to find minimum-wage labor in more promising markets, or perhaps tucked in to the luggage of a person flying between continents to seal a multi-billion-dollar deal.

The tendrils of cigarette smoke enter the most basic aspects of our daily lives, making cigarettes profitable and inescapable across all borders of legality. They can find their way to a bombed-out shop on the frontlines of a devastating war, and into the hands of a hungry street child seeking enough money to buy a piece of bread at the end of the day.

. . .

My interest in the powerful expanses of global il/legal economies — the intersections of the legal and the illegal — didn't begin with cigarettes. I met Okidi, the young war orphan, when I was charting "robber barons": those who trade for immense profits, most visible in international exchanges of resources (gold, diamonds, timber, humans, etc.) for arms. Military supplies are so expensive that few countries' tax bases can provide sufficient funds to purchase them. National currencies in warzones are generally shunned by financial markets: they tend to be weak and unpredictable monies that few urban industrial centers accept. Natural resources become the "hard currencies" of choice to raise the capital to run wars and countries. Given the pressures of international laws, sanctions, and national industry regulations, much of this commerce crosses the line of the law in the journey from source to profit.

In charting this trade, I realized that a veritable smorgasbord of goods travels these circuits: people have to eat, set up industries, and obtain computers, energy, entertainment systems, and life-saving pharmaceuticals. Immense profiteering exists in this trade, as well as that surrounding war supplies. The illegal is also sustained by a human desire for beauty. One can see this in bombed-out frontline markets. In these places, desperate people congregate to seek or sell pitifully small amounts of food or a handful of smuggled life-saving medicines, often carried over land-mined fields and under gunfire. Amidst these critical necessities, there is often something of beauty for sale: a delicate piece of cloth smuggled in from a neighboring country, an incongruous piece of art, or maybe a pair of counterfeit Nike shoes or the recording of a beloved musician, carried across the trenches of hell and outside the law, only, it would seem, to remind us of our spark of humanity.

And cigarettes. The fire that flares from the match lighting a smuggled Marlboro clearly illuminates the entire global flow of il/legal commodities and the power regimes behind them.

STREET MARKET. MULEQUE, ANGOLA.

CHAPTER 2

THE BOMBED-OUT SHOP

The boy went off to peddle his cigarettes. The shopkeeper, that prover-bial "uncle" of the abandoned and the orphaned, was nowhere to be seen, but his wares were. Sonys from Japan glittered seductively from dusty wooden shelves, generators from China hulked on mud-splattered floors to power them. A DVD of an American blockbuster just released in exclu-sive urban cinemas was tossed casually on the counter. Bottles of Scotch whisky stood clustered on a shelf, supposedly imported from Scotland, but more likely counterfeit in a factory in Southern Africa. You could buy the Mercedes parked out front, though how you could drive it on the land-mined roads under the predatory eyes of soldiers, rebels, and ban-dits wasn't clear. In point of fact, driving isn't the key consideration. A vehicle like a Mercedes is money in the bank, capable of being sold, bartered, or exchanged for profit and patronage. "Special" wares sat unseen underneath the counters and in the back room. Wares that guar-anteed hard currency, international access, and financial survival amid competing militaries and collapsed economies. Computers, communica-tions systems, diamonds, arms, dollars.

As a shop owner, Kadonga stood at a crossroads of power and profit, though this wasn't immediately obvious. His store looked more demol-ished than functional, yet in one of the profound ironies of market glob-alization, Sonys might be easier to get there than construction materials. Wood was far too valuable to use for covering windows that had lost their glass to bombs or looting troops. In a place where all travel was curtailed by land mines, rogue bandits, soldiers, government controls, or lack of vehicles and gasoline, thieves would be more likely to steal the wood than to steal the Sonys inside. Besides, how would someone pass off a hot Sony unnoticed? Kadonga's store was dark and dusty; a pile of money from small purchases sat in an open bucket beside the simple wooden counter. A tattered red plastic flower that looked as much a war casualty as the town's occupants graced the front shelf.

How did this entrepreneurial irony come to inhabit the frontlines?

The world's core resources tend to lie well beyond urban cityscapes and industrial sprawl. Minerals and agricultural goods, people exploited for undocumented labor, flora and fauna from poppies to ivory, energy sources, and raw industrial products generally reside in the frontiers.

A frontier combines (often immense) freedom, danger, and profit. This explains why resource-rich countries are four times more likely to be engaged in political conflict than more normally endowed states. The political instability of war is a boon to "commerce lords," legitimate and otherwise. As these resources move to industrial centers to fuel enterprise, the products they produce move back to the frontiers — Kadonga's "Sonys" — all the scintillating treasures of twenty-first century urbanism — for sale at exorbitant prices. It's a flow of tremendous, and largely unregulated, proportions.

A man whose shop draws everyone from the child cigarette vendor to the business and military elite capable of buying his Sonys has his fingers on the pulse of such profits.

Kadonga and shops like his sit on the frontlines of a war that left Angola's infrastructure in ruins: virtually all industry had collapsed; the kwanza was worthless outside the country; banks were but empty depositories. Trade routes had been ground away under the heel of violence and deprivation: rail lines were defunct, roads the haunt of human predators, vehicles and the gasoline to fuel them a luxury available to the exclusive few. Communications systems had collapsed, energy sources dried up, and corruption had become endemic. Whether a pauper or a billionaire, you can't buy a Sony using kwanza. You need dollars, pounds, marks, yen, or the resources that fuel the world's industrial centers.

"Scotch from Scotland—that's a luxury," I said to the shopkeeper.

Yeah, fine stuff it is, *said Kadonga.*

"Come from Scotland?"

Sure, *he says with a wink.*

"Label looks a wee bit blurred to me," I suggest.

Well, perhaps it comes from a good little factory I know of that makes its own labels.

"In Africa?"

He smiles.

"The Sonys?"

Real. The real thing. Or so I assume; I don't check every internal part to see if anything's counterfeit. I have a friend who tells me there are more counterfeited parts in the electronics in UK than here.

"I won't even ask about the Mercedes."

I was referring to the common knowledge that carjacking and cross-border smuggling are major industries in Southern Africa. Even if a car isn't stolen, the customs tariffs and government taxes are so high that only the most foolish bring in their cars entirely legally.

No need to.

"Many diamonds passing this way these days?"

Enough. Lots of people grab the lightest things of value they can carry as they flee attacks. They arrive here in the city with nothing but some stones, looking for food and necessities. Arrive by the thousands. Poor miners wander out of the bush looking for cash and a meal. Traders pass through carrying them as barter chips. Troops at the gem sites come to town and secretly trade for the stones they have pocketed. Business is done. Big business, small business.

Here, the word *business* refers to the core of an economy, often crossing lines of legality. It is how things are done. It can entail a handful of clothing or pharmaceuticals — or millions in gems. "Business" is economic life at its fullest.

For an outsider unschooled in the intricacies and mysteries of local commerce, it's hard to know how extensive Kadonga's holdings are. To the locals, it's easy. For them, all possibility flows from the people who have resources. The businesspeople represent bosses, bankers, grocers, police, and potential warlords. They are, so to speak, the transport systems, the entryway to resources, the font of communications, the ticket to a brighter future. This "uncle" to the street children may also own the local bar, have access to gem-mining areas, control truck routes to neighboring countries to move goods and people, and enjoy military backing ensuring that his trucks make it to their destination. He may be quietly amassing land in the area, holding it for a better day when war gives way to a stable economy. The more fortunate — giving resonance to the root *fortune* — have large and far-flung families and fictive kin, which can translate into large and far-flung holdings, as another, equally successful, shopkeeper in town explained to me:

The most successful of us have a cousin—and, mind you, here "cousin" is used loosely—up in, say, the north of the country. We are talking with them all the time: What goods do you have up there? Gold, arms, Nikes, people flowing? How's the exchange rate up there this morning, got currency? Is there a flight heading this way? I'll send up some X if you load up some Y and send it down here.

And another cousin, or brother, or niece, or distant relative on your mother's side down in the south, and so it goes. Each of these places from north to south has connections with other borders, other goods. And each "cousin" has a whole network of cousins of their own, which are now yours too. The best off have a sibling in the capital city, in government, in business, in the military. With connections. With information. With access.

Then there's the wife's sister's husband's cousin in the neighboring country, and then one in London, or Bucharest, or Bombay. International access. Guaranteed.

Teoría

There is a popular notion that cosmopolitan centers have cosmopolitan goods, and the farther you get from these centers, the farther you get from these goods. Like black holes, industrial centers are seen as nodal points of gravity, pulling in people, commodities, and the promise of advancement without ever releasing them. These ideas have been developed by people who have never visited war-weary towns like Muleque, walked with its street children, or talked with its businesspeople.

Just off the main street, with its bombed-out banks and government buildings, was Muleque's central market. Most of the buyers and sellers abandoned the town's battered buildings to set up in an open space, overtaking roadways, decimated building sites, and what might once have been front yards. Here, you could find tins of margarine from India, batteries from China, and vacuum-sealed packets of sausage from someplace in Eastern Europe or the Philippines. Alcohol from all over the world flowed in abundance. Among the largest selections were pharmaceuticals. Hawked from wooden tables half the size of a door, these elixirs promised to treat anything from gunshot wounds to tuberculosis; from a bacteriological infection to malaria. Scores of these tables graced the markets. The local hospital operated largely without medicines: a cash-strapped government, corruption, and a debilitated national infrastructure made even the most basic resources a luxury. The town boasted one local doctor who was away "indefinitely." No formal pharmacies operated. But life-saving drugs were available informally, at a price.

Food was at a premium, both in price and availability. The scorched-earth policies of the competing militaries had reduced croplands to smoldering ashes ringed with land mines. Hundreds of thousands of homeless people moved from one supposedly safe place to another in search of the simplest of things that would make life possible for another day. Three potatoes cost the equivalent of $3. This represented a substantial portion of a grunt soldier's or hospital nurse's monthly wages, and most had not seen a salary for the better part of a year. The vacuum-packed sausages would cost several months' salary. Dazzling promises, just out of reach. Even if the populace were to unexpectedly come into money, the amount of food was limited. With the croplands barely functioning, basic foods had to be imported from abroad. From the farms and factories of India, Iowa, and Indonesia came food whose price continually escalated to meet the demands of international transport, tariffs and taxes, and a seemingly infinite number of middlemen seeking grease to keep the machine of survival going. Potatoes, grains, and tomatoes sometimes fetch a higher price than arms, drugs, and technology. In the more remote and war-ravaged locales, you could get a Sony and a Mercedes to take it home in, but not life's necessities.

In conditions such as these the concept of "law" takes on new, often creative, and generally extra-legal definitions. Even in countries at peace, as Manuel Castells (1998: 178) notes, there is a "thin line between criminal traffic and government-inspired trade."

To put this in perspective: economists at the UN office in Luanda told me they estimate that over three-quarters of the economy runs outside of formal state and legal channels in Angola.

·   ·   ·

Kadonga leaned against the pockmarked counter of his little shop, lit a cigarette, blew out a ring of smoke thoughtfully, and continued:

> This is my home, and because it is, I can do things here others can't. I know people, I know what works, I know what doesn't. I know who's in charge, and who's not. I know how to get things; I know how to get things done. The easiest "security," for rich and for poor, is gems and gold. You want to start a new industry, a gem can get you started. You work in some god-awful mining area and you want a better future, just one good gem can do it. Thousands of refugees running from the war come through here. And if they are lucky, they have managed a gem, smuggled out of some mining area without being caught and killed. Local boys, running from poverty, may carry a gem, a piece of hope, and come through town. These people don't know who or how to sell these stones. The guys in Luanda haven't got a clue how to get these stones out here. Local "business" makes the connections. They [he smiles, meaning "we"] give refugees and locals the means to keep alive. We have contacts that move the gems up the line to Luanda and out to Europe. We get a cut, everybody's taken care of.

It's not just gems and gold. We know the situation. We know what routes are being attacked, what's safe. We know how to "market" a lorry-load of food or clothing. How to move the things that "fall off the military wagon." No commander who finds he has "excess" medicines or beer or whatever is going to move these things to market himself. And of course, none of us do any business at all if we are not connected; you know, the government.

Accounts such as these are social. Each person in a community adds a piece, has an important perspective. Later, another Angolan business-man — recently unemployed — added a piece to the puzzle of how international routes work by sketching out a map as we talked over a cup of coffee. I was familiar with one route he showed me because, thanks to the UN representative in the area and some surprisingly accommodating military officials at the front, I had just taken a trip there a few days before. It was at the extreme perimeter of the security zone; the military perimeter was marked by a river. On one side was a zone where road travel was theoretically possible with military clearance. On the other were the no-go lands where battles raged, communities were razed, and thousands of civilians stumbled out, often too weak and traumatized to tell their stories. The bridge across the river was so war-ravaged that no vehicle could navigate it. Or so I assumed. I walked the bridge and saw why it marked the perimeter: no transit except by foot seemed even remotely possible. I took pictures of dead tanks lying on their sides in the river just off the bridge. "Anything pass this way?" I asked the military commander escorting me. "No way," he said, "how could it?"

Back in Muleque several days later, I asked the unemployed business-man to map critical trade routes for me. I was trying to figure out how people got the medicines, canned meats, and the rest of the flotsam and jetsam of war-torn markets in town. The war had seemingly closed all trade routes. The man took a piece of scratch paper and drew several routes, linking Muleque to the capital city of Luanda, to major cosmo-politan sites in the region, and then one across the perimeter I had visited: across the bridge, through to the next province, and then on to the Democratic Republic of Congo.

"This is a trade route? Now?" I asked in surprise.

Of course, an important one.

"What travels along these lines?"

Anything. Everything. What people need to live. Food, supplies . . . "Business."

"But how? I've been to the river. The bridge is impassable. The war is wip-ing out hundreds of communities on the other side."

He gave me a look: how could I not know? His expression enjoined me to read the implications behind his words: think trade, and then keep thinking, think of local powers, militaries, government officials, warlords, international wildcatters.

> How? It goes. It always goes. It goes by vehicle, and if it can't go like that it goes by air, or by foot, or by however a person can get from here to there. It goes across the bridge, and it goes across the battles and into the next towns and provinces to trade for the different items and necessities there, and it goes into the next countries and so it keeps going. Don't kid yourself, everyone here knows it goes across no-go zones. This is a major trade route.

These stories, and others like them in upcoming chapters, show that here in this remote town, situated amid fragile hope and the desolate landscapes of violence and poverty, stands one of the principal intersections of raw resources and cosmopolitan goods. This reality is all the more powerful given the extremes of wealth and poverty, of extensive resources and demolished infrastructure, that define it. International wildcatters — those who profit on the frontiers of legality, geography, and ethics — amass fortunes here, while local citizens find even the most basic services beyond their grasp. A handful of businesspeople and politicians shape the course of the country, driven either by concern for the people or by deadly greed. Or, in the curious way of politics, both. Their populace survives by non-formal economies in the wake of collapsed formal systems.

But that isn't the whole story.

The man who fronts cigarettes to street children — from Africa through Asia to the Americas — is a lynchpin in the intersections of extra-legal transactions, business development, and political power. In a town like Muleque, Kadonga stands at an interesting nexus of linkages to international networks, informal economies, and formal state systems. With financial and business success, and with all their attendant alliances, this man, and those like him, can enjoy political power. As this book will show, he can back politicians, formulate policy through major state institutions, or stand for office directly. He can also work for international non-governmental organizations (INGOs), become a UN representative, sit on multilateral trade boards, or attend forums on international law. He isn't likely to give up his extra-legal alliances when he enters a formal state role. Why would he want to? As the young street child cigarette vendor reminded me: it's where he acquired money and power in the first place.

~~LOCAL~~ GLOBAL ADVERTISING: HOMELESS BOY. MATA'LO, ANGOLA.

CHAPTER 3

COCONUTS AND CIGARETTES
SOME DEFINITIONS

Perhaps we can't predict economies' trajectories because we don't know what an economy is.

Legal. Regulated. Formal. Legitimate. Recorded.

Illegal. Informal. Illicit. Unregulated. Unrecorded. Extra-state. Extra-legal. Parallel. Second economy. Gray market. Brown market. Illegitimate. Underground. Subterranean. Clandestine. Shadows.

What words apply to the intersections of the il/legal? *Power? State? Chaos? Invisible empires?* Formal published analyses generally fail here. The answer is perhaps most evident in everyday experience — a conversation I had on a cargo plane carrying supplies to the frontlines:

> The pilot handed me an (undeclared/untaxed) Marlboro before takeoff. I had been smoking (informal economy/untaxed) cigarettes with names like "Life" from the local markets, and they were usually moldy and full of bugs. Sitting around with friends, pulling bugs out of my cigarettes, I often felt like a chimpanzee grooming my nicotine habit.
>
> The flight was a humanitarian one: some wild pilot was risking life and limb in questionably airworthy planes to take life's necessities across battle-zones full of armed soldiers who used the planes for target practice (variously using legal, proscribed, sanctioned, and smuggled arms) to land on (sanctions-violating) land-mined runways, sometimes to be attacked not by soldiers, but by desperate civilians trying to get a ride on the plane out to anywhere that wasn't under attack.
>
> The plane had been bought in a deal that avoided industry taxation

because of humanitarian status, registered in a country known for selling registrations, and based in yet another country supporting the rebels who were fighting the government the plane was flying for—by a man who was known, by insiders, to run "unregistered" commodities along with his humanitarian aid.

A man I didn't know joined me on the runway, carrying a bag of coconuts. The two of us (unregistered passengers, proscribed by law) climbed into the plane and settled on bags of flour destined for starving civilians at frontline villages. We moved aside as several generators (value underdeclared at customs) and drums of fuel ("lifted" without payment from industrial reserves) were moved onto the plane. A person from an INGO put on a box of critical pharmaceuticals "donated" (not legally authorized) for the clinic in the village they heard had been out of all medicines for weeks now. Someone slung on a bag of weapons (a second economy commodity that variously served as currency, power, barter product, and status symbol as well as weapon). Planes such as these were one of the only ways, and surely the safest one, to move people and goods from cosmopolitan centers out through the provinces and into the more remote (yet resource-rich) areas and back.

No one that I could see checked what was actually in all the tons of "flour" and aid going out.

"Coconuts?" I asked the man traveling with me.

"Of course," he responded, "There's no food out there; those with means will pay a fortune for a coconut."

"A fortune?"

"Yes," he smiled, "You know, a fortune, a small, bright, shining fortune."

Ah, I thought silently, gems for coconuts on a scoundrel owner's humanitarian flight carrying all manner of legal and illegal goods along with the aid that actually does save lives of people who desperately need the help.

Where was all this in my economic texts?

Many, probably most, research projects are born in the quiet, tweed-and-blue-jeans bustle of the urban academy, along hallowed halls splattered with cheap coffee, in vast libraries of revered tomes. Like all human communities, the university has its distinct cultures. Cultures are multifaceted, but one defining characteristic of the academy is categorization. We study disciplines by category: physics, economics, anthropology, theater. We find books in libraries by categorical reference: science, politics, literature, business. We publish in journals and books identified by topic, and go to conferences with those of our ilk.

Our theories are constructed to fit the narrow confines of our discipline. We may even begin to think in neat units of analysis. These categories make perfect sense unless we try to apply them to the way people actually live their lives.

Had I begun this research into il/licit economies in the neutral grounds of the university, I would have been prompted to see this world in discrete phyla: there is the legal world, and the illegal one. In the illegal world, there are distinct sub-universes:

Dangerous illegalities: narcotics, illegal weapons

Immoral illegalities: child prostitution and enslaved labor

Threatening illegalities: violent criminal actions

Intrusive illegalities: property crimes, theft

Quietly corrupt illegalities: corporate crime

Expected but seemingly victimless illegalities: tax evasion

Unreasonable illegalities: trade in body parts, unrecorded child adoption

Nonviolent cosmopolitan "reasonable" illegalities: pirated software, films, information technology

Purely economic illegalities: smuggled cigarettes, food, gas, alcohol

Aristocratic profiteering illegalities: smuggled artworks, antiquities, jewelry

Grudgingly respected industry illegalities: gems, gold, securities, currency speculation

Informal but not true illegalities: barter, subsistence market goods, survival technologies;

and so on . . .

Each category becomes a distinct research domain, its own empire. Each is its own field of study, like the disciplines of the academy, published according to topic, shelved in libraries by subject matter.

Many of these studies are excellent, yet taken as a whole, they give three misleading impressions:

– The world acts according to these categories and divisions.

– The sum total of these discrete analyses adds up to an encompassing reality.

– There is a discernible line between legal and illegal, between acceptable and illicit, between legal development and criminal intent.

Return, by way of example, to Okidi, the war-orphan Marlboro vendor, and his "uncle" Kadonga, the shop owner. On one level, the lives of the poor child and the shop owner unfold as parables of the tragedies of war, the poverty of development, and the riddles of morality. Is the shop owner exploiting the child? Or providing a little dignity to one of thousands of homeless children by giving him the means to make some money honestly and control his destiny? Let's say the shop owner obtains the hard currency to buy these cigarettes through the unregistered trade in diamonds. Is he a criminal or a man seeking to develop his community without taking his profits offshore, like his more powerful compatriots? These questions have no easy answers, but following the global life of these cigarettes and diamonds provides clues.

At this larger, macro level, the same riddles of development and morality persist. Perhaps these are etched into the fabric of the very state and the economic foundations upon which it rests.

The "travels" a cigarette might enjoy on its way from production to consumption, and its ordinariness, its very centrality in everyday life, is a window on this. As I noted earlier, 50 percent of all cigarettes are smuggled. It is a quiet flow, unlikely to ever stir the public censure that smuggled narcotics and human trafficking do. It is a flow that gains support from corporate centers, as much as they would prefer this story to remain unspoken. As Rich Cookson (2001: 5) writes in an article entitled "Tobacco Firm: We Want Smugglers to Buy Our Fags,"

A UK tobacco manufacturer has for the first time admitted that it wants smugglers to buy its brands.

"We don't want smuggling to happen at all," Imperial Tobacco spokesman Paul Sadler said last week. "But if brands are being smuggled in we see no advantage to anybody if they are just foreign brands. If it is going on, we don't want our brands to be excluded."

UK tobacco companies are facilitating smuggling by exporting billions of cigarettes to countries where almost no one smokes them. The cigarettes then enter the black market and are smuggled back into the UK . . .

[Sadler said] "We don't want any smuggling to be going on. But we have no choice from the point of view of our jobs and our shareholders but to sell our goods to these places."

The smuggling trade costs the taxpayer 2.5 billion UK pounds every year in lost taxes — enough to run more than 60,000 hospital beds . . .

Ten billion Imperial cigarettes may be smuggled into the UK this year — more than half the amount the company exported last year.

Customs officials say large-scale tobacco smuggling is organized by criminal gangs, including the mafia, and profits are used to fund other serious crimes like drug smuggling and gun running.

In the vast schemes of illegal economies — in the hundreds of billions of dollars of drug money that flow from hungry users into the bank accounts of powerful cartels; in the millions of tons of illicit weapons that buy authority and wreak violence; in the massive corruption that props up the governing power of kleptocracies, how serious can cigarette smuggling be? The answer may not be self-evident.

Detective Richard Flynn of Scotland Yard was telling me about the many forms of illicit and informal commerce in the UK, and I asked him, "Of all the non-legal commodities and services found in the UK, which is the most serious, the most dangerous?" Without a pause, he responded:

> Cigarettes.
>
> "Cigarettes?"
>
> Yes, cigarettes. That simple, everyday packet of tobacco that you see in about 40 percent of the population's pockets. Because they flow in from everywhere: on the ferry from France, in the car from Holland, in the container from Bulgaria, on the plane from India or the States. Vendors sell them out of car boots. Take a walk in the local street markets, guys line the streets with cartons of every brand name. They sell them from under the counters of the local corner store. They are absolutely everywhere, in the middle of everything.
>
> Cigarettes show every porous hole in our borders, our customs, our laws, and our ability to enforce the laws. It's not just the cigarettes, it's what they move with: the routes of cigarettes, their flow into just about every conceivable corner of a country—just about every dangerous commodity moves along these same channels, moves with cigarettes. And at the end of the day, millions in taxes are lost yearly to cigarette smuggling.

As cigarettes — a synecdoche here for commodities in general — cross countless legal borders, they intersect with the legal world in myriad places: customs, police, tariffs and taxes, licensing, shipping and inspection, border control, purchase and sales records, audits, government accounting, the courts.[1]

In a world where the legal and illegal are neatly divided into clear categories, attaching values, whether moral or monetary, is relatively easy. Such neat divisions make both research and policy straightforward. Except that such research and policy don't match the realities of the economic world. Illegal narcotics pay off industrial development costs; militaries import contraband; lifesaving medicines are hawked by gold profiteers. Criminal organizations working in hospitals steal pharmaceuticals and sell them on the streets to people who might not otherwise be able to gain access to them, while also engaging in protection rackets, credit card fraud, and prostitution. Multinational corporations secure major bids on important oil-producing blocks by providing weapons contracts and hefty monetary "gifts" to governments waging wars with dubious human rights records. Which of the many transactions are illegal? Illicit? Informal? How does each shape economic growth or decay for a country? And at the level of coconut smuggling and a street child's cigarettes, the activities that coalesce around shops like Kadonga's are variously legal and illegal, illicit and allowed, informal and legitimate; and these run the full spectrum of values both moral and monetary.[2]

These examples aren't the exceptions to the rule of economy. They are the economy.

CITYSCAPE. DOWNTOWN MATA'LO, ANGOLA.

CHAPTER 4

THE GOV'NOR'S RED TRACTORS

Let me tell you the story of a small Angolan town I will call "Mata'lo." It is a study in the building of countries and personal empires; an insight into development and deadly profiteering; a postmortem formal economic studies tend to keep silent.

It is also a story of brand-new, bright-red tractors.

FIVE YEARS LATER

Before I get to the Gov'nor's red tractor, let me set the stage.

I returned to Okidi's hometown five years after I first met him. The war continued to take untold numbers of lives, wipe out entire communities, and provide a few with immense fortunes. Every time I walked on the streets, I looked for the boy with his coins and his Marlboros. Okidi would just be entering his teenage years now, if he were still alive. Sadly, I never saw him, but I ran into hundreds following his footsteps.

The military violence was worse than it had been five years before. The rebels had been ousted from their main base and forced into the bush, where they turned increasingly to guerrilla tactics. But this very mobility, combined with a history of severe human rights abuses, led rebel troops — however ill-advised — to rely more on violence than on "winning hearts and minds" in controlling local populations. The government troops matched this reputation for excessive violence. Civilians were caught in the crosshairs. Their villages were attacked, and government forces took them to relocation camps. People's goods were "confiscated," their livestock slaughtered, and their croplands burned to ensure they couldn't return to their homes and thus assist the enemy, even inadvertently. Land mines barred any attempt to return and rebuild.

MATA'LO—OR HOW TO STEAL A TOWN

I was told that I should try to make the trip out to "Mata'lo," which was on the security perimeter of the frontlines. People said it personified the war these days, a war grown ugly.[1]

Towns like these — far removed from the media eye and far too rich in resources — live and die on the frontlines. Not just the populations, but entire towns. Mata'lo had gained notoriety several months before I arrived when fighting in outlying areas beyond the township produced huge IDP (internally displaced people) flows. In response to the rebels' violence, the government engaged in "relocation" for security purposes, a nice word for a harsh reality: people were rounded up and taken to a "secure" area — in this case, the areas around Mata'lo. It was a town full of ghosts and the sharp remnants of terror. Locals accustomed to years of war said it stood out as a time of horror: the starving and the ill would literally fall and die in the streets. Bodies were visible everywhere. There was no food to give the living, no medicines to treat the sick and wounded. People agreed that the helplessness permeating the horror made it doubly traumatic.

The military, and by extension the government, could now put their stamp of ownership on the region. Literally, in some cases, as we will see. The ability to muster international humanitarian aid was a lynchpin in this process. This aid kept people alive (barely), but it also provided a buffer zone. The rebels were unlikely to launch any significant attack on Médecins Sans Frontières, Concern, Care, or the United Nations. Blowing up a humanitarian team known worldwide only hurts a force's international support.

More importantly, humanitarian effort equals infrastructure. To bring in food and medical aid, organizations need roads, vehicles, gasoline, airstrips, planes, communications systems, distribution centers, orderly populations, and a host of bureaucratic measures.[2] And in this way, the government extended its control over Mata'lo as much through the trucks of the humanitarian organizations as through bullets.

All this could be read, if any economic specialists were there to read it, in the incongruities of the local market, sitting at the crossroads of horrific deprivation and need. Enlisting humanitarian aid here was a strategic move in more ways than one. Mata'lo sits on the crossroads of a strong east-west trade route and a major north-south route that links Angola both internally and with neighboring countries, and ultimately with the continent's major ports. War had reduced roads to crumbling skeletons, but it hadn't reduced the flow of people or the need for goods these pathways were first created to carry.

THE GOV'NOR'S RED TRACTOR—OR HOW TO STEAL AN ECONOMY (AND GET A HUMANITARIAN AWARD FOR DOING IT)

As I rode in the local UN jeep toward Mata'lo, bouncing down a line of connected potholes and bomb craters someone jokingly called a road, I looked across the raw and broken countryside, saddened by the escalation of violence. My eye was adjusted to destruction — it was the norm here. Warzones are disordered: No neat rows of houses, streets, or farmlands give meaning to the landscape. We passed by deserted communities, shelled houses, and looted farms. So I was startled when a lush, well-ordered farm came into sight, appearing like a scene out of a Fellini film — a fantasia so incongruous that it was jarring. A gleaming, bright-red tractor was parked by the roadside. How did it get there?

The answer begins with the government settling the IDPs that they had forcibly relocated to the lands around Mata'lo. Officials told the displaced that the lands were theirs to develop. They were encouraged to clear the land, build houses, plant and harvest their crops. This place, "free from war," would be their new, secure home.

A curious dialogue ensued:

When INGO representatives said the lands needed to be de-mined before the people could move there, both military and political officials said this wasn't necessary.

The INGOs, pointing out the massive number of land mines buried in this country, and the especially high percentage in this location, stressed that they had de-mining teams available in the area.

The officials said land mines were no threat.

How so? inquired the INGOs.

We have maps of the land-mined fields, responded the military.

The INGOs noted that these maps had never before been available to de-mining teams in the area, and that even if they were available, they couldn't be completely accurate, as they wouldn't account for rebel-laid mines.

The military ended the dialogue: Case closed. No de-mining would take place.

The relocated people were turned out onto their new lands. After losing their homes and loved ones, they faced the new day with a combination of grief, shock, betrayal, and resignation. Those responsible for displacing them are part of a system so large that revenge is incomprehensible. As the displaced in Mata'lo told me, tomorrow is a distant dream, maybe an illusive one; making it through the day is the only realistic goal to hold on to.

And they hold on to each other. The eyes of the children I met walking through Mata'lo held knowledge and experience too great for their years — and parents, aware of this, held them closely, as if they could ward off further disaster with an arm around their child's shoulder. The promise of new land was a light in the darkness that people could believe in. But they had nothing to start with. When they fled, they left behind their crop seeds, livestock, vehicles, tools, household goods, and valuables. They also were forced to leave behind their claim to these things. Stories of their homes reached the displaced in Mata'lo, if at all, like feathers blowing unpredictably on the winds. Passersby — a new wave of displaced, itinerant traders braving the dangers of these battlezones (someone has to move all the goods looted from these families on the frontlines), a soldier related by family or friendship — carry bits of information, interlaced with tall tales and legends, to the relocated. The news was always the same: their homes were gone. To return home, or to move elsewhere, was to "violate security."

So the displaced venture onto lands that have not been de-mined to clear them, plant crops, and build houses. Humanitarian aid provided the basic means: seeds and simple tools. As the aid agencies opened roads, runways, and other infrastructural support, they also opened up the fundamentals of trade routes and avenues of military control. As we will see, these did not benefit the displaced, whose hopes would be shattered on the waves of global profiteering. Larger plans were in motion.

Just as the lands of the displaced began to bear the fruits of their labor and they completed their houses, one of the leading government officials stepped in to say:

I'm so sorry, a mistake has been made.
These are my lands; someone has located you here in error.
You must move.

So the peasants are once again forcibly relocated from the lands they
de-mined with their footsteps, the farms they cleared and planted by hand
because their equipment was lost to the first relocation, from the homes
they built from scratch.

The officials, and most notoriously, the Gov'nor, "legalize" their new
holdings. They, not the poor displaced peasants, control the courts, the
land registry, and the official channels to property titles and deeds. They
are now the owners of prime, developed real estate ready to bear fruit
(and vegetables) that are readily transportable, sitting, as they happen to
be, on a critical trade route.

But the story doesn't end here.

The now twice-displaced people are moved onto new land that is neither cleared nor planted. They are now again in need of humanitarian aid.
But this time, there is "work" for them: they can work the Gov'nor's
lands. Land that had been theirs. In aid parlance, this is "food for work."
The INGOs fear that aid recipients will prefer to grow fat and lazy on
"handouts" rather than become self-sustaining. I can only assume this idea
has developed among people who have never spent time in IDP or
refugee camps. Few people choose to live at the fringes of survival, on
handouts that are often accompanied by humiliating treatment and a trau-
matizing lack of control over their lives. But the fear remains, and it
shapes policy. There is a reasonable side to the food-for-work programs.
Given the choice between simply providing food aid to people who have
no employment opportunities (money, land, jobs, resources, etc.) and
providing food aid in return for work that will ultimately develop the area
(building of schools, roads, agricultural production, waterways, etc.),
most would choose the latter — under ideal circumstances. But in places
like Mata'lo, the developmental work is all going into the lands (and the
pockets) of private ownership for the elite few. People like the Gov'nor.

From the aid agencies' point of view, it looks as if the displaced are
being given a chance at a new life. To the peasants, they are once again
being forcibly relocated, but onto land that is now generally poor, without the seeds or tools to develop it. In order to achieve even the minimum
of survival, they must now work someone else's land, getting only food
in return. All the profits go to the new owners, the politically connected.

Even if the displaced have the time to work their own land after working on someone else's, they don't have the means — the seeds and tools — to do so. The food-for-work program makes sure of that.

The Gov'nor gets free labor, free resources to develop his land, and the development of infrastructure right to his doorstep. He gains pure profit at no expense.

The ironies of "development" continue. In a country largely dependent on imports to feed its population, and in a country so debilitated by war that any infrastructural development is deemed desirable, the Gov'nor's projects look like a godsend: he is developing agricultural land, providing a home and work for desperate displaced families, and building essential commerce. These projects not only address the needs of the country — they are undertaken at the frontlines, where development can actually stimulate the peace process, and where few are willing to risk such investments.

And now, because he is providing jobs for IDPs, because he is providing critical food and labor to a starving country, and because these provide an oasis of peace and national security in a war-ravaged country, he is eligible to receive aid monies, agricultural supplies, and — my personal favorite — state-of-the-art red tractors, with the gas and parts to run them and support for the technicians who drive them. And technology for irrigation and communication; materials to construct transport systems; and the trucks and planes to navigate them. Pure gold in gold-rich lands.

This is only one acquisition in a string of such successes for the Gov'nor. Industries have come into his hands and those of his compatriots in same way these farmlands have. For most of the people who survived the bloody fighting that took tens of thousands of lives in the region, running their enterprises was little more than a cherished dream. Buildings lay in ruins — bare husks with their internal organs long since ripped out and looted. New equipment, and the money to buy it with, were out of the grasp of all but the most politically connected. Ownership in such times and places is a fluid concept, which can pave the way for creative gain or for autocratic profiteering.

New opportunities emerge out of these conditions, made possible by the complex interconnections between politics (government), security (military), and economics (commerce). For example, at this time a story was circulating that the Gov'nor had connections with people bringing in medicines for the provincial hospital — which everyone knew had no medicines. Because the national hospitals have no medicines and few staff (who were so poorly underpaid they had to work other jobs to survive), private clinics do a booming business. Private clinics in the capital are veritable gold mines — servicing not only the country's elite but also the many ex-patriots, all of whom pay in dollars, not kwanza. The Gov'nor, people explained, "rerouted" the entire stock of government-purchased drugs intended for the provincial hospital to the private clinic he owned in Luanda.

THE GOV'NOR'S GIRLFRIENDS — OR HOW TO OWN YOUR NEW ECONOMY

"But how," I asked, "can the Gov'nor keep acquiring industries and properties, businesses and commerce routes without someone, somewhere with some power saying 'Hey, this guy and his friends are gobbling up a whole country?'"

His girlfriends, *came the answer.*

"His girlfriends?"

Well, life can be incredibly difficult here. But some women have done extremely well for themselves.

"I don't get it."

The Gov'nor's girlfriends. He puts his holdings in their names.

"Outright ownership?" I asked.

He puts business holdings in their names.

"They run these businesses, the girlfriends?"

Yes, and they do a damn good job. They are hardheaded businesswomen.

"What kind of ownership? What if he breaks up with them? What if they want to get married and break up with him? What if they have a fight and the woman wants to strike out on her own? Does she keep the business because it's in her name?"

Carolyn . . . *with a smiling shake of the head, implying: You just don't get it.* Think! It's how it works.

THE GOV'NOR'S TOMATOES — OR HOW TO GO GLOBAL AND ACHIEVE PURE PROFIT

This is a form of capitalism that offers pure profit. No personal investment is made: all investment is public; all profit is personal. Profit, in this way, translates beyond commercial and financial power into dominion, into the ability to control governance.

But the story still doesn't end.

This isn't a simple account of national corruption; it's a story of global profiteering. What happens to the Gov'nor's tomatoes? — and by "tomatoes" I mean all the goods and resources gained in the cycles explained in this chapter. While some of the produce and the resources can be sold in Angola and in Africa, the greatest profits are to be made in Europe.

Follow for a moment a seemingly unrelated set of events. Relatively few people fly in and out of countries at war. At the level of passengers, Angola doesn't seem a prime commercial airline routing site. But the massive amounts of military supplies flown in and the extensive resources flown out make countries like Angola desirable to well-known international airlines. The profit margin on air cargo is a carrot dangling in front of airline executives; and that carrot can illuminate the business ethics of large corporations. A number of airlines were, at this time, bidding for the rights to service the country.

The Gov'nor's tomatoes figure centrally in this set of negotiations. As one of Angola's leading elites, this man and his ilk negotiated deals with airlines to provide certain services in exchange for the rights to routes into Luanda. One such deal was that the airlines fly the Gov'nor's produce and goods to Europe. Timber can travel by ship; it won't rot before it reaches its destination. But food perishes rapidly, and Europeans expect their culinary treats to be fresh. Air shipping is the only reasonable answer, and it is far more expensive than ground freight. A free flight yields a considerable profit margin.

I spoke with several European ambassadors who were involved with these negotiations. Their views coincided: most major airlines agreed to these kinds of deals. The one declining said it smacked of corruption and unfair business practice — not just for the country, but for the airlines. The other airlines saw not only profit, but development: they were assisting a war-torn country to get on its feet economically by providing free services, and they were helping their fellow Europeans by bringing in excellent, low-cost food supplies.

No one talks about the fact that the Europeans sitting down to a nice, reasonably priced salad with tomatoes from Africa were linked by their purchase to military battles and the forced relocation of poor villagers who were then transformed into a desperate, unpaid workforce; to aid and development monies provided free for the governing elite; and to deals with airlines to provide free transportation for the fruits of this labor. The profit on these goods is 100 percent, because land, workforce, supplies, equipment, and transport are all free. No duties, tariffs, or taxes are paid. Because of this, a virtual monopoly is created: those who benefit from these advantages can undercut any competition (who, in normal fashion, must lay out cash to develop their businesses). The very concept of development takes on a whole new meaning.

The information provided in this chapter is not unknown to people working in humanitarian aid, development, and industry at the ground level — on the frontlines, so to speak. I was able to piece together the account presented here through many travels with humanitarian organizations working at the front; from relaxed, late-night conversations with aid and de-mining experts; across numerous business meetings with people in industry; and on long walks or quiet interviews with political officials. Many were surprisingly forthcoming with information and analysis. But few ever discussed these issues professionally or publicly. I would ask these people, especially those working in INGOs and humanitarian organizations, "Who tells these stories?" And they invariably answered, "People like you, I guess; it's not our mandate."

In the final accounting, this entire system *is* the site, the management, and the exploitation of twenty-first-century frontiers. It *is* the rapid creation of powerful empires. These, as we will see, are modern versions of the robber barons of previous centuries — the robber barons whose names now grace the large corporations and leading philanthropic organizations of the world.

GENERAL'S HIGHWAY: MAJOR INTERSTATE TRADE ROUTE. ANGOLA.

CHAPTER 5

MILITARY TAKEOVERS
(OR, HOW TO OWN A COUNTRY)

There are many truths and many fables defining militaries; this is just one of them. As Vietnam veteran Tim O'Brien writes in *The Things They Carried:*

In many cases a true war story cannot be believed. If you believe it, be skeptical. Often the crazy stuff is true and the normal stuff isn't, because the normal stuff is necessary to make you believe the truly incredible craziness. (O'Brien 1990: 70)

This account complements that of the Gov'nor,[1] but it speaks to more than military control and is about more than profit. It's the story of owning a country. There is one thing everyone doing business in Angola knows, from the Marlboro-vending youth to the diamond-rich merchants: if you aren't on the military's good side, you don't do business. The ultimate CEOs of the nation's industries are its commanding officers.

CEO OF RESOURCES

Yet it's in the mines and faraway resource reserves — not in the corridors of urban power — that the story of owning a nation unfolds.[2] In war, and as we will see, in peace as well, diamonds and other resources like oil, minerals, timber, and seafood fuel dreams and guide strategies, some empyrean, some nightmarish. Without resources, soldiers can't be fed and clothed, armed aggressions fought, countries developed, and political systems sustained. While fierce fighting was common in resource-rich areas during Angola's war years, with control passing back and forth to the victor of the moment, many areas established an enduring equilibrium. In diamond areas, for example, the government worked a set of mines on one side of an arbitrary "no-man's-land," and the rebels the other. They may be within shouting distance of each other. A truce of sorts develops, a truce achieved on the ground and far from the offices of diplomats who see only accounts of "the battles" of "opposing forces." Soldiers may call out greetings to one another across mining/political divides, perhaps sharing information or critical supplies. They may use the same brokers for laundering their acquisitions up the ladder to European or Asian markets. And they may pick up weapons against one another when something breaks the fragile truce. As a local NGO worker involved in resource development in these frontline locales explained to me:

> Oh, we all know how the government troops mine on one side of the river, and the rebel forces on the other—each has made a pact with the other about not attacking them, or their transport lines. You do your business, I'll do mine; and the war just goes along this way.
>
> Sure, there are intrigues and blow-ups: one side sees the chance to rout the other and gain a foothold on better mining land; maybe they see a chance to extend their control over the region. But there is always the recognition that if they attack, they'll get attacked back, which will interfere with their ability to "get on with business."

It's here we can most visibly see that while resources matter in war, they aren't the complete explanation. Christian Dietrich commented on this in relation to his research on diamond profiteering: "In a 'resource war,'" he asked, "why aren't they fighting consistently about resources?"[3]

If red tractors are the symbolic entryway into the study of the Gov'nor's power, basic staples of life are the answer to Dietrich's question and the entry into larger systems of military control.

CEO OF EATING

A large set of subsidiary businesses springs up to supply the lucrative industry of resource extraction. Soldiers, miners, middlemen, and concessionaires need mechanics, cooks, technical experts, shopkeepers, repair services, communications specialists, prostitutes. And all of these people need food, cigarettes, alcohol, clothing, medicines, entertainment, tools,

household or camping goods, transportation, and a host of related necessities and pleasures.

The magnitude of extra-state transactions in these mundane areas is
often overlooked. What, for example, does the trade in life's quotidian
necessities add up to in terms of global markets? What does it mean to
control this trade? Who would think that this humble trade is the lynchpin in a financial dominion that equates to a form of national governance?

To explain: businesses that transport people, equipment, and commodities often rely on military-controlled travel. Sometimes these businesses are simply military entities in civilian guise. In fact, the very
notion of a discrete line marking where "the military" begins and ends in
relation to commerce and industry is defied by everyday reality. Airports
and roads are arenas of national security. Airspace and transport are
under military jurisdiction. Those who use them are granted access; they
don't assume it. Flights and convoys — and by extension, airplanes and
vehicles — are always military matters. This is especially true in embattled
resource-rich areas and military-controlled zones.

"TRAVEL AGENCIES"

Those who supply the concessionaires — the "travel agencies," as they are
fancifully called in Angola — may work out of small, unpainted one-room
buildings near the airport; and they may reap millions of dollars worth of
profit annually. The more successful also own the industries producing or
importing essential commodities. Without the military's OK, one entre-
preneur told me, "you are run out burned out or killed out."

The man who told me this was sitting on a bag of potatoes at the airport, waiting, as I was, for a ride. I had been lucky enough to secure a
flight on a World Food Program transit out to one of the hard-hit battlezones. The flight left early in the morning, not my favorite time of day. I
had gotten up before dawn to hitch a ride to the airport with some bois-
terous de-miners heading out to help in heavy IDP (internally displaced
people) areas. A sleepy man from a local NGO was driving. The approach
to the airport was lined with the little "travel agencies" — one-room clap-
board buildings with cheerful touristic pictures of palm trees and signs
like "tourist travel" affixed to their dilapidated storefronts. In these dark
early hours, the travel agencies were more brightly lit and bustling than
the airport itself.

"What's the story behind these places?" I asked the driver.

Well, we don't have any tourists these days, *he replied.*

"Huh?" I mumbled in early morning shorthand.

Unless you call food and guns and petrol and all "tourists." *The man snorted in laughter at his joke. Then he grew serious again and continued:*

Everything that moves out of here to anywhere moves out of these "travel agencies."

At the airport, waiting to be called for my flight, I sat next to the man on the bag of potatoes and watched "everything" being loaded onto airplanes. All under the watchful eye, the bottomless pockets, and the unspoken ownership of the military. Through these tiny "travel agencies" and these planes, an entire country was being fed, clothed, ministered to, controlled, born, and buried. What kind of money did this add up to for those that controlled the flow? I asked the man next to me, and he replied with a shake of his head:

Money beyond counting.
Almost beyond thinking.
Money like you own a country.

CEO OF THE COUNTRY

The number of trucks and planes traveling the country with everyday necessities like food, fuel, clothing, and medicines — selling in city stores and village shops, at the sides of roadways and unregulated markets — stretched out in my mind's eye. It linked with what must have been hundreds of thousands of local markets selling to the country's population. To millions of people. Daily. The sum total of revenues generated from the untaxed goods that changed economic hands daily had to be staggering. When all the unregulated extra-state daily transactions of life's necessities are totaled in, the figure of $1 million a day in illicit diamond sales pales by comparison. As Christian Dietrich said to me: "In the final tally: are you really making profits from diamonds or from all the soap and petrol and food and essentials that people need?"[4]

Such commodity networks are lifelines for a country. They anchor the complex interplay of economic development and profiteering: that kind of money can buy soldiers, sway politicians, even undermine governments; it can shape the course of development and of national policy. What military, what government, would allow anyone who was not fully allied with them such access? In the hands of the opposition, it could threaten the ruling party itself. At the same time, why would the government and the military allow access to allies without some kind of meaningful return? Return in monetary compensation, in support, in loyalty. Tight control over access to national infrastructure — where right of entry is reserved for an exclusive in-group — isn't (merely) about militaries controlling wars, nor protecting national security.

This is the creation of empires. Subtle, international, unconditionally twenty-first century systems of wealth and authority . . . but empires nonetheless.

CREATING MULTINATIONALS—FORGING TRADE ROUTES (AND GOVERNANCE)

If battles erupt around resources, they also mark trade routes. Commanders and politicians, like shop owners, need reasonably secure routes to convey supplies and people to resources and to carry those resources out to larger international venues. By way of example, let's return to Muleque, the home of Okidi and his shopkeeper patron. During the war, most transit routes were dangerous at best, and impossible to navigate at worst. The highway east was effectively closed to vehicles because of bombed-out bridges and severe fighting. No direct route moves goods north; the highway to the south was somewhat functional physically, but fraught with the dangers of severe fighting and banditry, and large stretches were closed by the military. Ground travel, then, tended to move west to pick up the single quasi-safe north-south artery.

One day I was shown a map of some of the new fighting areas. The hot spots appeared to follow the military-restricted thoroughfares straight south across rich timber, agriculture, livestock, and mining areas of the country to neighboring countries like Namibia, Zambia, and DR Congo, which serve as major trade outlets.

> "A trade route?" I asked.
> But of course, *was the reply.*

Battles to open up transportation routes shouldn't be viewed merely as exercises in military control.

Diamonds don't need much in the way of ground transport. A handful of diamonds can hitch a ride on a cargo plane, in a diplomatic pouch, with an itinerant barefoot trader walking the byways of war. But the produce from the Gov'nor's farms needs to get to markets capable of returning a serious profit, and the military needs routes capable of supplying their burgeoning private commercial domains as well as the war effort. The shop owner needs functioning routes to acquire (hot) Mercedes, (unregistered) Sonys, and (pirated) software. The street vendor relies on Marlboros, which, like water, find the easiest path to him or her — wads of tobacco wrapped in stale paper and dreams so enticing people will smuggle them around the world and across warzones to make a profit.

As the war orphan and his cigarettes demonstrated, commodities do not tend to travel the extra-legal pathways alone. In this case, diamonds and tomatoes pick up other strange bedfellows on this route south. Bedfellows that continue to carve areas of de facto governance. Decades of political unrest and population displacement have left vast stretches of virgin timber — timber that is very valuable on international markets. Some of the military commanders who have wrested control of these timber areas have set up profitable logging industries — using their soldiers to help with labor and transport. These remote regions are far from the critical eyes of disapproving government representatives, probing media, and vocal international organizations. They log timber, pack it onto convoys traveling across international borders to transport worldwide. Warlords become commerce-lords.[5]

A MATTER OF BEING LUCKI

After seeing the map of the new military hot zones, seemingly opening up a new commodity transport corridor, I began to try to put the facts together — and had the good fortune to meet Lucki. He was ostensibly in "development and humanitarian aid" — which meant he had found a seat on the commodity flow chain where he could help his community and himself at the same time. Lucki was handsome and jovial — life had been treating him well these days, he said. He wore a new cut of Levi's and Nikes graced his feet — a product of global supermarkets whose tentacles reach to the most remote parts of the planet. He was an Angolan civilian who had managed to develop military contacts. Maybe in his earlier days he had been military. Maybe he still was. He could now join in, he said with a smile, "building the country." That meant access to key resources, and the means to move them. It also meant access to information. He was, he said, lucky, and he knew it.

Lucki was relaxed and forthcoming in his descriptions of the military and the extra-legal. He had been told, he said with a quiet smile, to take care of me. I wondered who my benefactor was — research often takes place beyond the pale of explanation. Lucki spoke with a quick and penetrating intelligence; I remember thinking that if he were in the USA, I would ask him to guest lecture in my class. He might have had a secondary-level education at best, but his grasp of political science and economics matched the brightest of my colleagues. In the midst of explaining the development work taking place in the area, he began telling me about the military's plan to open a north-south route to the international borders, and how this would allow timber logged by the military to reach global destinations, where it would produce huge profits. Curious about his reaction, I asked him:

> "If the military, who forge key aspects of national-security policy, have access to resources by virtue of being military, use military means to harvest these resources, use military vehicles to transport these resources to national borders, and the military's 'right' to move them across the borders without paying taxes or levies, tariffs, or duties—as formal military—does this constitute legal actions or non-legal ones?"

Like Egypt

The question was somewhat loaded. Lucki had been explaining to me that he, like everyone, did business with the military's blessing, or not at all. The military was the only game in town: the final source of permits, vehicles, fuel, transport, and transit. Ultimately, asking about the military's cross-border activities was asking about everyone's activities. Lucki leaned back in his chair and smiled with mirth, delighted with the ironies of honesty:

> Legal or not—now what do you think? Of course it's not legal.

PURE PROFIT

At the most basic level, militaries can carry just about anyone or anything, and they do so for a price. But at a more sophisticated level, militaries can argue that, for example, gem mining is in the interest of national security and development. Buying, selling, and transporting everything from food and expensive machinery to professionals and prostitutes are thus in the interest of the country, which is in the guardianship of the military. In addition, these supplies generally come to the military through international channels, paid for by government taxes. These can be "diverted" in bulk to supply private demands. At the end of the day, with little to no investment of personal finances, militaries control a productive empire that spans from diamonds through provisions of critical goods to core trade and commodity industries.

This entire cycle generates pure profit.

Ultimately, in the flux that defines ownership, the victors can plant their personal flags on real estate that, in addition to being resource rich, will likely be the postwar homes to new cities, large industries, agricultural centers, and transport routes. Or they can partner with others who will do the actual developmental work, while they provide security, supplies, and transit for the price of partnership. For years and perhaps decades to come.

The shop owner, the Gov'nor, and certain military commanders are forging suzerainty. When the war is over, whoever has de facto control over resource areas will likely keep it. With peace accords, the successful military officers become commercial magnates. Power resides, not in governance, but in governing. Harnessing the very war is a resource.

AMPUTEES AND STREET MARKETS. ANGOLA.

CHAPTER 6

THE UNTOLD STORY OF THE AMPUTEES

UN-ARMED

The truckers quietly moved their diamonds out and loudly moved their beer and commodities into town. The Gov'nor shipped his tomatoes abroad without worrying about how quietly or noisily he worked. The shopkeeper and the street child went about their business, holding down the town's center of commercial gravity. Amid this swirl of activity, other groups of people were redefining the economic landscapes of the country and its worldwide links in ways rarely recognized in business analyses.

These latter business ventures — challenging established notions of legality and nationality, of the divides between civil society, NGOs, and development — are best summed up for me in the example of a group of women amputees I met in Muleque.

The story starts, not with these women, but with the belief that land mines are a military weapon. The mythology of land mines, which is sold along with the mines themselves, is that these explosives deter soldiers and protect sensitive sites. But the truth is that the most common victims are average civilians looking for food, water, and work. From country to country across the world's militarized zones the same statistics emerge: children playing or going to school, women doing their daily chores, and men engaged in nonmilitary work are those most likely to step on the little metal and plastic units that blow off bits of humanity.

Many people's lives are defined not by whether war continues or peace emerges, but by a chance encounter with violence. A woman who loses her family to attack or a limb to a land mine, finds herself struggling to survive in war and peace alike. These tragedies can happen at the acme of war or long after a peace accord has been signed. In either instance, staying alive suddenly becomes far more tenuous.

> Look at me, *the woman said,* I am incomplete for this world. I have no leg, not much of an arm. My heart is strong, and my spirit good. But heart and spirit don't carry water from the river for drinking or firewood for cooking; heart and spirit don't go out and put seeds in the field, get water to irrigate my crops, tend them, and then harvest them. Have you ever tried to do these things with one leg and arm? I have no husband; he left. If I don't do these things, I starve and die. There are no wheelchairs out here, no way to get them even if there were. If I have to crawl to carry water, I crawl.
>
> *She spits in disgust.* This they call war? I won't get into that. There are thousands of us like me around here. But we are going to make a difference.

BUT NOT DEFENSELESS

The group of amputees around Muleque began to congregate, to pool resources, and to help one another. An Irish INGO provided support: seeds and tools, a workshop, and other critical help. The first time I met the women, they had come from far and wide to attend a meeting and seed distribution at their center in town. Walking the long kilometers was the only means of travel they had — a tough ordeal for people who have lost limbs to explosions. The range and barbarity of the land mines available on the world's market was visible in the wounds the women carried. Some had barely the remnants of a leg. Others were missing arms. Some were scarred from face to torso by the shards of metal packed into shrapnel mines. A crutch was generally an impossible luxury; neither the crutches nor the money to buy them were available.

At the center, the women showed me a play they were working on — they had decided to use theater to educate people about land mines. They enacted despair and hope, support and a will to live. They sang of the difficulties of no longer fitting the ideal of a woman — whole in body, capable in limbs, desirable in womanhood — and of the families and men who had stayed to help, and those who had abandoned them; of the suffering and sanguinity entailed in creating a new kind of community of women, with and without families, helping each other. The performance didn't shy away from raw emotions or painful truths. But there was one topic that was left unspoken. Either a person is in the know, or isn't; and thus the knowledge is best left unsaid.

COMING BACK FROM THE DEAD: INFORMAL ECONOMIES AND FORMAL DEVELOPMENT

These women had developed survival skills: they cleared farmland and planted crops, built places to live, and established market and barter systems to gain essentials. These are the "informal economies" that governments and INGOs reckon keep the poor alive and the basics of a society intact. This is what the International Labor Organization deems small-scale, low-tech, low-income. But the women had larger plans. They didn't want to eke out the rest of their days hobbling to tiny fields, raising just enough food to keep body and soul together until a drought ended their hopes. They wanted the option to buy prostheses, build decent homes, go into business, and gain the kinds of power that could buy permits and sock away money to cushion them against life's unexpected upheavals.

The Muleque women had several money-making enterprises in mind. They operated what women throughout Southern Africa depend on: a self-run informal banking system. Women who know each other form a group based on stability, trust, and economics. Each month, all the members of the group put a predetermined amount of money into a communal pot, and one woman gets the entire pot that month. The next month the next woman on the rotation gains the entire amount, and so on, throughout the membership cycle. There are no laws or mechanisms to ensure that a member doesn't take her turn to get all the money and then leave the group. That these women's banks are so widespread and enduring is a testimony to the systems of trust and allegiance that can underscore informal economic networks.

With the proceeds of their banking investments, the women amputees were beginning to reap profits: some had been successful at farming and had surplus food. Some began to link into the secondhand clothing industry. And some had plans to begin producing small items to sell, from crafts to business components.

> The trick, of course, is to broaden our markets, *they explained.* Oh, we can sell here. But this is a limited market. We will reach a certain volume and then that's it. We won't grow. We need to be able to sell our products to larger cities. We need to be able to reach Luanda, the capital. We have things that people across the border could use. With these connections, we can really make a go of it.

But as to how they could reach these markets, they remained silent. These were devastatingly poor women, women for whom many days went by when they couldn't scrape together enough to eat. Their impaired mobility made the normally difficult task of walking and trying to hitch rides across the country seemingly impossible. As women, they didn't have the networks of access that men who work in government, transport, or mining and industry have — networks where a friend who is making a flight or a truck run might let him bring his products along. To find the money to pay for such "help" was a distant dream.

The women's silence wasn't due to lack of ideas, but discretion. The story unfolded only when I sat talking to a local coordinator for an INGO working with the amputees. This woman, whom I'll call "Leli," had lived her whole life in the Muleque area and knew it well. She wasn't sure why she had escaped stepping on a mine or stopping a bullet, but she threw herself into helping these women and her community tirelessly. She was a font of enthusiasm, hard work, and dedicated vision. Leli and the hundreds of thousands like her who work beyond the pale of CNN and the *Times* of London give lie to tossed-off statements by Westerners that humanitarian aid produces complacent and dependent populations. I spoke to Leli in the small mud-walled room where she worked. She leaned across the rickety wooden table that served as her desk, taking my hand periodically as if to envelop me in the vitality of her work:

> These are the women who are not supposed to make it—the women who fall off the margins. How does a woman make it in this kind of life. . . . a life where a healthy woman with all her limbs finds it hard. There are few precedents for women breaking out of traditional roles and forging new communities of all-women support. So these land-mine victims are sort of expected to fall off the map. But they don't.
>
> They start up farming and making small things they can barter for essentials. And then they start up with the ideas. They have talked with every trader who comes through here, and they know the markets in the next big city, in Luanda, across the border in Congo. They know what is available, what is desirable, and what the prices are. They have tailored their enterprises and products to suit these markets. And they are ready to sell. All they need is transport.
>
> They have come to me to ask if I can take their goods on a flight to Luanda. They know that because I work with the INGO, I have access to flights and cargo rights. They know these flights are safe. And they know they can trust me. They have offered to cut me in on the business for this. I think it's an excellent idea. I am proud of the women. In truth, these INGO flights bring in seeds and tools to keep these women alive. But this is sheer subsistence. They give only enough to keep people alive. They live at the minimum. There is no real way in this scheme to improve, to grow, to gain

some prosperity. If the INGO closes shop and moves, these people are left at the margins.

To use my rights as a worker for an INGO, to carry these women's products to the capital, this is development. Now these women have a real chance. I am really moved by what they are doing, they are succeeding where no one expects them to. I'm glad to be a part of it. Now women in my hometown may actually make it.

The women's ambition to group together, form banking and entrepreneurial systems, and move from local and subsistence to inter/national profit making is part of a larger ethos. It is neither haphazard nor reactionary; it follows a carefully crafted plan of development. It is not that the women just want to create a new market for their goods. The market is not the goal, but the means to expanding one's business, one's options, and one's opportunities.

DOMINGAS'S STORY: FROM RAGS TO RICHES

After speaking with Leli, I grew increasingly curious about women, survival, and the intricacies of enterprise. At a UN program office for health and education, I spoke with Domingas, the only local woman on staff. Domingas exuded the same vibrant concern for her work and her people as Leli did. Both had seen the worst of war and poverty: Leli in the broken bodies left behind, Domingas in seven-day work weeks dedicated to broken families, communities, and economies.

"How do women and societies on the brink of existence make it?" I asked. It is one and the same thing, *she said with a smile.*

Women, Domingas explained, are the invisible center of gravity of the society. Gravity, because while men move more fluidly, women *are* families, in times when men are there and when they are not. As such, they forge the basic links of society: producing food, daily necessities, communal networks, market systems. Where families are centered, infrastructure, health, education, and trade emerge. Invisibly, because women's role in this is generally overlooked.

If women don't make it, families crumble and communities collapse. And perhaps, she added, economies collapse too; one could argue that the foundations of the economy spin out from here. "Let me give you an example," Domingas said:

No one starts out in this place with anything. Well, if you're a woman that's for sure. They start out below the bottom. They carry water for a penny. You see these poor, hungry women in rags carrying a beaten-up old bucket of water for someone, and you think, "There goes a person all of life has forgotten, a person who will live and die carrying that bucket."

But it is not so. She struggles down the road with a plan. When she scrapes together a few pennies, she will begin to make and sell charcoal.

Domingas grabbed a piece of paper and a pencil and began to draw on it. Her formal "professional in an interview with a stranger" demeanor relaxed into informality; she pushed up her shirt sleeves and hiked a foot up on the rung of her chair as she began to draw, and then stopped to chew thoughtfully on her pencil: "Did I," she wanted to know, "really want to understand the whole thing, the way the economy really worked?" She emphasized the word *really*. Her enthusiasm for her work, and her ideas, was contagious. I remember thinking even a stone would say yes to her question. She began her description, outlining it in a flow chart on paper as she explained it in words:

OK, here's the sequence:

1. You begin with carrying water, or some such hard labor.
2. And then move on to making a product to sell at a little "marketplace"—a patch of swept dirt by the roadside or a spot on the ground in the local open market. Maybe you go out and collect wood and make charcoal, or find food, herbal medicines, whatever, in the bush to sell.
3. You scrape together some few pennies. Enough to get by. Enough to join in a women's informal bank.
4. When your turn comes for the whole banking pot, you invest in a bit of farmland and begin harvesting produce to sell. Bananas, for example. Bananas open the door for you to actually make some money. You start selling in the local markets, reinvesting everything you can to grow. You check out what they are desperate for in the next country. In the places where the "tourist agencies" fly to. And you begin to plan for that trip.
5. You work the markets, trading and selling, bartering and speculating, to get the dollars to pay for that flight to the neighboring country. One hundred bucks per person per flight, 90 cents a kilo for cargo.

"You know the prices?" I asked.

You're missing the point if you ask this. Of course I know the prices. Everyone knows the prices. The bent-over woman in rags carrying that bucket of water knows the prices. This is where we live our lives. It is the stuff of survival.

6. And then you make the trip into the next country.

"Do you worry about visas, permits, taxes?"

Domingas seemed surprised by my question. The system was so well known that the question seemed irrelevant.

This has nothing to do with that kind of economy. This is informal. Daily life. It works because it is not formal. Entire infrastructures work on this.

7. In the neighboring country, you use the profits of your sales to buy what people need and will spend money for at home. Then you fly back home, sell, and continue the cycle, growing at each turn.

8. At some point, you begin to see real wealth. You build a decent house. You buy a car, hire a driver. You begin to put money into your community, provide jobs, develop the place. You give out goods for poor kids to sell in the streets so they can put together enough money at the end of the day to buy some food to eat. You care about schools and clinics for your kids. Your banking group really carries some weight now.

9. Your horizons expand, and you begin to make flights on commercial airlines to Europe to buy more expensive items to sell to those with real money in your community and country. Often, you bring back suitcases of goods and sell them out of your house.

10. And finally, you purchase a boutique and set up a formal business. You begin to pay some formal taxes. You invest in better education and social development for your country and your home region. But you don't give up your networks. You work them all. You send your children to private schools. And you make your own decisions: you have boyfriends, no husband. Like the Gov'nor's girlfriends who run their own businesses under his "protection."

OK, only the lucky make it all the way down this line, *Domingas added.* But people do. It is how we make the system work. How women make it.

Domingas leaned back in her chair and took a deep breath, saying she could use a cup of coffee. As we strolled over to the rustic kitchen in the UN office to make coffee, she confided that she didn't normally take time out of her demanding workday to talk to outsiders. "But this needs to be told." Like Leli, she cared deeply about finding solutions. While we were making coffee we ruminated over the process Domingas had just outlined. I asked her if it was only at the end of this, at point 10, that any of these transactions moved into the formal economy. "Of course," she replied. Points 1 through 9 are invisible to all formal economic reckoning.

Coffee in hand, we walked out to sit on the front stoop of the building. As we looked out over the town — the muddy dirt roads carrying nameless dreams, the women wrapped in bright African cloth hauling heavy burdens on their heads and in their hearts, the children trotting along at their sides — Domingas finished her explanation:

A huge economy forms the foundations of this country, and much of it runs along these lines—along what people call "informal." Consider: $250 billion of imports comes into this country through the informal economy yearly. Those are UN estimates. What does this say about determining economies? About the way people work? About the impact of women?

And the truth is, while the world talks about diamonds and oil, food and clothing are the real profits. These are where the biggest gains are. Remember: along that line of development from carrying water to a boutique, the leap in profits, the juncture where one can finally move from subsistence to capital ventures, is here—it is food and clothing that builds the houses, buys the cars, and launches the businesses.

Pictures of women who have stepped on land mines and lost limbs — women eking out a subsistence living by farming a small plot of land with a hoe and a crutch — are used worldwide to elicit outrage at perfidious weapons, sympathy for the victims, and money for the organizations helping them. The bananas, or charcoal, they sell constitute another stereotypic image of Africa: women on the margins of the economy offering a small homegrown harvest in neatly arranged piles on a mat in a local open-air market. Their earnings are counted up in single-digit figures, their impact left largely uncalculated because of indifference.

Why their stories, their earnings, their networks, and their contributions to development are not added up becomes an interesting question when we take the UN estimate that $250 billion in informal import earnings is made yearly in the country. The $1 million a day in unauthorized diamond earnings in this country pales in comparison. So too does the $1 billion a year lost from oil profits. Indeed, $250 billion rivals the entire GDPs of the countries of this region of the world.

It would seem the amputee women, and all the women working diligently to earn the money to support their families, are central to the economy. Where, then, are the margins?

And where do we place development? Illicit oil and diamond revenues can be easily channeled into foreign bank accounts and businesses, offering little to help this nation. But in the most basic sense, the work of these women is developing the country. Survival follows their footsteps; infrastructure settles in the imprints they make. They move food, clothing, household and industrial goods, and energy supplies. They set up local and international transport routes, and forge markets across borders and countries.

What they do may be deemed informal and even illegal. It is here that the very notion of "extra-state" becomes most interesting: it would seem that real profits, and real development, are to be found in the places economic analysts are not looking. Perhaps we don't look because we would have to reassess our most fundamental — and cherished — ideas about power, and about the morality and the legality of economics and development.   *Read on . . .*

THE FORTUNE OF WAR.

CHAPTER 7

ROBBER BARONS

Tony Hodges and I were sitting having a cup of coffee in Luanda in 2002, talking about his new book, *Angola from Afro-Stalinism to Petro-Diamond Capitalism*. It is an excellent book on the intersections of national wars, resource plundering, and elite profiteering in Angola. I complimented Hodges on the model he had employed in his book and said I was interested in how such dynamics played across not only a single country, but the world in general. He asked, confused:

What are you talking about?

I explained I was looking at how all kinds of economic enterprises variously spurred development and exploited markets by crossing lines of ethics or legality.
Tony responded, shaking his head:

That can't be true. There is just no way that any significant proportion of the world's economy can be moving along non-formal lines.

As Hodges and I spoke, the United States was beginning to face its string of early twenty-first-century corporate scandals. It is much more clear now, after Enron, WorldCom, Xerox (as well as a host of other large corporations such as Adelphia Communications, Qwest Communications, Peregrine Systems, Dynegy, Imclone, Tyco International, Global Crossing), how unlawful practices can permeate the most respected of economic institutions. Amid the reverberations of the fall of so many corporate giants, Joseph Stiglitz, Nobel Laureate in Economics, wrote in *The Guardian:*

Of late, there has been much discussion of corruption in the public sector of many developing countries. It was the inevitable corruption of public servants that, in part, made it important to privatize in developing countries. Privatization also lauded the private sector's ability to compete. But I'm not sure these private sector advocates quite had in mind the abilities that American corporate capitalism has demonstrated so amply recently: corruption on an almost unfathomable scale. They put to shame those petty government bureaucrats who stole a few thousand or even a few million. The numbers bandied about in the Enron, WorldCom and other scandals are in the billions, greater than the GNP of many countries. (July 4, 2002: 15)

. . .

In its monitoring of entrepreneurial integrity, Global Witness estimates that more than $1 billion a year disappears from oil revenues into the pockets of leading political figures in Angola. This flow of government revenues into private hands carries a simple word: *corruption*.

The term both clarifies and obscures a good deal of the reality of global money flows. Analyses of corruption generally stop at the national level. In truth, corruption is about transnational profiteering — it entails a highly cosmopolitan, twenty-first-century form of international warlordism.

Certainly the word *corruption* fits the Gov'nor, who profits from war, the free labor of displaced people, land grants, and the political power needed to develop provincial fiefdoms. It also fits the generals who run diamond and timber concessions and use their soldiers for labor. But they can't operate without international business partners linked within the same systems of (unregulated) values and (corrupt) business practices.

A great deal of attention is paid to corruption in Africa. Analysts explain that it's not merely about accumulation of wealth, but about creating strong foundations of patronage, of consolidating control over resources and thus governance, of creating empires of wealth that assure entry into the international elite. The more negative analyses label such pursuits cults of personality, megalomania, kleptocracies, and the supreme abuse of privilege. Analyses of corruption generally focus on the offshore flows of illicit gains. The money diverted to private interests at the highest levels of government and military is seldom seen to benefit the country: it moves to cosmopolitan centers to buy superb education for the children, elegant villas for the family, luxury commodities for investment and enjoyment, and offshore bank accounts for posterity.[1]

Corruption, then, is seen as a personal endeavor. But, as chapter 5 suggested, it's about far more. It's not just the story of bleeding a country. It's about owning it. This is a fact that even the poorest of locals recognize, perhaps more clearly than international analysts. A woman administrator, a businessman, and a poor peasant in Angola all told me the same thing (here I use the words of the administrator):

> You must appreciate that more than anything, it's the family that explains this the best. The whole country follows the model of a family. Control of the family rests in the hands of parents overseeing the resources, and they make decisions for everyone in their care. The political and military leaders of the country hold this position, a position they have created. Nothing happens without their knowledge or express permission. Everything coming into or out of the country moves with their blessings. No decision can be made without their approval. The family follows the lead of the parent, the country that of the model of the family. Parents don't squander resources, they control them.

This image of taking care of a "family" — of running a familial country — provides a justification for those feeding at the national trough. In my experience, few people see themselves as morally compromised. From torturers to criminals, from corrupt elites to wildcat profiteers, people devise explanations that smooth their actions into acceptability. Here are three examples: a military commander, a politician, and a businessman.

THE COMMANDER

I was speaking to a military commander in the informal setting — that curious limbo — between the frontlines and the formal urban institutions of military command. Sitting on a rickety chair, the commander's only concession to relaxing his military posture was to throw a leg out casually to the side and lean back to look out over his domain. The man exuded an aura of authority, and as usual I wondered briefly how soldiers in muddy remote locations could have uniforms that were immaculately clean and pressed. After just a day of traveling in the area, I was covered from head to toe in indelible red-brown mud etched into permanent wrinkles in my clothing. The commander was the start and the end of anything that happened in the region, from war to business, and it was general (however unpublished) knowledge that he was using his position to run mining concessions, control transport in the region, and regulate access to the region's major enterprises.

What I do, I do for the good of this country. We're fighting a war. To do that, we need resources, supplies, structures. The government can't do this by itself; what government can fight a war all on its own? Everyone has allies. How do you think we get the stuff we need? How does anybody? It's what's essential to fighting this war, to keeping the government stable.

And my own gain? My control over prime business locations? That is how we keep control, and keep out trouble. You can't let just anyone have access to setting up business—the wrong people can turn their gain over to those who fight us; they can be against good government. Those of us who know the military, who have been here all along, we know what's going on. We oversee things in the interests of keeping the country stable.

THE POLITICIAN

The politician was in some ways the mirror image of the commander, but unlike his military counterpart, he worked to give off an air of casualness; his only concession to formality was a subtle strength of posture that commanded the space. He was soft-spoken, gracious, and seemingly sincere. Our conversation covered myriad topics, and he had an answer for everything. When I asked why it was acceptable to divert most of Angola's education budget to scholarships for a few elite children to study at leading private schools and universities in the world, his answer was immediate:

> This nation desperately needs the best minds it has to solve its problems, and to do this effectively, these bright people need the best education they can receive. They need the most sophisticated training they can get, and as well, they need the contacts, the networks of work and support, the international links that any person, and any country, needs to make it. It's only as these talented young people move into leadership positions and our country develops that we gain the ability to construct successful educational, health, and social services.

And when I asked why politicians purchased expensive villas in Paris with diverted funds:

> There is only one way to succeed at the world's political game, and that is to play the same game as the rest. Since the time of kings, people have associated power with grandeur: audiences in impressive locations, traveling with large retinues, having access to sophisticated technology. The better able we are to have a voice in world strategies on trade, pricing, resource allocation, policy, and international law, the stronger our country as a whole becomes.

THE BUSINESSMAN

This man, trying to gain a foothold in the difficult flux of transitional development and political turmoil, would never consider himself a smuggler or a criminal. In fact, he sees people like himself as central to the development of Angola.

> I am helping my country, *he says with sincerity.* We all try to work in the midst of endless strangleholds. Ruined infrastructure, land mines, corruption, excessive taxes, contradictory regulations, inefficient bureaucracy, loaded international trade policies, patronage, you name it, we struggle with it. If you wanted to make sure a country has problems developing, you'd invent this.
>
> Without development, this country dies; the people starve. We make things work; we're bringing in goods, industry, employment. We're setting up trade, kicking up production, getting essentials into the country. We're providing work and jobs. Honestly, the way we work is a whole lot more organized than the government we work with.

I bumped into this man at a local corner snack shop. We sat talking at a little wooden table pockmarked by poverty and flaking blue paint chips. Unlike his military and politician friends, this man gave little thought to projecting a polished appearance. His simple slacks, slightly rumpled open-neck shirt, and somewhat unruly hair gave the appearance of a man working hard to get a day's work done. He sprawled more than commanded the space, casually sipping on a soft drink from the bottle. He settled comfortably into his story:

> I love this country. Hey, it's suffered a terrible war, but it's home. I'm not packing up and looking for greener pastures. But that doesn't mean it's simple. God, no. So I'm trying to start this manufacturing plant up-country. Do you have any idea what that means? First I have to get the materials to build what I need. Nothing available here at the corner store. I have to get Chinese construction materials, European machinery, Indian software, a reliable source of energy, just to keep going. I need to cut deals all over the place to get this stuff.
>
> Then a friend says, hey, we need some X, Y, or Z from the next country, or some young hustler comes up with a deal to sell books or antibiotics or global positioning systems and he's got a hot deal in the same country I'm bringing in a load of industrial equipment. Can I bring in the stuff with my goods? And then we are bringing in everything from ball bearings to software to some goddamn weird new wine press someone thinks can make a fortune here—and we've got to arm a small army just to keep all this safe.
>
> Then I have to get all these materials into the country. Coming in formally is a death sentence. Taxes and all are bad enough, but honestly, that isn't

the real consideration. I have businesses to run, I have to get things done. I don't have time for endless paperwork and payment rules and meetings and whatnot. Get it across the border and get to work. I tell you, what a headache.

So I need vehicles, and petrol, and mechanics. Now I have to get all this too. I have to get dollars to pay for this. Who in the international markets is asking for our local currency? I have to make sure I have other businesses that get the dollars. I'm moving goods out of the country to get dollars to get this other stuff in.

The stories just go on. It's a constant juggle. I'm buying and selling everything across borders: we have this here, they don't have that there; we have dollars today, tomorrow we don't—the exchange rates move by the minute. I'm off just now to see about a shipment coming in across the border, you know, grease the way.

GLOBAL PLAYERS IN THE OIL GAME

These are not mere stories of warlordism. They represent modern-day empires in the same sense that the Carnegies, MacArthurs, and Stanfords viewed them. Behind the European villas and offshore accounts, the truly enterprising amass land and industries, transport routes, and monopolies over core commodity and service sectors.[2]

Importantly, this system of state/extra-state transactions moves out internationally, through wildcat profiteers, powerful international businesses, multinational enterprises, and other governments. It's here that the profoundly international character of what is so easily termed "corruption" can be seen.

Picking the diamond industry as an example is too easy: diamonds exist, it might seem, to be bought, sold, and smuggled. Instead, consider the oil industry. I was struck by an interview with an oil executive who told me that his industry was so closely monitored that legality was ensured — that it was tamper proof. After all, you can't put a few carats of oil in your pocket and walk across the border. He pulled no punches: some of the highest signature bonuses in the entire industry had recently been paid by the leading companies in the oil field to the government to secure blocks.

But we do this in every country, *he stressed.* No one tells us not to offer signature bonuses to the Queen of England. It's the way things are done. Who are we to say how the government is to handle this money? What business tells a government how to handle money paid to it?

The rest, he assured me, was all above board.

Conversation after conversation gave the lie to this claim. These exchanges often emerge in informal settings, like backyard barbecues. In one such setting, upon hearing of my research interests, the head of a company in the oil business, a Westerner I'll call "Richard," leaned forward and said:

> I simply can't do business here without doing illegal things. There's just no way around it. I bribe. Everyone does.
>
> Listen, I'm good at what I do, perhaps the best. But there are ten, twenty other companies from around the world breathing down my neck to get my contracts. People here don't necessarily know who is best, who can deliver the goods, who is reliable. Government officials come and go, new industries pop up all the time. Who has the background to know the best in the field?
>
> So I'm there first thing in the morning and last thing at night, and I bribe my way into getting the contracts. Whatever it takes, I give it. Or I go bust. I'm from the States; I've been promoted up the ladder from sites all over the world. Because I get things done. If I don't, they give my job to someone who can.

Sitting next to us at the barbecue was "Dian," the economic officer of the local U.S. embassy. She covered her ears in mock consternation and said:

> Would you stop talking like this! This is illegal, and the embassy can't support such behavior. The embassy is here to support legitimate business practices. We can't condone anything else. You are putting us on the spot talking like this.

Richard responded:

> But what I'm saying is true. It's true for everyone here. It's the reality of doing business. How can you support business here and not deal with the realities?

Dian grinned, and then said seriously:

> Look, I know the game, but I'm embassy, and that's a reality too. Just shut up here, would you?

I asked Richard if I could talk with him about this another time, and he agreed. At our next meeting, he was forthright on how "deals" are done. But perhaps my favorite part of the discussion came when I asked him about getting things in through customs. My data suggested that nearly everybody, from small wildcatters to large respectable multinationals, fudged on customs declarations, sanctioned goods, and tax payments.

Of course, that's how it's done, Richard said with a laugh. I even smuggle things out of customs myself. I'll put in for a shipment, and about the time it's to arrive, I call daily to find out its whereabouts, if it has docked. I have my "friends" at the port—people who have made a little extra for helping me in the past. They let me know when it's in and where it is; and when I arrive at the port, they let me in and turn their heads while I get what I need. I even put important packages under my seat and drive out the port gates like that. Smuggle, you might call it. And I wave to all my friends from other businesses who are doing the same.

Richard was the head of a business that employs nearly two hundred people in this one African country alone. It's part of a respected multinational corporation with offices worldwide. He is one of the younger people in his business to head up a country to date, and says casually it's because he's smart, easygoing, and knows how to play the game and get things done.

I asked Richard if things were different when he worked in the United States and Europe, whether he had to smuggle and bribe there as well.

Different? No, it's not qualitatively different. Not in the USA, nor anywhere. That's why we can all travel and work anywhere in the world. The game is played roughly the same everywhere. You just fine-tune it for the specific cultures of the country you are in at any given time. The only difference I find in the USA is that I have to pay much higher bribes. It just costs a lot more there.

If business is about knowing how to play the game, research is sometimes a game played for fun as well as information. For the next several weeks, it became something of a research game for me to try and figure out the ways in which the world's leading oil companies stepped across the penalty lines of legality without getting caught. To date, I haven't found a company that doesn't stack the game at least a little. The following conversation catches the dynamics of the game.

I was speaking to a respected top executive of one of the world's leading oil companies. It is not a conversation "Zachery" would appreciate having his name and that of his company attached to. Research bonanzas are curious and often inexplicable: perhaps Zachery talked to me because he loved "the game"; or perhaps because it seemed he was suffering the pangs of unrequited love for a friend of mine. Aside from his affairs of the heart, Zachery was urbane and articulate, and unable to hide his swift intellect and mischievous grin. Conversations, like business, are about "knowing"; if you know enough to ask the right questions, you know enough to warrant a serious answer. If you can't ask a question with enough insider information, you get "public affairs officer" answers. Zachery let me know that he was open for "playing." He wouldn't disclose less-than-legal activities, but he would let me guess:

> "Is there anything slipped along with the signature bonuses that is less than declared?" I asked.
>
> Oh sure, handshakes, nods, and winks. But it's not necessary at that level: we make so many millions available that a few more are overkill. Point is, we hand over the money, and they can do with it as they like. Accepted practice worldwide.
>
> "OK, how about the equipment you bring in. Do you declare everything?"
>
> Irrelevant. We set up deals whereby all equipment is brought in tax free. We partner with government or local representatives, and all this will go to them ultimately as part of our development packages.
>
> "Computers, software, business necessities, office supplies, do you buy and bring everything through customs with full disclosure?"
>
> Again, irrelevant. All supplies, by the agreements we sign with the government, are tax free as we leave everything to them when we no longer need it. Customs just isn't a problem.

The last sentence was a statement, and also a hint. I had been following postal services and smuggling routes, and asked:

> "What about DHL, the global air courier service?"
> *Zachery smiled, and said,* Good.
> "How much DHL do you get a day?"

He laughed. The game had gone well:

> Oh, over three hundred packages *a day.*

I had interviewed one of the United States Postal Service regional postmasters, and knew that in a country with as strict a monitoring standard as the USA, at very best 5 percent of all regular international postal packages were checked. Like postal services, courier services moved massive amounts of goods without inspection.

I told Zachery that a colleague of his, the country representative of another of the world's leading oil companies, had said the oil industry was largely "tamper proof." Zachery shook his head and laughed. I asked how much of the industry worldwide he would estimate ran extra-state.

> Oh, at least 20 percent, *he answered.*

THE AMBASSADOR'S STORY: PEACE IN PROFIT(EERING)

By reading the patterns of alliances, trade, and profiteering (in light of the more intangible dynamics of identity and ethos), I have had success predicting whether political violence in a country will worsen or abate. My predictions are generally 180 degrees opposite to those made by political scientists, diplomats, and INGO specialists. At the height of the most recent bout of severe warring in Angola, most analysts were pessimistic: they cited the massive gains leaders on all sides could enjoy in war — gains that could easily disappear with peace. But the patterns of social relationships and extra/state activities made me optimistic. At the height of the war, I read its demise. Five months later, a peace accord was signed, and it has held for some years now. This kind of analysis isn't unique. During severe days of war in 2001, I spoke with a European ambassador widely recognized as one of the brightest in the country. She told me she would give me her frank opinion, off the record:

> In all conflicts, someone is making money. People worry that the war is kept going to keep making money. This may be cynical, and this may not be the predominate factor, but it's a factor: if we are looking for solutions we must go to "the respectables" [i.e., the generals] and talk to them, say, "Hey, you are a remarkable part of society, you can do well in a legal economy, and here is how . . ."[3]
>
> We all know about the concessions, the control of trade, the channeling of military stores into private markets. I love the example of fuel, also controlled by the military. Of course, there is an embargo on fuel to the rebels — anyone caught selling fuel to them is a traitor. Military fuel convoys start out to traverse the country, and the trip takes three times as long as it should: the trucks stop pretty well every few kilometers to trade with the rebels. The rebels come up with everything from tankers to pots and fill up. The military isn't ambushed, and everyone is fat in the end. It's not just the military; all the governors have "businesses." Some care about helping their communities, some more about helping themselves. And this moves all the way down the line: if people don't have salaries to sustain life at a reasonable level, the whole system will become corrupt. Government employees are allowed to stay "in business" so their pay can be kept low. People must be corrupt to survive, so the question in the system becomes, "How corrupt are you?" In all, the elite have a stranglehold on the economy.[4]
>
> But here is a key — and here is why I am more optimistic than my colleagues about the prospects for peace. There is something of a break-even point. During war, the elites are able to consolidate control. Now, they are finding stability useful. That means peace is becoming useful.
>
> There are lots of other forces going on that have a bearing on this. You have the same people on top who have been on top since the colonial strug-

gles, and at the same time you have new people who want to come in. For example, these old-guard elites have sent their children all over the world to excellent schools and universities: they have received a global education, and a good dose of liberal education. Some remain abroad, but some want to come home and make a difference in their country. These are the 40-somethings; they haven't been formed in a colonial environment, but in a postcolonial world. They honestly care about their country, they want to be able to say, "I'm from X country" and have people respect their country and what they have been able to accomplish. They want to join their international colleagues in global business ventures with a strong economy. These children know what their parents control, and they are now saying, "Hey, Dad, it's a big world out there, and no one is impressed when I say what country I am from. But with our country's wealth, we can change that; we can become a leader in Africa; we can bring in technology and skills and really make a difference."

Both the old guard and the newer generations of the elite are recognizing that while chaos allowed vast accumulations, at the break-even point, chaos can become destabilizing. Keeping a stable power system going will open up opportunities without losing control of it all. And that means winding down the war, going for elections, settling in a democratic process that further consolidates strength in international markets and politics. Sadly, that tends to mean a more repressive security system so that the elites can maintain their control. But on the positive side, it also means bringing more people, more stakeholders, into government and business. In sum, it means legitimacy now begins to outweigh the gains of war.

And, by this reckoning, you can see the transition in place already.

The ambassador and I were in agreement: in war, the leaders could divide up a country. But the very instability that can produce such gains, once industry begins to develop, becomes detrimental in the long term. To bring such gains to fruition, stable bases of politics, trade, and internationalization become desirable. At the break-even point, peace becomes a resource more useful than war. The robber barons are in place.

INTERNATIONAL

TRUCKERS. SOUTHERN AFRICA.

CHAPTER 8

THE BORDER POST–A BILLION-DOLLAR TRUCK STOP
(GOING INTERNATIONAL)

We stood at the border looking across the no-man's-lands into Angola, the country of the war orphan, his benefactor the shopkeeper, and the businessman's benefactors, the Gov'nor and the generals. I was there to do some fieldwork at the intersections of war and peace, commerce and transition, fortune hunters and scoundrels, to see how the tomatoes and diamonds moved from remote corners of production into global flows. The border was the first step out into the larger world.

"Gina," a friend who teaches at the local university, had offered to take me on the long drive to the border. Her thirty-year-old Mercedes was built like a tank, and equally roadworthy. Gina had devotedly nursed it through tropical heat and rugged back roads, and equipped it with sleeping bags, charcoal, and water to comfortably survive the frequent breakdowns. A fashionable pair of sunglasses dangled from the visor.

There was nothing for us to see across the border except a line of cars and trucks waiting and a broad expanse of scrub plain. Waiting for merchandise, waiting to cross, waiting to meet contacts, waiting to return to supply the war or peace, whichever came first. The story was here on this side of the border.

The town on the border that I call Truck Stop is a kind of giant warehouse. Gina and I had visited here five years before. Then, a few warehouses, some beer halls and rustic restaurants, and an open-air market spilled out along the main road in a somewhat haphazard, low-key way. The "story" back then was the new hospital that had just been constructed, and the mission station that provided education, jobs, and vocational training as well as religious services. There was no hotel in town, and the mission allowed us to stay in an empty room and cook outside over a fire. Located just a few kilometers from the border post, with its steel gates and security fences, the mission taught classes to students from Angola who crossed the border every day from the rural hamlets deprived of social services by the war. In the eyes of the nation-state, the students crossed an international border illegally to get an education. The students just saw a dusty footpath from their village to the school, where at one point they stepped over a wire strung between sagging wooden posts.

Today, Truck Stop boasts a hotel, scores of immense warehouses, tiny beer joints, and "supermarkets" that sell everything from food to toilets — all lining a single main road running right up to the border post. Hundreds of trucks of every conceivable size and make are parked along the road, in front of bars and warehouses, beside supermarkets, and in front of the only hotel. The town seemed to consist of truckers in blue jeans, young women, and businesspeople from every continent. Beyond the town's perimeter, empty savanna bush stretches in every direction. A gigantic truck stop warehouse in a sea of sand and bush. A single thread of commerce connecting the riches made and lost in war and politics from all points of the world.

Along this thread of commerce flow millions of dollars. Daily. Truck Stop isn't a remote point on the world's financial maps; it's a geyser. Here, the term *dollars* isn't used figuratively. Business is done in dollars. The local currency isn't accepted, nor is Angola's kwanza. To stimulate trade, many of the warehouses are duty free, and a duty-free manufacturing zone ostensibly exists, though it appears to be more of a warehouse jobber — moving goods internationally rather than engaging in manufacturing. As warehouse manager after manager explained to me:

> Everything, everything is done in dollars.
> "What about German marks, Japanese yen, English pounds?" I asked.
> Dollars. Only dollars.
> "What about national currency, from either side of the border?"

The men just smiled and shook their heads at the obvious. No answer was needed. One of the men conceded:

> Listen, dollars aren't a currency here, they're a fact. Well, dollars and diamonds.

This simple conversation points out a core dynamic in commerce and nation building. Neither of the two countries at this border post has a currency that exchanges on international markets. Neither can use the fruits of its own economy to get dollars. To obtain the international goods they need to survive, they have to find something that people with dollars are willing to give up dollars for. By hook, by genius, by hard work, or by crook.

Commerce went one way in this town: dollars came across the border, and goods went back. Goods accumulated at this border from all the world's continents. Dollars provided the government and businesspeople in this peacetime country with much-needed foreign exchange; goods kept the war-weary Angolan population from slipping off the UN quality-of-life charts completely.

Truckers kept the flow moving. Conversations, like goods, flowed around them as well. Information is one of the most important commodities in this line of work. Gina and I were sitting on the verandah of a beer joint talking with a group of truckers who had just come across the border with dollars to load up on supplies to take back to Angola. The men spoke Portuguese, but like many of their fellow truckers, didn't speak the language of this country or English, the language of commerce. Gina didn't speak Portuguese. Our conversation was a jovial mix of simultaneous translation and pantomime between Gina and the truckers. We asked them about their trade, and they explained their routes and the products they ferried:

> Beer, beer and whiskey. This beer here—*he holds up the bottle of the locally produced national beer he is drinking*—this beer that costs about 60 cents here, I can sell this for $10 US a bottle in the eastern province. So beer and liquor and soft drinks, that's probably the first thing. Then anything else you can name: tables—*he pats the plastic table we are sitting at*—medicines—*he holds his stomach in mock distress*—refrigerators—*he points to the cooler keeping the drinks cool at the counter, indicating the gamut of goods moved on their trucks*—building supplies, machines, food, televisions, clothing, biscuits . . .
>
> I've been waiting here two weeks for biscuits to come in, *another man chimed in.* I'm waiting to buy fifteen tons of biscuits. That's less than half my load. Everything else I want, I've been able to get here in a moment, but you think I can get those damn biscuits?
>
> . . . housewares, *the first man continued,* furniture, engines, cars . . .
>
> I'm here to buy a Mercedes truck, *another man at the table added casually.*

I looked at him and realized how much money changed hands here with a promise and a handshake. A Mercedes truck of the kind he referred to costs hundreds of thousands of dollars. These dollars didn't pass through banks, a topic I would return to later in my conversations here in Truck Stop.

> "OK," I said. "You buy a truck, you load it up with, let's say, beer. How many tons can you carry?"
>
> Depends on the truck, *he replied.* Thirty to forty, some up to fifty tons.
>
> "That's a pretty big outlay of cash," I said.
>
> But you don't think in terms of one truck, *another man added.* You think in terms of fifty, a hundred trucks all sent by the same guy to make a run. Think of fifty trucks—like two thousand tons—of beer, or whatever it is you're carrying.
>
> Yes, but look at our route. We cross the border and then hit . . .
>
> *The first speaker listed off their route city by city, across the provinces of Angola.* The entire trip takes us about seventy days. Seventy days, can you imagine? We really suffer, this trucking is a life of suffering. A hard life.

The man charted out a route across the border and through Angola to Luanda that made a complete circle of the country — across both the only open and somewhat safe corridor linking the major urban and industrial cities along the western coast, held largely by the government, and swinging across resource-rich but embattled provinces and diamond areas, as well as large tracts of rebel-held territories in the eastern part of the country. They then completed their trip swinging back across rough lands held as much by bandits as by government and rebel forces to the border post, to the beginning of another cycle.

The description of the route was in part just that: an explanation of a trucker's existence. But it was also a deeper comment on the kinds of ironies that attend to this life, and to the very nature of commerce. The truckers supplied the entire country, moved resources, serviced both/all sides, and also linked into larger regional and international trade flows. Some of the goods they picked up here at the border post could well be off-loaded at another border or port and shipped to, say, Europe or Latin America, in the curious set of exchanges that marks global exchange, tariff-skirting, and extra-legal profiting.

> "Don't you worry about attacks, problems, troops?" I asked.
>
> I am military, *replied the man who had charted the route for me. He swept his eyes along the hot, dusty street and the metal and plaster warehouses that shimmered in the desert sun like mirages, and then looked out beyond the town to some distant place invisible to the rest of us and said:*
>
> I spent a year in Spain, taking a course with the police. God, I love that place.

.   .   .

Gina and I gave the truckers nicknames, both to keep anyone in earshot from knowing who we were talking about and also to capture some of the flavor of their lives. That commerce, development, profiteering, and the questionably il/legal were combined in these people's lives isn't a far analytical reach. But perhaps, in a world fed on cheap gangster movies where the "underworld" survives by intimidation and violence — where miners, truckers, "traders," and profiteers are portrayed as uneducated toughs with bad clothes and profane monosyllabic utterances — the nicknames pointed toward the larger realities shaping people's lives.

The military man who charted the trucking route for me gained his nickname soon after that discussion. After he explained their seventy-day trip, I asked what they brought back to this country from their own in this trade circuit.

> Dollars.
>
> "Dollars, that's it?" I asked.
>
> It's tough, there's not a whole lot our country produces to sell on the open market. *The men paused in thought.* Sandals, *one replied. And everyone chorused,* Oh yeah, some really good sandals.
>
> I asked where the sandals were made, and when they told me the city on the coast in central Angola, I knew the products; I had met some of the men who made them, and had bought a pair myself earlier in the year.
>
> Sandals, ah, sandals, and . . . and . . . Hey, want to see the sandals? *the military trucker asked me.*
>
> "Sure," I said.

The trucker and I walked over to his truck. He opened the door to the cab, climbed in, and reached behind the seat to grab a plastic bag with two mismatched used sandals. They were definitely the same manufacture of sandals I had encountered previously. But clearly these were not the story. The trucker turned to finish his earlier sentence:

> Ah, sandals, and diamonds.

He pulled a tissue out of his pocket, unwrapped a diamond, and handed it to me.

> I have ten in my pocket now like this.

"Business," for the players, is done as simply as that.

As I handed the diamond back to him after admiring it, I looked at

him sitting in his cab and mentioned that he looked like he was in his
home.

God, no. It's a hard life, *he replied.*

It was hard, I realized. He had the telltale sores that marked AIDS.
This was one of the tragedies of trade: commodities that made life easier,
sexually transmitted diseases, and the medicines that cured them or
promised illusory treatments all traveled together. In this region of the
world, a third of the population is HIV positive. Among the trucking
population and along the trade routes, the figures are generally much
higher. What would happen to these economies when one-third of the
adult workforce succumbed to this illness?

It's a life that's hard on you, he repeated as he climbed down from the
cab.
"Do you have children back home that you are missing?"
No, *he replied softly.* No family. I just work. I'm traveling and working, sav-
ing up money.
"What are your plans, what do you want to do with the money? Give up
the hard life and settle down?"
No, not that really. I think I would like to save up enough money to go to
Spain and live out my days there. It's such a good place, *he said with a dis-
tant look in his eyes, looking across time to Spain.*

Then he stopped and turned to look at me, dropping his guard for a
moment to convey to me what he knew to be true: he was a man
doomed by a microbe he would never see. He would never have a family, and he wouldn't live in denial and try to lie his way into making one.
He would make the money he could while he could, and then try to retire
and die in the most peaceful place he knew.

We returned to the beer joint and rejoined the group. Just as we sat
down, the man with the diamonds pointed to the front pocket of his
jeans, a reminder to me that if I changed my mind and wanted to do
"business," just let him know. Gina, who had remained behind, and who
spoke neither the language of the men nor that of smuggling, saw a man
who clearly had AIDS return from his truck with me and point to what
she assumed was his crotch. "Rocks," I said to her in English. The first
nickname.

Undeterred by the fact that she and the men at the table shared no
common language, Gina had been trying to ask them what people in the
region thought of Jonas Savimbi's death. The infamous head of the

Angolan rebel group UNITA, Savimbi had been shot to death by government troops that month. A picture of his corpse graced the front pages of newspapers from Cape Town to Cairo. A soft-spoken man was responding to Gina's question and asked me to translate for her. He had explained earlier that he was married to a German woman who taught agronomy at the university in his hometown across the border. Gina and I had seen the man walking down the road the night before and had commented that he was cutting-edge fashionable: he looked like a musician or MTV model and was wearing a great-looking pair of boots, arguably the only ones in the town. We dubbed him "Boots."

> This isn't just about Savimbi, nor is it just about the war in Angola. In fact, it isn't just about war. It's about superpowers, and it's about business. Savimbi's death isn't a national reality, it's an international negotiation. America is the only real superpower player these days. Back when it served America's interests, they supported Savimbi directly. For a while thereafter, it served America's interests to have the war, to have Savimbi.
>
> But that has changed. Now, as an uncontested superpower, America has found a friend in the Angolan government.

The man was referring to the fact that in Cold War days the Marxist government with its links to the communist block was a nemesis to the USA. With the end of cold-war contestations, American oil companies were doing a booming business with the "socialist democratic" government of Angola.

> America doesn't have time to play around now, it's ready to do business, big business, oil business. Savimbi no longer offers a return on the investment. The war, once profitable, is now a nuisance. America is more interested in a stable environment to do business. The Americans helped take Savimbi out of the equation.
> "Savimbi became obsolete," Gina said.
> Business. Savimbi died of international business, *the trucker smiled. He swept his hands wide to gesture to the bustle of commerce all about.* But, *he added in a gentle voice,* Angola has lived in sadness, and this sadness, for now, still marks her people. The sadness of bearing these hardships of war on their flesh.

Gina and I expanded the speaker's name to "Boots — The Philosopher," because he would have been as equally at home on an MTV set or in a university coffeehouse discussing economic theory.

A third member of this group got his nickname later that evening when Gina and I moved down the road to a pool hall where I could "continue interviews," truck-stop style. Gina turned out to be a pool shark, which is a boon to any anthropological investigation. "American Vacation," as we soon called him, sauntered up to talk and play a game of pool.

> I'm thinking of taking a vacation in America, in the USA, *he said.* It's a bit hard for us to figure prices here. Do you think $20,000 would be enough for a visit? That, and my diamonds, of course.
> "Ah, yes, I think that will get you there and back. How long does it take you to get that kind of money trucking?" I asked.
> Not long. Couple of months max. Money, *he shrugged, indicating it was something insubstantial,* dollars, it's just dollars. I have $6,000 in the cab of my truck now. Just there. No big deal.
> "Don't you ever worry about being robbed?"

It was a question that would occur to me time and again, as I began to realize the kinds of hard cash that people hand-carried through this border post.

> Naw, *he said casually.*

Robbery really did seem to be a distant possibility to the people here. Gina and I had walked through every nook and cranny of the town, both day and night, and had encountered nothing but calm in the midst of millions of dollars. But the truckers didn't take risks:

> Of course I'm always armed, *he added.*
> "Big arms," I asked, meaning assault weapons, "or small?"
> Small, a gun. *He patted his stomach, indicating the gun tucked in his jeans.*

I realized that like every man in the place, he had a long and somewhat baggy T-shirt hanging out over pants. Fashion wear for guns.

American Vacation was taken with Gina's pool-playing abilities. With good-humored banter, he said:

> Hey, ask your friend if she wants to come to the USA with me. Tell her I have $30,000 and five diamonds this size *(indicating most of the top knuckle of his finger)* at my house across the border. If Gina will come to the USA with me, I'll give her two of the diamonds and $10,000.

I translated for Gina, and they fell into light-hearted market-haggling repartee in sign language about a trip to America. At one point "American Vacation" turned to me and said seriously:

> You know, if you two really want to go, we can pop across the border and collect the money and diamonds; I really could use a vacation.

There was no doubt in my mind that he had this kind of money sitting at his house, and the networks to gain a "valid" passport and visa.

. . .

Camaraderie and dollars. The two key themes of this chapter, and the two key themes that explain why unregulated flows work.

Much of the currency the truckers and businesspeople carry is unregulated. Quite simply, unregulated money can't pass through formal banking systems, wire transfers, bank drafts, checks, or any other means of paper or electronically "safe" exchange. That means people use informal banking systems or carry dollars. Given the amount of buying and selling done at this one border post alone, that's a lot of dollars — a theme summed up in a conversation with a warehouse manager:

> "What all do you take as payment?" I asked.
> Dollars, dollars, or dollars, *he laughed.*

We were walking through his warehouse, and I stopped to look at a mountain of packaged beer and soft drinks.

> "Thirty or forty tons of beer is a lot of dollars," I noted. "Do people just walk in and hand you the cash, or do they ever use banks?"
> People are scared of the banks. *He smiled and winked: the money, clearly, couldn't go through banking systems.* They come in with cash.
> "But that, quite physically, is a huge amount of cash. Do people walk in with suitcases, boxes, trunks of dollars, and hand them to you for payment?"
> Of course, *the manager answered.*
> "Doesn't anyone find this unusual? Aren't people scared to be walking around with this kind of money?"

My question, it seems, was the only thing the manager found unusual.

It was the day after American Vacation had tried to take my pool-playing friend to the USA, and we ran into the entire group as we left the warehouse and walked down the street. They were at a new beer joint, where they called to us to join them; they were buying several tons of whiskey. With dollars. The transaction was done at a plastic table sitting in the sand outside the tiny, pink-colored bar to catch the few cool breezes that swirled past. One of their trucks, sitting beside the bar, dwarfed the place in size.

> "You are walking around with enough dollars to buy several tons of whiskey?"

They all nodded absently. It was as if I had asked if they walked in with shoes on. I expanded the question:

> "You are all traveling with enough money to do all your business here?"

I turned to Rocks:

> "You carry enough money to buy a Mercedes truck and all the merchandise to fill it?"

They nodded again, bored with the obvious.

> "Aren't you scared of being attacked?"
> Attacked, why? *They look confused.*
> "You know, robbed?"
> No, *they said simply, as they shared money, plans, and beer together.*

I realized the answer rested in the fact that the men had confidence in one another, and in the rules of the game. They knew who to do business with, how to do it, where to do it, and when. Only those stupid enough to try to do business without knowing the ropes get in trouble. Or those who break the rules.

Camaraderie is a glue that holds the networks together.

Rocks, Boots — The Philosopher, American Vacation, and their group were always together when we saw them doing business. They traveled together, ate and drank together, bought tons of whiskey and new Mercedes trucks together. And, as American Vacation had reminded me, they were all armed. People like Rocks were with the military and thus could call on a much larger and more dangerous set of backups. This equation is repeated many times in traveling back through the battlezones of their own country, where predatory factions from either side, as well as roving groups of armed bandits, could find looting trucks more profitable then looting entire villages. Rocks asked:

> Do you know how many trucks travel together on the run we will make back on Friday? One hundred and forty.

Diamonds

Raw resources and hot dollars meet up with cool goods that come, quite literally, from all parts of the globe to fuel international economies with hundreds of men, thousands of arms, millions of dollars, and tons of commodities congregating at dusty isolated border posts and inching their way along endless kilometers of remote, pot-holed, battle-scarred roads.

CHAPTER 9

ROMANCING THE STONE
BORDERS AND BUSINESSPEOPLE

While "American Vacation" and Gina were playing pool, a businessman joined me. I asked him:

"Which would you rather have, diamonds or tomatoes?"

It was a question I had been grappling with since seeing the Gov'nor's farm across the border. I didn't expect the question would mean a great deal to someone who didn't know what I was interested in, so I was surprised when he replied:

Depends on what kind of tomatoes.

The businessman had come with his own nickname: "Nod." He had gotten it from his friends, who said he was always smiling and nodding in agreement. He explained the nickname went back to when he was growing up in Mata'lo. Noting the coincidence, I said I had been in that town recently. Nod replied:

I was born in the hospital just down the road from the center of Mata'lo . . .
He gave his birth date. Then he looked me in the eye and said easily, the same year you were born.

To the best of my knowledge, neither Nod nor anyone else in town knew my name, much less the year I was born. I had long since learned that information is the most valuable commodity of all, bar none. The best traders are adept at negotiating both tangible goods and ephemeral knowledge. That people like Nod could know me so well is disconcerting, but I had long since learned it's unavoidable. At least he had accurate information about me — preferable to misinformation, which could lead to potentially dangerous speculation. To balance things a bit, he outlined some of his own history:

> As I said, I was born outside Mata'lo. The hospital was new in those days. Grand. The lands were so rich. We lived well. It's hard to believe, looking at the place today.
>
> The only thing that has not changed is that the province is one of the most diamond rich in the region. And the quality of the gems is very high. In truth, the province boasts the best diamonds.
>
> With the political turmoil and war, we lost everything. Anything and everything we had so carefully accumulated over the years and generations was gone in the blink of an eye. I fled the violence with nothing. I moved through several countries and made and lost several fortunes before sort of settling here at the border. I suppose my heart is still with Mata'lo, but the money is here.

He paused and looked outside at the bustle of commerce and the many trucks parked in the sand near the building.

> Do you have any idea how much money passes through this border post? How many dollars? How many millions? This small place, this town, this is the most important commercial point in the whole country. It's the "dollar generator."

Laughing, he added:

> And it's not even the diamonds. This is not a major route for diamonds. They travel a different route. I tell you, I know. I buy diamonds.

I returned to my original question:

> "OK, since you're from Mata'lo, you know the Gov'nor's farms, and you know the realities of the diamonds. Would you rather have a mining concession, or the farms and the produce—the tomatoes, so to speak?"
>
> That's a tough one. You know, it's difficult to say. Truth is, you can make a lot of money on tomatoes. And with tomatoes, you have other things. You have potatoes. You have all the things that link in. It's not just the tomatoes that sell. It's all this. You have gains on so many other things. And then you expand out from there. With this, you have trade, and through this you develop structures. And then you find this leads to development: you get schools, a hospital. You get so many possibilities.

I asked where the Gov'nor's "tomatoes" were sold. It was common knowledge that most staples were imported into the country, and that with some 60 percent of the population suffering some form of food deprivation, many relied on international food aid programs for survival. Did the Gov'nor's tomatoes remain in the country? Or were they exported? Did Nod see them coming down this way? Nod snapped his fingers:

> Out. Out of the country. Gone. Fast. No questions. To Europe. Mostly Europe, a bit to South Africa. But mostly to France, Portugal, Switzerland.

He explained, his voice turning soft:

> Listen, the Gov'nor's power is absolute. Complete. Consider what this means. Nothing moves without his approval. He puts his tomatoes on an Air France, or TAP, or you name it flight, and that is it. Period. Gone. Sold. Sold for real profit.

I pondered Nod's statement that nothing moved without the Gov'nor's approval. Was he saying, between the lines, that I should understand that airlines themselves felt vulnerable, and were thus linked in to the Gov'nor's networks, however many shells of legality provided an acceptable aura of legitimacy? He continued:

> The Gov'nor knows everyone. He knows control. He *is* access.
> It's like the military in Angola, in the region, and the trade that passes through this border post. The trucks that come down across the border, the dollars they bring, the commodities they buy and transport back to sell . . . this is all done by the military. The military controls the trade. Oh, it's not like direct military control: it's an ownership. Business. Trucks, trade, profits, these may not be in a general's name directly. There are ways these things are done. He may be a step back from direct recognition. But it's his.
> And remember, you are talking about trade of sizable proportions. It's not one truck, trading. A run is fifty, seventy-five, a hundred trucks. All sent by the same general. And that's just a single run.

I thought back to the man I had spoken with in Mata'lo who did "business." He had carefully explained to me that doing business meant doing business with the military:

> If you don't have the military's blessings—that is to say, if you are not partnered with them—your trucks will be burned. Period.

"Doing business" involves intricate relationships. In a diamond-rich area across the border, I had heard that a local United Nations representative was running diamonds — but also doing a good job at his human-itarian work. I asked Nod if he had heard of this.

Of course, *he nodded—and smiled.*

. . .

Fragment

The snapshot of the border post and the truckers who bring it to life is only a small sliver of the story surrounding the commodities they carry.

Consider the process whereby hyper–twenty-first-century global cap-ital and the extra-legal are infused in the proverbial "anywhere":

NCR
– *Governments may allow business "irregularities" for the sake of national profits. Places like the border post accommodate this trade.* Governments need foreign exchange, and they need access to international markets. Duty-free zones, economic processing zones, free trade zones, non-bank dollar licenses, and trade deals (which reduce taxes for national social services) are common answers. Governments may be willing to turn a blind eye to the realities that accompany these zones: unregulated trade, illicit dol-lars, undeclared goods, smuggling, currency speculation, money laundering, and innovative forms of profiteering.

It's here, in these vast sets of intersections of local and international trade, complex tax regulations, and negotiations over the very nature of legal-ity that a country's fortunes are made.

– *The dollar-for-goods system is customized for speculation and profiteer-ing.* The warehouse managers told me their exchange rate for dol-lars was 3 to 5 percent below the official bank rate. But, as they told me earlier, "People doing business here are scared of banks." Banks represent tariffs, regulations, monitoring, and control. Less scrupu-lous bankers can blackmail or divert funds. Armed truckers can fend off masked bandits; they have far less ability to fend off the impersonal institutional bureaucracy of banking systems and any bandits these might harbor.

– *Extra-state speculation reaps far-reaching rewards.* Businesspeople can take their foreign currency straight to the bank — exchanging for local currency reaps an immediate profit. But that locks them into formal economy regulations and leaves their profits open to

how do we get past the fragment

investigation. Or they can speculate on the open market, using their cash variously to purchase more international goods, to manipulate legal markets invisibly, to trade in unregulated commodities, to provide "loan services," to make offshore investments, and to engage in currency speculation and conversion.

The chief detective for fraud investigation in the country hosting the border post told me that one of the unit's major activities was busting currency speculators:

> We are always making a raid. And it's always someone's house. The Chinese are major players. We go out to some guy's house, some big nice house in town or out in a peaceful suburb neighborhood, and we raid it. You go in and open up any cupboard, any closet, like you walk into the kitchen and open up the pantry, and it's filled bottom to top with piles of cash. They buy and sell money. People just go round and exchange whatever they need and have a cup of tea. You can't believe the amount of money you can find in a single house. And there are tons of these places. We bust one and they just pack up and move down the block and open up shop again in another house. It's huge business. We make raids and we make more raids, and we don't put a dent in the business.

Apparently, currency speculation is far more profitable than the average economic textbooks on commodity trade indicate. Economists in the region explained to me that centuries ago when international ships plied trade across the world's major continents, they found the resources of Africa extremely profitable and the need for urban goods great. But the real profits lay in the buying and selling of currencies.

The fact that money is exchanged out of suburban houses or that trade takes place at exchanges in remote locales does not mean they are isolated in terms of global economies. The money traded out of someone's kitchen pantry may have arrived from anywhere in the world. It will be used to buy products from an equally wide range of production sites. The notion that ethnic groups constitute mafias that work unto themselves is hopelessly outdated. Certainly, people sharing a common language and heritage, like the truckers, may work together and protect one another. But, like multinationals, profit is in international exchange, complex partnerships, extended networks of alliance, and a working knowledge of global finance.

Rational behavior

The final point in this process is the somewhat radical notion that, in actual economies (those not reckoned solely in terms of formal legal

Magnitude / Fragmentary images.

*exchanges but in terms of all exchange, regardless of legality), every loca-
tion — the proverbial everywhere — simultaneously serves as offshore
investment and local development.* The dollars the truckers bring
across the border fuel local development, international currency
speculation, and global commodity acquisition. . . . and then they
are reinvested back into the same cycle of commerce at a profoundly local site.

.   .   .

At every point in this process, the commercially legal, the criminally illegal, and the merely mundane intersect. The fraud detective who told me
about money speculation turned to a topic I heard every time I visited this
country:

> We are having a real problem with people stealing copper wiring. It's really
> harming our telecommunications industry. Long stretches of isolated wiring
> are ripe for the plucking by thieves.

He then added the international flavor:

> One of the biggest scrap-metal dealers in the country has a house the
> likes of which you can't believe. Beautiful. Luxurious. Built on shady deals.
> I'm not saying anything, but he has run into the law. All that copper wiring
> has to get out somehow. Useless unless a person can sell it. And let me tell
> you, the good ones have a lot to sell. Scrap metal comes from all kinds of
> places, some legal, some illegal. The scrap-metal merchant is supposed to
> get all the proper certificates. But a huge amount of metal passes through
> his gates. Can he check it all? Is he likely to? Does he want to?
>
> You say scrap metal, and it doesn't seem like such a big deal, but he
> makes a fortune. He gathers the metal, bulks it, ferries it to the coast, packs
> it in containers, and sends it worldwide. Great way to launder out all kinds
> of stolen stuff into the world.
>
> Speaking of moving stuff, a huge amount of furniture moves across the
> borders of this country, people moving in, moving out, moving furniture to
> sell. They pack it on these huge lorries and head out across the border. And
> then the guys doing the moving pack drugs in between the furniture and
> carry it across the borders. You have a large amount of trucks crossing the
> border posts daily, hourly. How can you tear apart every furniture lorry?

For the fraud detective, currency speculation, stealing copper wiring,
and drugs packed into everyday trucking items are all major headaches.

He would be, he admitted, hard-pressed to say where the greatest gains emerge, where economic power is kindled, or what practices most undermine the formal economy and the health of the nation.

Business is done in the ebb and flow of il/legalities. These are so basic to commerce that only the smallest percentage is captured by the law. This is in part because law officials can't, so to speak, empty the ocean with a cup. But it's also because the unregulated is intrinsically interwoven into formal business in a way that judicial systems can't easily separate. Even determining where the lines of the il/licit can or should be drawn is a judicial challenge. To attack certain fonts of unregulated trade would be to attack some of the fonts of the economy in general — and the business leaders who control them. This point can be illustrated in the stories of two average businessmen, two friends — Nod and Tiago, at two border posts — one official and one unofficial.

· · ·

The day Gina and I were leaving Truck Stop, I ran into Nod. I mentioned that we were heading to a town down the road I'll call "Kalunga." It too was a border town, but one without any formal or legal border post. Nod pulled out his cell phone, punched a number, and told his friend, "Tiago": "I'm sending two women your way; give them a hand." He then gave us directions to Tiago's shop in Kalunga. And thus, in the soft ring of a cell phone, networks are forged. Perhaps Nod made a second call; or perhaps Tiago had an Internet and intelligence system as sophisticated as Nod's. Shortly after I met Tiago, he mentioned the year he was born. I noted that it was the same year his friend Nod was born.

I know, *Tiago replied.* The same year you were born.

Borders run the length of a nation's politics and the gamut of its business practices. Whereas Truck Stop openly services transregional routes, Kalunga sits on a more informal channel for supplies and the diamonds and dollars that pay for them. As no legal border post existed in the area, all border crossings were unauthorized, and all cross-border trade unregulated and untaxed. People walked, drove, and flew commodities and arms across the border. To allies, this constitutes important aid. To traders, this is good business. To international law enforcement, this is illegal. Decades of war in the region have given rise to well-established supply routes that merge from points across the globe to sites such as Kalunga — facilitating exchanges that can be as lucrative and as dynamic as those in Truck Stop — just not as legal.

Kalunga is very different from Truck Stop. No road crosses the border. No large tracts of warehouses define the town center. No bustle of non-stop commercial activity marks its streets. It is, by outward appearances, a rather sleepy hamlet. Deals done under the cover of night, at uncharted airstrips, along unmarked border crossings in the bush, and through unlicensed dealers deliver less clearly visible profits. But the profits come at a price, Tiago explained:

> When the government troops were preparing for the attack on the [rebel-held] town across the border, they brought the largest cargo planes they had, flew them across the border here to Kalunga, filled them with stocks from the warehouse, then flew all this booty back to their country to sell.
> But it wasn't easy: these guys came in swaggering, throwing their weight around. Demanding this, taking that, not wanting to pay. "Do you know who we are?" they would demand. "Who do you think you're dealing with?"

I asked about a story I had heard in Angola earlier that year. I had been told that government troops had been paid in beer, and a lot of this had been brought in from Kalunga. The payment of troops has long been a sore point: months would go by without soldiers receiving any remuneration. The prevailing opinion was that troops were encouraged to get money by fleecing or looting the populace. Beer was an interesting development on this.

> Of course, *he replied.* Soldiers would rather have beer than local currency. They can drink it, they can barter it, they can sell it, even for dollars if they want.

So, it seemed, the military flew into Kalunga, filled their largest military cargo planes with every conceivable good, and purchased beer to pay their troops.

Again, the story does not begin and end with diamonds and military supplies. In Kalunga, "tomato" profits are quietly amassed in numerous ways. Cattle and other herd animals are big business: meat graces the tables of most people in the world. In the interstices of war — in the wide stretches of sparsely populated land no army easily controls — herders raise prime stock, stock that easily walks across borders. "Mechanical stock" — vehicles — also move easily across unmarked border routes. A trucker explained to me that stolen vehicles from South Africa were taken to Angola and then moved across the border here, even though a more direct route existed from South Africa:

> It's stupid to drive stolen cars from South Africa directly to their destination. People prefer to route them to my country and then just drive them here to sell again. It's really easy. In the many kilometers of border between these two countries, long stretches of empty bush, there are a couple crossing points that are popular. My friends drive across cars, my brothers drive their trucks on full hauls. It all works. Everyone grows rich.

Tomatoes, cattle, and cars — and of course the Sonys, furniture, medicines, and industrial equipment that travel alongside these — don't make the front pages of *Le Monde* or the *Wall Street Journal,* nor do we hear the term *blood cows,* as we do for diamonds. While there are attempts to calculate illicit diamond routings and earnings, little is done to chart highly profitable exchanges "on the hoof."

Tiago laughingly lamented the fact that in the Truck Stop area, one often saw people with tiny little stores driving fabulous new expensive cars, talking on the world's most sophisticated cell phones, and dressed in the latest fashions from Europe. They had all the fortune, he implied: the right locale, the right contacts, the right political support, the right stuff. In contrast, Kalunga was lost in the midst of the overgrown stretches of border, lacking any formal posts or transit routes.

This conversation took on added meaning the day Gina and I tried to leave Kalunga. On the way out of town, her car broke down, and we were unable to travel. It was a national holiday, and every business in town was closed. We went to ask Tiago for advice, and he said he happened to have the parts we needed. We stopped by his house to get some tools. A simple wall enclosed the unprepossessing premises. But upon entering the gate, we saw a driveway with two European sports cars, two fully loaded 4 × 4s, three of the small trucks Africans call "bakkies," and a brand-new luxury car that sells for more than $100,000. Not to mention the dirt bikes and the family car his wife had at home, plus the SUV Tiago was driving. All sitting in the shade of blossoming fruit trees outside a gracious villa. I remembered his comment about people in Truck Stop with small stores and fancy cars.

Staring at the scene, I asked Tiago if he had ever seen the movie *Romancing the Stone.* In it, Michael Douglas and Kathleen Turner knock on the door of a seemingly simple farmhouse with a small, dusty wooden porch, and are then ushered into a stunning villa.

Tiago just smiled. He had seen the movie.

INTERNATIONAL BORDER (AND THE QUESTION OF SECURITY). SOUTHERN AFRICA.

CHAPTER 10

THE WASHING MACHINE
LAUNDERING, PART ONE

> In reality, there is no shifting frontier of money laundering. From the very beginning, money laundering occurred using exactly the same methods, and passing through exactly the same institutions, as legitimate finance. As a result, it isn't only extremely difficult to detect and deter, but attempting to do so imposes a regulatory burden whose social costs probably now far exceed any benefits in terms of crime control.
>
> NAYLOR (2002: 194)

Dirty money — generated outside of the formal economy — is useless. Money that can't buy property, construct businesses, enter banking systems, purchase commodities, or speculate on equities is worth no more than a piece of paper. A diamond that can't be sold doesn't even make a good paperweight.

A VIAL OF GOLD

A casual comment made in what Africans call a "cool drink shop" sparked this analysis of laundering. The place was nothing fancy: it boasted a single plastic table and four chairs and stood on a dirt lane off the only tarred road in town. Rogue winds and passing cars blew dust across the doorstep. The bush winds were the greatest threat; few cars passed by. The hamlet was a fraction of the size of Truck Stop or Kalunga. Like those much bigger towns, it nestles up against the border, but no formal border post exists. A simple outdoor market, a few small shops and restaurants, and a decent range of social services — schools, clinics, churches — dot the area. It seems a sleepy remote village by any definition. I asked the woman serving Fanta and sandwiches if many people came across the border to do business.

> Sure, *she replied casually.*
> "How do they pay?" I continued.
> Anything: dollars, diamonds, gold . . . We see it all.

A man in his twenties standing at the counter came over to join the conversation. He was casually dressed in expensive Nikes, a Chicago Bulls shirt, stylish shorts that looked like J. Crew, and a good-looking gold watch.

> A lot. *He paused to underscore the significance of his comment.* I mean a lot of money passes through here. This is a very rich town. I mean very rich.
> Payments, you ask. One of the most popular are the small glass vials— he pulled one out of his pocket—filled with gold. This tells you a lot. This town is very rich.

I asked the man what he did in the town.

> Oh, business. That, and I'm in the police.

Gold is mined throughout Southern Africa, and it is anyone's guess if it flows more easily along legal or illegal channels. For example, Peter Gastrow (2001b) estimates that 35.6 tons of gold were stolen *per year* from South African mines from 1994 to 1998.

For me, this comment about payments in little glass vials of gold catalyzed a more complex view of laundering. Recent conversations I'd been having about economic activities intersected:

- Dollars *are* business.
- People are scared of banks.
- People with simple little shops drive expensive cars.
- Truckers can cross the legitimate border post to purchase goods and then at the end of their run cross back via an unmarked border road.
- Everyone talks gems, but the untaxed trade in cattle is huge.
- The military paid the troops in beer.

– The detectives in the fraud unit may spend more time trying to bust people who steal copper wire than they do trying to bust people engaged in currency fraud and drug dealing.

These conversations now made more sense — and the conventional wisdom I had heard on money laundering was turned on its head. The prevailing analyses were far too restricted and simplistic to meet the real challenges of the business world of the twenty-first century. A conversation in Kalunga, again in a cool drink shop, illuminated the deeper realities of the world of laundering. Curiously, it is here, on dusty streets and cool drink shops, amid the hustle of commerce both legal and illegal, that I found the core dynamics of laundering — not in banks and money-laundering laws.[1]

TIAGO'S REFRIGERATORS

It was late afternoon, and I was sitting in Tiago's shop. Usually a popular hangout, the place was empty except for us. The phone rang, and when Tiago answered it, his face became serious. He put down the phone and explained that a convoy of trucks was coming down an unmarked border road carrying a consignment of commodities for him, and one of the trucks had disappeared. I didn't ask if he thought the driver had tried to abscond with a truckload of goods, if he was running from bandits or border guards, or if he had just had a blowout and was off the radar screen. Tiago might have had his suspicions, but as a good businessman, he kept his options open. He needed to be able to provide help in a moment if the truck was in danger, or quick retribution if the driver was stealing. But he did explain why it was important: the truck was carrying a cargo worth over $65,000 wholesale (extra-legal), worth much more on the street.

Tiago's response was immediate. He first contacted an international group of associates by cell phone and sat-com (satellite communication) gear. He pulled up his computer to check transit, flow, and routing channels. All this was at his fingertips, just behind the counter. He swore as the computer booted up and he encountered a glitch in the system. His son had a degree from a leading British university, he explained, and kept him in the latest technology and upgraded software programs — creatively tailored to suit his needs. But his son was out of town. Juggling his new computer, sat-com gear, cell phone, and a sheaf of printouts, he called his son. He explained the situation and said that he had to get online immediately to track this problem. An animated dialogue ensued about how to find the best information on the truck and who to contact to get help as the son walked his father through the computer repair. In the midst of all this, Tiago sent an e-mail to his lawyer, located in a major urban city, and to his financial consultant.

I realized Tiago was talking to people both nationally and internationally. The networks he could activate at a moment's notice were powerful and they were global. I smiled to myself at the irony: here was Tiago, wearing torn jeans and a tattered T-shirt, leaning against the counter of the local hangout in a dusty little African town far from any officially recognized commercial routes. The average passerby might wonder if the electricity worked with any consistency in this town, never guessing that the rough bars and cafés held state-of-the-art electronics and communications gear that the computer professors at my university would be happy to own.

Tiago got his computer up and running, gathered the information he needed, sent several messages, told his son the latest family gossip and a joke, and then took a moment to grab a Pepsi and fill me in on what was going on.

First of all, the missing truck had been carrying refrigerators. They'd been picked up that day at Truck Stop and were being transported to Kalunga. In the first phone call he received, he was told that the truck had crashed and the driver had disappeared. He had no way of knowing if that was the truth or not. Was the truck really damaged, or did the driver abscond with it? If it was damaged, had the driver been attacked by renegade troops or bandits? Did he crash it himself to make off with the merchandise, or was it really an accident? Each possibility demanded a different and very politically nuanced set of responses. Errors of judgment could be lethal. With a smile, Tiago said that if the trucker thought he could just disappear with a fortune of commodities on a lonely stretch of outback savanna, he was seriously mistaken.

I asked Tiago if he had any insurance; he just looked at me.

The pieces of the puzzle gradually fell into place: Tiago was buying from the dollar-only warehouses at Truck Stop, where Nod, Rocks, Boots — The Philosopher, and American Vacation did their business. By law, only foreigners could do business at these commercial duty-free zones, and Tiago was a local. Imported cosmopolitan goods command hefty tariffs and taxes in most countries in Africa. Thus, those available duty free (and illegally) are treasures in their own right. Tiago bought duty-free merchandise with dollars — and along unrecorded channels —

from the border post warehouses. To get the dollars, he had to work the extra-legal markets: arms for diamonds for food for gas for international commodities for . . . refrigerators. To complete this set of business circuits, he couldn't simply send his trucks along the bumpy washed-out road from Truck Stop to Kalunga. So his drivers crossed the border into Angola; traded merchandise for diamonds for dollars; journeyed along roads wrecked by years of war; then drove back across the border at an unmarked spot, taking the poorly guarded back roads to Kalunga. Common practice, and completely illegal.

REWRITING THE TEXTBOOKS ON LAUNDERING

Men such as Tiago and their "offices" provide a window on how unregulated economies have grown into a multi-trillion-dollar global phenomenon, and they are a key to understanding money laundering in the twenty-first century.

Tiago is a textbook on laundering — one that all law enforcement personnel should read. While authorities are trying to bust laundering by looking for large sums of cash entering banking and financial systems from "shady" sources, the Tiagos of the world — the vast bulk of launderers — are using far more sophisticated systems that no one is monitoring. Quietly and efficiently they are amassing invisible fortunes. No wonder so little progress is made in curbing laundering.

Laundering is seldom a linear set of transactions moving illicitly earned cash directly into licit banking and business systems. The sheer complexity that can mark laundering renders the process almost impossible to chart, much less curtail.

Tiago's is the story of millions of businesspeople. He owns several legitimate businesses. Some stores deal in commodities, which justifies buying trucks, brokering merchandise, setting up financial and investment networks. These stores can move goods across the boundaries of the law with relative ease. Some of his other legitimate businesses deal in service and entertainment, businesses long known as easy means of moving unrecorded monies into formal economies. Restaurants, bars, hotels, casinos, tourist services, currency exchanges, and the like are efficient laundering points. Finally, some of his businesses deal with production: farming, mechanics shops, and light industry. Sites of enterprise that bespeak the salt of the earth. Few investigations of laundering scrutinize farms or auto repair shops.

Tiago's many business interests necessarily involve politics. He must survive the vicissitudes of political upheaval, changing political regimes, war, the ironies of development, and natural disasters. To some, he is a hero: he has been known to run arms to desperate troops across the border. To others, this makes him a scoundrel. Arms and refrigerators. Perhaps the latter is the more profitable in the long run. And, while it may defy conventional wisdom, running household commodities is just as nerve-wracking as running weapons.

Tiago doesn't think in terms of being legal or illegal; he thinks in terms of development. What works best, given the circumstances at hand? He juggles numerous currencies, multiple businesses, complex commodity flows, convoluted transport systems. In the course of a normal day, he breaks and honors laws from many nations. A host of financial advisors, lawyers, accountants, friends, family members, and assorted colleagues assist him. He is an upstanding member of the community: his businesses bring in critical taxes and resources; he is reliable and hardworking. He is part of the commercial dynamism of the community as it struggles to develop. He has banks in-country and in Europe. He buys globally. Money moves into his banks, through his accounts, around his holdings, across continents. Banks love him; he is good business.

No bank would see his deposits as indications of laundering. Tiago himself doesn't think of this as laundering. It's just business.

If you follow precious commodities instead of people, the story is the same. Little glass vials of gold are unlikely to be laundered directly up a chain of middlemen to government stores or retail outlets. Instead, they find their way to sleepy little towns down dusty side roads, towns on unmarked border crossings. They can be traded for stolen cars coming across the border, with enough left over to buy the necessary papers conferring legality. Gold buys food, a stake in a dollar-only warehouse, or cutting-edge digital equipment. A connection with a legitimate business lends an aura of legitimacy to these transactions.

Latin American drug cartels have found it useful to send shipments of narcotics intended for Europe through these Southern African countries. While they escalate their risk by increasing the number of ports, borders, and checkpoints they must cross, they gain access to goods from Africa, including vials of gold and trade routes that follow inconspicuous shipments of food, beer, furniture, and diamonds. Gold can be traded for refrigerators that can be traded for generators and fuel that powers a remote tourist lodge, which is useful for laundering cash as well. Gold travels back with the empty trucks to the international ports and out to destinations worldwide, where sailors, shippers, and businesspeople have whisked the shiny treasure across lines of authority for millennia.

A shopkeeper smiles at the quality of the gold he is handed, tens of thousands of kilometers from the sleepy unmarked border post where it crossed an undisclosed number of hands, nestled in among tomatoes and copper wire. A little vial of gold is discreetly slipped into a traveler's suit pocket and moves undisclosed across customs. It provides a means to skirt restrictions on the amount of foreign currency that can be taken out of the traveler's home country and will be exchanged, along a complex set of transactions that start with a friend of a friend in Europe, into money to invest in a European business and to pay the traveler's daughter's tuition at an expensive university. Gold that crosses palms to buy beer for the troops will ultimately link into the circuit of sales that diamonds travel as they make their way to metropolitan dealers. The cattle herder in ragged shorts and sandals made of old tire rubber who refuses to recognize national borders on principle sells some of his cattle in Angola for gold, and then carries it back to his village on an unmarked road too small for cars. He uses his cell phone to call the capital city to see when his cousin can manage a shipment of construction materials for his village and its enterprises — for a little vial of gold.

These are the everyday truths of laundering.

Of course, this isn't just the story of gold. It is the reality of il/licit flows. In a very real sense, they represent hope for better days as well as profiteering. As Kadonga sells Sonys and Mercedes, Marlboros and beer, he fulfills his dreams of becoming a businessman. He might even end up a government official, INGO country representative, or military supplier. Who would question his Sonys? They are a boon, not a problem. Perhaps he sells them back across the border to a businessman in Kalunga, along with a shipment of refrigerators and a few diamonds. The rest he keeps to pay for his son's trip to Europe or Asia to do "business."

Businesses like Tiago's and Kadonga's dot the landscapes of development. They stand in zones of transformation, political uncertainty, and need; they represent anchors of stability, economic growth, and exploitation.

Neither moral assessments nor objective comparisons come easily in considering the impact of the extra-legal on a country. Legality (as it has been since the times of prestate empires and robber barons) is a wagon pulled by "progress"; it isn't the engine. Both Kadonga and Tiago profit by acting outside the law. And while they clearly benefit personally, their actions often bring development to their communities. In areas where

infrastructure is weak and governments can provide little in the way of social services, it is people like them who help rebuild regional industry, donate to health and education, and bring in critical resources for the citizenry. This is the ultimate contradiction defining the extra-legal: it can act as both harmful profiteering and positive development — sometimes simultaneously. If fully 80 to 90 percent of Angola's population at the war's end relied exclusively on extra-state resources to survive, then the Kadongas and Tiagos of the country personify this paradox. Yet they do not represent all extra-state players: for example, whereas these men exploit resources and trade routes, the Gov'nor exploits internally displaced people as well. The former tend to reinvest more of their proceeds back into their communities and country than the latter, who tends to invest more in international markets. What legal, ethical, and practical concerns arise in these comparisons? The playing field of global economics isn't equal, and access comes along these complicated networks of truck stops and gold exchanges.

THE UNWRITTEN AD: BANKS LOVE SUCCESSFUL LAUNDERERS

I spoke with several people responsible for laundering-detection programs at leading banks in Europe. Some were responsible for programs teaching financial institutions worldwide about safeguarding against laundering. Their primary concerns were shaped by classical orientations toward laundering: looking for large sums of money entering accounts from unknown sources, from sources without a history of such transfers, from questionable locations, from sources unattached to recognized commercial or financial institutions. They looked for money moved in and out of accounts within a few days, or letters of explanation that offered rewards or percentages to the banks for their services. I asked if banks in cosmopolitan centers of the world would find any reason to question, or investigate, funds coming from an established tourist complex, a respected industry, a viable farm, or a transport company in Southern Africa.

> Of course not; many of our clients come from such locations and backgrounds. In fact, sometimes we send people down to the region to meet the larger clients so as to make the process of international banking and investments more personal; to make it easier for the clients to utilize our services.

I met with a banking team from the United Kingdom that traveled to Southern Africa to maintain good working relationships with their clients there. They were also on tour to teach about laundering. In the course of a relaxed conversation, I asked about their valued customers, describing people like Tiago. They said:

> These people are some of our best customers. So good, in fact, that we travel down here yearly from Europe. We have had good banking relations with these people that span decades, sometimes generations.
>
> "Do you ever worry about laundering with these people?" I asked. "Check them out?"
>
> Good Lord, no. Why would we?

Developer, or
smuggler?

GLOBAL

HOOTERS INTERNATIONAL. RURAL NAMIBIA.

CHAPTER 11

DIAMONDS AND FISH
GOING GLOBAL

A FISH STORY

Before I began this study into the intersections of un/regulated economies, I had absolutely no interest in seafood, other than to eat it. But if you study smuggling and the extra-legal, it seems you can't get away from fish.

On the southern coast of Africa, a number of drug gangs have moved from running illegal narcotics to fish smuggling. Abalone and its cousins are illegally harvested and sold worldwide, but my favorite story is the one about the Patagonian Toothfish.

The Toothfish is an endangered Antarctic sea bass that fetches hundreds of dollars per kilo in the world's markets. Because *Dissostichus eleginoides* is such a mouthful, the fish is sometimes called "white gold" — and this certainly doesn't refer to its looks. The Toothfish represents the classic endangered species/expensive markets cycle. A delicacy in Asia and to some extent North America, it has been fished to dangerously low levels in its natural habitats, and to extinction in some sites. As the prices for smuggled seafood go up, gangs leave less lucrative work, narcotics for example, to get into the fish trade.

Fish don't usually conjure up images of murder and mayhem, but Melanie Gosling, a Cape Town journalist for the *Weekend Argus* who follows the Patagonian Toothfish trade, tells of smugglers and shoot-outs. Shortly before we talked, the police had tried to stop a group of fish and abalone smugglers, and some of the officers had been wounded in the ensuing gun battle.

Gosling explained that poached abalone, crayfish, and Patagonian Toothfish are involved in massive international smuggling networks. The gangs that harvest the fish transfer their products to contacts in other countries who work with freight, customs, and transport personnel to move the goods across international borders. These people then work with middlemen in the purchasing countries to get the proscribed goods to wholesalers and retailers. Without this complex internationalization, the fish would not be endangered. I continued to encounter fish stories as I researched the extra-legal. Each turned out to be a step in my growing understanding of how local economies, smuggling, profiteering, and globalization shape markets and politics — all the way to the United Nations.

BIGGER FISH

John, a South African computer executive, told me the following story. Eight of us were sitting around the dinner table of a leading academic in Johannesburg. John was in his thirties, the product of an urban upbringing and an excellent education: cosmopolitan, witty, intelligent. The people at the table all knew John and his ex-girlfriend, and threw in comments as he told his tale. It was funny to everyone there, but not unusual: these stories were the stuff of everyday life.

My old girlfriend got involved big-time with fish. Profitable, but none too legal. After we broke up, she met a European in the fishing industry, and moved to Namibia, where he was based. He ran a fleet of trawlers, and packed the fish up to the European markets. He made decent money in the coastal waters of Namibia, but it was too regulated for him. Like so many others from all over the world, he ran his trawlers up into Angolan waters. Because Angola has been at war for so long, the national fishing industry has all but dried up, and until all these trawlers arrived, the waters off the coast were teeming with fish.

My old girlfriend's new guy kept running deals up in Angola, and looking for "big" backing. Finally he scored: he partnered up with a general, and somehow managed the sole concession for fishing rights in an impressively large expanse of coastal waters. Because of his partnership, he's exempt from the normal rules, regulations, taxes, and monitoring. Basically, he is working outside the law with an official OK.

That's when things got wild, and I started getting lots of calls from my old girlfriend asking me what she should do. Angola's a wild frontier. Her boyfriend was fishing the place out and running all these scams getting the fish packed and sent to Europe. When someone would come into this guy's turf, he'd call the general, and the general would come along and blast the guys out of the water. National security, and all. It's like something out of the old Wild West movies, and this boyfriend is buying into the whole thing, acting like a cowboy warlord.

I'm told John's ex-girlfriend's boyfriend has been able to retire at a young age with a tidy fortune. And while the world's key diamond producers meet time and again to draft legislation controlling the diamond industry, fish smuggling barely gets a line in a local newspaper.

DIAMONDS ARE A FISH'S BEST FRIEND

Fish don't tend to travel alone. If there is a shipment of drugs to move out, they can easily travel with fish — as can Marlboros, beer, diamonds, and col-tan, the hot mineral critical to cell phones and Sony PlayStations. It isn't uncommon to hear of drugs, diamonds, or even priceless art objects being shipped with fish. What, I began to wonder, did trawlers carry on their way *to* the fishing grounds? Ostensibly, they would be empty — but trawlers kept cropping up in my exploration of the world of extra-legal goods. A leading official at the World Customs Organization headquarters in Brussels, Belgium, offered some insight.

> "When the empty trawlers are heading out to the fishing sites, do they carry commodities?" I asked.
>
> Sure, why would a good businessperson sail empty half the way?
>
> "Are these legal transactions?"
>
> Sometimes, *he said.*
>
> "Are trawlers expected to call at ports and go through legal monitoring in the countries they work in?"
>
> Of course, and some do. But that's not really the point. Ships can stop anywhere at sea, meet up with any other ship at sea, exchange just about anything with anyone at sea — and who is there to monitor? They're floating supermarkets. This is huge — and I can't underscore enough the word *huge* — business.

The linkages kept expanding. In Angola, a man explained to me the human side of diamond smuggling. He told me about average poor citizens caught on the frontlines who had to mine for the military and the concessionaires. Paid a pittance, some were able to pocket a good gem, the promise of some relief in their lives.

I asked him how the stones got from the landlocked marketplace in central Angola to the gem dealers in Europe, for example.

> Well, what comes into town? Food. This food comes in from Portugal. Portugal's connections are stronger here in this area than in other areas, where trade with South Africa is more developed.
>
> This is because of the enduring nature of the old trade routes forged in colonial times and still in place—not because these routes are better or more efficient or smarter or smoother, but because they are in place; habit. So stones follow this old trade routing, Bíe—Luanda—Portugal—Europe.

FISH AND GLOBAL POWER REGIMES

The final piece of the expanding story of fish, politics, and globalization came from a conversation with several senior United Nations economists. I had run into a fascinating conundrum in my research. By UN estimates, Angola's economy in the late 1990s was 90 percent non-formal. But it was impossible to find out empirically how the non-formal economy worked, or the quality and degree of its impact on the nation as a whole. When I asked for reports, indices, and statistics from the United Nations and the World Bank, only formal data were included — without exception. To me, this very *lack* of data was a research goldmine. How could an accurate understanding of a country's economic health — much less viable development programs — be implemented using only one-tenth of a country's economic data? It was a question I put to several leading UN economists.

> People like my friends and myself here will do everything we can to support your work.
>
> "But you have excellent people on the ground in your UN offices worldwide. I've spoken with them and they would love to do this kind of work."
>
> It isn't something we as the UN do.
>
> "Why?" I began to add that their on-site economists had better access than I did.
>
> It's not how we are set up. It's not what we do. It's not in our mandate.
>
> "So, why not change the mandate?"

The senior person in the room stopped for a moment to look at me. He took off his glasses and rubbed his head, signaling that the tone of the conversation was about to change. He leaned across the table toward me and opened his palms in a gesture indicating that he was opening up a difficult truth:

Look, we at the UN have to follow the mandates set out for us, and as important as studying economies outside the formal sector may be, these issues fall outside the realm of our mandate. Period.

He held up his hand to stave off any more questions from me, took a deep breath, and continued:

And why? Look where the mandates come from. They come from the leaders forging UN policy. They come from the leading countries in the world. And think about it, think about all that seafood illegally harvested off the coasts of Africa, for example, and sold around the world. Who do you think is doing that harvesting? Who do you think is selling and eating all that seafood?

You are talking about a huge international set of businesses. About significant profits. About food that graces the tables of millions of citizens in scores of major countries. The citizens of the countries forging our mandates.

Multiply these considerations when it comes to the mined resources of Southern Africa. Then extend that equation out to other "non-formal" goods and services worldwide. Then ask yourself why the UN is specifically not given a mandate to study non-formal economies.

What if we had a mandate to study this, to publish the linkages between informal markets, non-legal resource profiteering, the respected multinational industries of our world's powers, and getting affordable food to their citizens' tables?

who loves?

A VIEW FROM THE TOP: THE ELITE CORPORATE PERSPECTIVE

From the Gov'nor's tomatoes to the flood of illegal weapons, from little Okidi's Marlboros to the shiny Sonys in bombed-out villages, each commodity that moves outside formal channels represents profit for an industry and the country that hosts it.

Extra-state economies are good for business.

Most of Africa relies heavily on non-formal business. More than half of the continent's economies run outside of formal reckoning. But this isn't unusual: half of the economies of Italy, Russia, and Peru are extra-state as well. And they are linked. As the head of Imperial Cigarettes in United Kingdom said, to stay competitive in business, their cigarettes have to be smuggled competitively. So too with weapons, pharmaceuticals, industrial supplies, and currency.

A conversation with the chief financial officer of a well-known multinational corporation — famous in world markets for over two centuries —

gave me an idea of the complexities of the intersections of un/regulated business activities. I was surprised when I entered the corporate lounge and met the man: he seemed too young and too fashionable to be the CFO of such a large and prestigious corporation. "Franklin" looked to be in his early forties and had an easy air about him. He was funny, open, and articulate. He graciously spent several hours talking with me in Johannesburg. He said he would speak honestly as long as I agreed not to use his name or that of his corporation in any deleterious way.

I made it clear from the start that I was interested in gaining a better understanding of how large-scale transnational industries dealt with the realms of the non/formal. During our conversation, Franklin would begin a discussion of this and then move to talk about more formal (legal) issues. He talked about material that was sensitive and restricted, but veered away from actually addressing non-formal activities. He recognized this and, laughing, acknowledged that there was an unspoken but powerful ethic in business that the unregulated — like any taboo topic — is discussed only in certain specific contexts. A formal interview in the imposing corporate lounge is the domain of the public and the published; backyard barbecues, restaurants, clubs, and unofficial office chats are the accepted venue for delving into less-than-formal activities. Finally, he loosened his tie, relaxed in his chair, and said:

> OK, there are many aspects to this. Informal—sure, it's a fact of life. But let's start at the top. I'm responsible for the final economic work of this corporation. I believe in what this company is doing; I'm not going to jimmy the accounts at this level.
>
> But you ask about non-formal activities, and I have to respond. The truth is, look at the guy at each level going out to the field. Start at the top: we have to go into a new country to work a deal with the government and partner business ventures to get a site up and going. This is infinitely more difficult and complex than most realize.

Franklin explained the seemingly endless departments and people you have to work through to get anything done. He warmed to the topic: some, he said, wanted to develop their country legitimately; others wanted personal bribes, kickbacks, larger business venture partnerships. Governments can impose regulations and restrictions that shackle the company from doing what it needs to do to make a profit, or, he said pantomiming consternation, force the company into competition or partnerships with other multinational interests it doesn't want to be associated with. "Like?" I asked. "The real scoundrels," he answered.

We have to juggle all of this. Our people doing these negotiations are on the frontlines, so to speak: they meet at government offices, in boardrooms, at private meetings, behind closed doors. They spend days, weeks, months working out acceptable deals. They come back to us, to the officers, to the board and tell us the final word on what they have managed, and we forge our response. We develop an approach that can meet public scrutiny. But what goes on behind those closed doors, that's their business, their work.

Walk it down a level. So a project gets started in some country. Some guy is out on a production site and he has to get things done. He has to get parts, supplies, labor, contracts, transport, negotiations, you name it. He is beholden to us at corporate headquarters—he has to get things done, done on time, and done cost-effectively. And he is beholden to the conditions and the people out with him. He needs something, and the only way to get it is on the black market. He plays with customs; he crafts "creative" ways to get around policies; he greases the palms of people he depends on. That is how it works. But he doesn't send this to us in a report. He doesn't come up to headquarters or meet with an officer of the corporation and talk about these things. He does it and turns in the kinds of reports the system expects. He gets things done, or he risks losing his job.

You can walk this all the way down the line. The people working for this manager know they have to get the job done. If they don't, there are others willing to step in. And so they do it. And they don't write this up in reports for the site manager any more than he writes it up for us.

I guess we know it. I guess we know how it works. But we don't. Because this all works by not asking. We don't ask the site manger how he got a system up and running. He does, or he doesn't. We ask for the formal reports. We know not to ask for the, ah, details.

This is how the vast non-formal works—how it is both possible and undisclosed at the same time. It is a fact of all business.

The CFO's words capture the local "anywhere" of globalization and the illicit—the daily actions and decisions of a very specific someone in a very specific somewhere just trying to get through his day. The larger networks of business and politics depend on this.

Practicalities and invisibilities.

AND A VIEW FROM THE NEW CENTER: GLOBALIZATION AND A NEW CONCEPTUAL REALITY

These practicalities and invisibilities are larger than mere corporations. They are rooted in a series of political and economic transformations and in complex value systems shared across continents. I brought my questions on non/formal economies and globalization to Augusto Alfredo, the economic correspondent for the national Angolan newspaper, the *Jornal de Angola*. His words capture the underlying heartbeat of this complicated process:

> We are all seeking to regain the things we have lost: formal markets, social-
> ist conditions, fixed values, a life free of the ravages of inflation, the open-
> ing of markets.

Augusto was explaining that people were now living in the midst of tran-
sitions, from socialism to capitalism, across war and peace. With this came
the confusions of emerging forms of taxation, war deprivations, privatization — and new markets opening to cover what the government cannot.
That means — he smiled — they run the gamut of the informal.

> But hey, now we all drink Coca-Cola. The links are there — it's the life. A
> religion. Survival. What is the relevance of the legal and the informal to peo-
> ple in all this?
> To understand, you must think socially. In the city, people are preoccu-
> pied with image, with the imagined . . .

Here Augusto swept his hand around to capture the vast contradictions
that defined Luanda, pointing out his office window to the lean street
vendors and broken streets below, and then to the towering new buildings built with oil and commerce monies. This, he explained, is born of
the intersections of the desperate search for survival and globalization —
the shared dress, shared lifestyle; the influence of our imaginaries and our
imaginations.

> Take this a step further: a German, for example, goes to China. He sees
> the same sun, but everything is strange for him. One day, he finds a
> Mercedes car, and he is happy, delighted. Why does he have this sentiment?
> He identifies with these things, with these objects and objectives. He feels.
> The life is contained in one thing. So you have global people. Consume
> Coke, Big Macs. We eat these things, we watch these films, we drive these
> cars — and we feel the identity of the larger world. The familiar is globalized.
> The frontiers are diluted. If we eat the same food, we think about the same
> things, we have the same preoccupations, the same dreams.
> The desire.
> The global doesn't have a place. This allows people to make contacts
> across places; to consume culture. People become more open to others. It
> is hard to call a person a stranger when you share something.
> And it goes farther. When everything is available in the shops — things
> from worldwide, things shared across cultures — a person "meets" everything.

for food, shelter, mates... meaning purpose?

Looking, searching, is the base of life. This is what is permanent. The frontiers, the borders, are lost and broached. But this means people are more open to the perspectives of another. Sometimes in a person's personal life they have conflicts that are localized, and seem so difficult, and then when they run to another place—in war, in searching, in fleeing—it becomes possible to mediate these conflicts. You pass borders and share with others in a new place, share even the burden of your problems, and you begin to realize that others' cultures are no better or worse—that the solutions rest in the sharing. Globalization is a process of learning, of sharing, lives.

Fish personify the extra-legal; multinational business interests rely on corruption while deleting this fact from their corporate accounts; and for many, a Big Mac is as positive in twenty-first-century imaginaries as it is detrimental. And herein rests the answer as to why corruption is pandemic, multinationals are implicated in the full gamut of il/legal practices, and globalization is about more than power and its spreadsheets.

The roles of the military commanders and political officials are constructed in larger transglobal practices. Layers of in/formalization define interpersonal and intergovernmental trade and industrial relations alike. "Negotiations," signature bonuses, bribes, kickbacks, tax and policy manipulations, customs and excise latitude, layered organizational structures, and a generous notion of what constitutes a fair profit are international realities that shape local responses. Having the ability to define these economies internationally is the zenith of power. Who, making barely poverty-level wages and gaining a little extra informally, will blow the whistle on those at higher administrative levels who do the same, albeit for vastly larger sums?

But the conundrum is far more complicated. If this were simply a matter of skim-offs and kickbacks — personalized corruption — legal and developmental solutions would be straightforward. But, as the story of the shopkeeper Kadonga demonstrates, working around the formal legal system is also, for many, a way to develop, to survive amidst the stranglehold of excessive bureaucracy, onerous policy and taxation requirements, elite control, and fragile infrastructural and developmental systems. If globalization is a dangerous form of economic hegemony, it is also, as the journalist Augusto Alfredo notes, the means by which the displaced war refugee can — in the broadest sense — find the place to survive, and perhaps even flourish.

Globalization is about relationships? Networks, + sharing?!

SOUTH SEA FREIGHTER.

CHAPTER 12

PORTS

Some shores have been tamed, however temporarily, but beyond the horizon lies a place that refuses to submit. It's the wave maker, an anarchic expanse, the open ocean of the high seas. . . . Geographically, it isn't the exception to our planet, but by far its greatest defining feature. By political and social measures it is important too — not merely as a wilderness that has always existed or as a reminder of the world as it was before, but also quite possibly as a harbinger of a larger chaos to come. . . . At a time when every last patch of land is claimed by one government or another, and when citizenship is treated as an absolute condition of human existence, the ocean is a realm that remains radically free.

LANGEWIESCHE (2004)

The war orphan's cigarettes, the shop owner's wares, the military's weapons, the truckers' commodities all tend to journey through ports.

More than 90 percent of world trade is conducted by the international shipping industry. Around 50,000 ships registered in 150 countries are manned by more than a million sailors from virtually every country in the world.[1]

THE ONTOLOGY OF TRADE

To understand economic globalization, it is useful to see the world as traders always have. For them, the world is not neatly divided into sovereign states easily identified as unchanging landmasses with distinct borders and even more distinct rules, laws, and regulations.

Goods move. In the world of trade, goods have their own kind of sovereignty.

In a way, while traders and trade are situated in, and respect, specific local, national, and world contexts, they constitute their own unique — one might say sovereign-like — state. Movement is primary, borders are secondary. Laws, some might argue, are tertiary.

Traders see the uninterrupted flow of commodities, people, and services. Borders, to them, aren't regulated national institutions as much as they are unregulated opportunities. The seas are a broad expanse of profit outside of state jurisdiction, as dynamic a part of the commercial world as industrial centers. Transit is not just the time between two points, but a universe of meaning unto itself. Transport routes are arteries of commodity flow. Taxes and tariffs are obstacles, not obligations. This view is critical to understanding the intersections of il/legality. A state-based actor breaking a law must contend with a land-locked national response: codified laws upholding the canons of the state are backed up by security forces. The transgressor can be taken to a very real jail under national jurisdiction.

But for the trader moving on the high seas, on international rail and road links, walking across unmarked and unmanned borders, this sheer physicality bound to an overarching single sovereign governing system does not exist. A business may take raw fiber from one country, ship it to another to be made into fabric, then transport it to another to be sewn into clothing. It may then ship the clothing to be sold in a country where import taxes are low; but on the way, the ship stops in international waters, where part of the cargo is covertly transferred to yet another ship and smuggled to another country — one with high import taxes. What legal system, what governing body, is seen as an authority structure covering all these transnational exchanges? International law, however powerful its ideas and ideals, remains grounded in national authority. The intersection of fluid global networks and land-based sovereign states opens up a world of economics that falls outside the scope of state intervention.

Trade has always had its own special province, and providence. The fact that much of maritime law today is derived from Rhodian sea law is an indication of both the continuity and the power of the worldview of transnational commerce. The fact that much of our commercial and customary law today derives from ad hoc councils set up in marketplaces along major trade routes like the silk route in the middle ages shows that trade can trump political power. These market courts were revolutionary: in the era of royal rule and kingdoms, they circumvented both kingly control and country-specific interests. They also demonstrated that international associations of people with no formal governing controls could and did institute laws, courts, mediation mechanisms, regulations, and codes of conduct — ones capable of enduring centuries of change from wagon-based transport to cargo jets and massive container ships. In the final analysis, such examples suggest that while governing systems — from kingdoms through dictatorships to the modern state — change, trade practices hold constant.

COMING INTO CAPE TOWN

The cigarettes Okidi sold on the streets of Angola probably came to the continent by ship. So does over 80 percent of the region's goods. In 2002, when I conducted the interviews below, the seven major ports of South Africa handled nearly 200 million tons of cargo and over 14,000 vessel calls. In addition to bulk cargo like petroleum, timber, and coal, South Africa's ports handled approximately 2 million containers, or TEUs (Twenty-foot Equivalent Units), as they are called. These are the classic $20 \times 8 \times 8$–foot metal containers that are the foundations of modern shipping. Cape Town handled 6 percent of this cargo, and over 300,000 TEUs.

Bear with me as we work through the following numbers. They will illuminate the illusion of security and the world of smuggling:

- 3,010 vessels arrived in Cape Town in 2002. That's 250 a month, 58 a week, a little over 8 a day.

- The average small bulk transport ship docking in Cape Town can carry bulk cargo like grains or fertilizers, or 1,000 containers.

- The average container ships carry around 1,700 containers; the sturdier ones, up to 3,000. The large intercontinental ships carry 6,000 containers. New super ships, too big for the Panama Canal, can carry 8,000 to 12,000.

- A typical small ship arrives with 20,000 tons of cargo; a large cargo ship with 120,000 tons. (Legally declared tons, that is. Longshoremen around the world tell me they find single containers overloaded by up to 20 tons.)

To inspect a single container, South Africa National Port Authority representatives must

- bring the ship to berth, assuming one is available;
- bring cranes and stevedores to unload the container;
- put the contents on a vehicle;
- move the container to the container depot;
- make sure sufficient port officials, container depot crew and facilities, and ship or cargo owner's representatives are present to oversee the opening and inspection of the container; and
- unpack the container in the presence of the importer and the agent.

According to Customs and Excise officials, this work takes four to six hours per container for a cursory inspection. A complete inspection of all the goods inside a container can take over a day. If you figure five hours per container, a typical small ship would require 5,000 hours to have its containers inspected. A large ship would demand 30,000 work hours, which adds up to 1,250 days of round-the-clock work — a total of 3.42 years. Per ship.

In Cape Town, a relatively small port, about 10 ships were now arriving a day. There are 150 Customs and Excise staff in the entire port. What are the odds of them stopping even a tiny fraction of smuggled goods?

The most sophisticated ports in the world can inspect a maximum of only 5 percent of the cargo passing through customs, a figure that South Africa tries to match. One percent of the cargo is stopped at random. In South Africa, officials explained to me that of this 1 percent, they find something wrong with more than a third of them. This can range from underdeclaring the value of the goods, wrongly declaring what the goods are, incorrect papers, and improper practices — in other words, smuggling. In Cape Town, there are eight to ten ships in the harbor under arrest at any given time.

To those unfamiliar with the world of shipping, the 5 percent inspection rate may seem startlingly low: 95 percent of all shipments pass uninspected. But even the 5 percent figure is misleading. Nearly 2 million containers pass through South Africa's ports a year. The 1 percent random check covers 20,000 containers: at five hours per container, that adds up to 100,000 work hours, or 4,167 round-the-clock days.

As the harbormaster, and thus the leading Cape Town customs official, "Jonathon" explained:

> Theoretically, we could handle the stops; we could handle the containers. But then, what do we produce? I'll tell you. Gridlock. Total shipping gridlock, which is trade gridlock, which is economic gridlock.

Jonathon was a researcher's dream: he could explain the invisible and was willing to do so with patience and a wry grin. I had walked into the Cape Town harbor unannounced and asked for an interview. I was met with a graciousness I seldom encounter in similar situations in my own country. After being "vetted," first and most importantly by the secretary for the harbormaster's office, and then by the second in command, I was ushered in to the inner chamber to meet the man who oversees a global market flowing through his jurisdiction. I was first struck by his jovial mustache, and then by his forthcoming manner. It was this visit to Cape Town's port that taught me the basics of how to research the truths behind transnational commodity flows. Jonathon continued his explanation:

> If you hold up a ship in port, not only do you incur significant costs for the ship and for the port authority—which is taxpayer money—but you slow down trade altogether. The trade a country depends on to function. The trade business depends on to stay solvent. The trade people depend on for survival.
>
> Try holding a ship long enough to open all its containers, or try inspecting all the ships you have in port on any given day. You not only hold up these ships, but every other ship scheduled to arrive in port. Try holding up petrol that industries need, food that will rot, essentials like medicines, equipment that construction firms and factories require to operate.
>
> If you let 95 percent through unopened, why not 96 percent, or 97 percent? What is the greater threat, that, or gridlock?

The figure of a maximum of 5 percent inspections holds worldwide, but the volume of cargo differs widely. Major global routes intersect in hub ports like Dubai and Singapore. Where Cape Town has 350,000 containers coming into port yearly, Singapore has over 23 million a year. The world of shipping is a smuggler's paradise.

The media and popular culture focus on shadowy criminal organizations as the primary smugglers, but in fact legitimate businesses and multinational corporations are the biggest offenders. Underdeclaring and misrepresenting the goods they ship are basic tools of the trade. Jonathon's tone turned sarcastic for a moment, indicating his frustration, as harbormaster, with these truths:

> You want to know who we catch most often? Companies that sell the familiar everyday things in our lives, things so common we don't even think about them. The ketchup sitting on the table, the table itself, and the chairs. The paint on the walls, the clothes we wear, the parts for the vehicle we drive. Pick up the things around you and you'll be looking at what's smuggled.

I mentioned that the shipping agents I had been speaking with consistently estimated that 90 percent or more of all shipped goods are underdeclared or undeclared. One savvy agent who admitted to me he had been involved in smuggling in his younger seafaring days explained:

> It's in the mind-set of everyone. People go through the tariff books to find the cheapest possible rate. They will take sophisticated electronic items and find the cheapest component or metal they contain, then list the shipment as, say, some cheap metallic alloy or plastic. Cars may go as used spare parts. I've seen a Mirage plane come in listed as "air tools."

I told the harbormaster that my favorite quote to date came from a shipping and inspection agent who told me:

> The manifests and all the documents said "scrap metal," but it sure looked like a MIG fighter [jet] when it came out.

Jonathon leaned forward in his chair and said he would tell it like it is.

> It's a game.
> Tariff assessments are tremendously complicated. Scrap metal isn't assessed at the same price as weapons, or cars. You get a shipment of pieces of steel, it pays duty at a lower rate, and it looks like pieces of steel until you put it all together into a gun. People work the tariffs with amazing ingenuity: cheap canvas and scrap rubber are listed on the inventories, and in fact it's Nike shoes. And then you sometimes find drugs in the barrels of the guns or the heels of the shoes.
> But the continuous big evasions? Floor lamps [lower in tariffs] are declared when it's a shipment of major clothing consignments. Or you find symbolic associations, apparently intended to throw off any cursory spot-check: a shipment of "clothespins" which are really counterfeit cigarettes—about the same size and shape but decidedly different in taxation, and in legality.

Jonathon, like every other port official I asked, said that the most frequently "undeclared" (a nice word for smuggled) commodities are electronic equipment, clothing, shoes, textiles, engineering equipment, and a host of household and business brand names:

> Anything with high rates of duty; anything that can be disposed of quickly. The electronic field is the biggest; but in fact any product where high rates of duty create an incentive to smuggle. Cars; consider the fact that the rate of duty in South Africa is 65 percent of the value of the vehicle, inclusive. What greater incentive to smuggle is there? Also meat, flour, produce, daily products . . .

The harbormaster was about to continue his list when he caught himself, a serious look settling on his face. He took a deep breath and said:

> Consider the true impact: underdeclaration of goods creates a huge tax gap in South Africa. We figure we lose $1 billion a year.

Popular culture would have it that illegal drugs and arms shipments are the bane of customs and shipping and the ultimate threat to civilized trade. There is no doubt that untold fortunes are made and countless lives lost to harmful illegal commodities. Yet whether it's smuggled opium or tomato juice, the proceeds go directly into the hands of the traders: no taxes are paid, no tariffs levied, no duties or quality controls invoked. This, of course, is the true cost of smuggling: no money is available to build schools and clinics, improve trade infrastructure, and develop the country.

. . .

A secret lies at the core of the shipping industry. Even if it were possible to inspect every ship and every shipment coming into port, it would make little dent in smuggling. Everyone I talked to agreed.

A harbormaster:

> Once a ship is over the horizon, we don't know what they're doing.

A customs official:

> Ships meet up all the time in open waters. It's acceptable to move cargo and people from one ship to another on the high seas. As long as all the manifests, records, and paperwork are updated legally, this is no problem. But

would you like to guess how much is exchanged at sea that isn't
documented?

The head of British Customs and Excise:

To understand the truth of shipping, follow the unrecorded ship stops at sea.
But of course you can't follow them; that's the whole point.

A drug smuggler, introduced to me by his friend as the biggest one in the area:

Getting my merchandise is a breeze. A ship carrying the goods just stops
out on its normal route not too far from coast, and we send out little work
boats, meet up, transfer the goods, and bring them back to an empty stretch
of beach, pack it onto a truck, and head off to sell it.

I hear you're writing a piece on illicit economies. You should hear the stories of diamonds here.

I'm a scuba diver. We have a real culture here. We work the water-
diamond areas across several countries. Best for us are the places where
rivers dump gems in the ocean. We take gigs legally, and we work "unregistered" as well. Someone wants to work the field, buy diamonds, whatever. . . . well, there are the bars where we hang out. For my kind of specialty,
the best are on the coast. We're kind of a group, kind of a special culture.
You go to these places, you find out the score.

THE ARTFUL DODGER

Another example shows the difficulty of prosecuting maritime offenses.
It's the equivalent of prosecuting phantoms. In the port of Cape Town I
was shown a ship I'll call *"The Artful Dodger"* that had been tied up for
some weeks, under arrest. But *whom* to arrest became a real problem. The
case demonstrates how extensive illicit systems can operate with such
impunity.

The Artful Dodger was a former Russian Navy fleet replenishment vessel that had been "leased out" to a business plying international waters.
After leaving Russia and before arriving in Africa, the ship pulled into a
large hub port for repairs. But the Russian government wasn't able to
pay for the repairs, and the ship was arrested. The ship was given (by the
authorities of the arresting country) to the shipyard, where the repairs
were done under the provision that the ship could not be sublet. Before
the ink was dry on these papers, the ship was sublet to people who oper-

ate as part of a known criminal organization. The ship was reregistered in Belize. However, it was never deregistered from Russia. It was then run by a new company, and they chartered it out commercially to clients. They were not paying their debts, the crew's wages, or the charter fees.

The enterprise collapsed when *The Artful Dodger* was arrested in Cape Town, where I finally met her. At that time, I was told, the ship did not have much debt —"only about $5 million." This statement alone gives an indication of the kinds of monies that attach to shipping. But after the ship was arrested, a flood of other debts came out, from shipyards to charterers. While the investigation was taking place and the local courts were deciding what to do with the ship, South Africa had to pay all the expenses, which were substantial. Berthing rates alone are significant, and any ship that takes up berth space keeps out paying ships. Of course, even determining who owns the ship can be an exercise in futility. Assessing who is responsible for the debt can be next to impossible.

In maritime law, if a ship has broken the law or failed to meet its payments, a "sister ship" — a ship owned by the same company — can be arrested anywhere in the world and be held accountable for the debt. But proving who is a sister ship can be extremely difficult, as the example of *The Artful Dodger* shows. Maritime law takes these complexities and manipulations of ownership into account by following the "controlling mind." For example, if a director of company X is also a director for corporation Z, a sister ship from corporation Z can be impounded to satisfy the arrest of a ship from company X. But, as arresting maritime sheriffs told me, a legion of cases have been overturned because, in the myriad linkages of ownership, the authorities have not been able to correctly trace ship ownership for the arrested ships or the sister ships.

If this explanation alone causes headaches, it barely does justice to the realities of shipping law.

"Maritime law is a logic unto itself," explained the police officer in Cape Town who was investigating *The Artful Dodger.*

It's a sprawling, amazing field that bears little resemblance to sovereign, national, or international law. In this water-based world of law, fishing vessels aren't governed by the same rules as commercial vessels. Hundreds of years of commerce, survival, and tradition have produced these curious realities. Believe it or not, there are rules in force today that derive from the Lex Rhodia, or Rhodian sea law, a body of seventh-century regulations governing commercial trade and navigation in the Byzantine Empire.

Maritime law differs from land law in part because it's situated in the large fluid interstices of sovereignty, and in part because shipping figures so importantly in the running of transcontinental empires.

THE LARGER UNIVERSE OF SHIPPING

The story of unregulated transactions does not end with ships, their cargos, and their owners. When a ship comes into port, it deals with agents and requires stores, supplies, repairs, fuel, and a host of other things, necessities and luxuries alike. Virtually every exchange can be, and often is, grounded on "commissions" — skim-offs, presents, bribes, favors, kickbacks, backhands, and undocumented deals.

A European man who had been in sailing all his life, from military to private, and across all the seven seas, explained the system to me. He had seen most all there was to see, he said: he now had his captain's license, but he had spent many years working his way up the crewing ladder. He had grown up in a shipyard, sailed on working freighters, served in the navy, crewed billionaires' yachts.

> Skim-offs by the ship's crew are just a fact of life. We pull into port, and it's just a given that 15 percent is tacked on to the fuel charges. The owner pays the full price, none the wiser, and the crew splits the rest. The suppliers are in on this, and they get their cut. Everyone does this, and the owners never catch on. They're just too high and too far away from the daily grind of life. Maybe they care, maybe they just accept it, but it's the system. Same with stores: we buy food, materials, supplies, labor, repairs, whatever, and we add our take. Just about anywhere you go in the world, you know what the going skim-off percentages are: no one gouges, no one wants to get cheated of their fair share of skim-off. This is the legal world of shipping and sailing.

This conversation led me to talk with ship chandlers and suppliers for the land-based side of this skim-off equation. Many spoke openly with me. Typical figures for skim-offs in the international arena include the following:

A ship's master will get 15 percent in cash (undeclared).

The shipping agency gets 5–10 percent on top of payments (often declared in terms of tax/legal purposes, but unsupported by ship's owners), but any backhanders the agents get are undeclared.

An employment agency (service providers) gets 2–10 percent (undeclared).

Up to 30 percent is budgeted for agencies by contractors (legal but unethical), and 5–10 percent for repairs (undeclared).

Stevedores get presents to encourage certain kinds of "help" — anything from cash to a new Sony. As one told me, "You seldom walk away from any job without a little gift of some kind."

Fuel skim-offs aren't as common in the world of commercial shipping as they are in the yachting industry, but they happen. The fuelers and the ship's crew both profit from the skim-offs. In some cases, fuel is actually pumped off and resold elsewhere; in others the bills are merely jimmied. Considering the fact that an average-size commercial container ship requires 2,000 tons to fill, at $120 a ton for heavy-grade fuel, and uses about 60 tons a day, the money pocketed can be considerable.

These practices do vary by region and competition. Competition can be fierce in the world of shipping, and shipping agents told me that while many are happy with the 5–10 percent "commission" they take, they don't like turning a blind eye to misdeclared goods and other questionable practices. But they do it to get the business.

I was curious to see what response I would get if I walked unannounced into a ship supply agency in the USA and asked what the "cuts" were. I chose one at the Port of Los Angeles, walked in just before closing time, and asked to speak to someone who could "give me some decent information." I asked the harried man behind the desk what the typical "add-on" rate was.

Just a couple percent.

"That's low," I responded, with a surprised look.

Competition. Hey, most ships come in here are foreign owned, and they buy in their home countries.

"What can you provide?"

What can't we provide? You need it, you tell me, we'll get it. And I'll get out there personally and get it fast. No questions asked. Twenty-four hours a day, every day, no exception.

"Wow," I said, fascinated with this workload. "Don't you burn out?"

I'm young, but I can't handle this forever. More than anything, I want to be a longshoreman here. I'd make a much better salary, and really have a life.

Here I was, a stranger walking in off the street with no introduction, and in this short exchange, I was told:

– This man is willing to take a small, "couple percentage cut" and I, "the buyer," can pocket the rest of the skim-off.

– He will get me anything I need, indicating his willingness to negotiate prices, commodities, and services across legalities.

– He'll do the work himself, insuring confidentiality.

– A system is in place that has rules, prices, and codes of conduct that I, the buyer, can trust.

On board the ships, the crew is often running moneymaking schemes from legal to illegal. They may buy clothing in one port cheaply and sell in another where the prices are much higher, or trade for other items of value. They may barter ship's stores for valuable commodities. They may move pirated DVDs or drugs. They may carry new computer components or bring in banned pornography. As one port agent, formerly a sailor, told me:

> It's so institutionalized that it's symbolically enacted each time a customs official or port authority boards a ship. When they come on board, they're almost always handed a carton of cigarettes by the captain. You might say it's a ritual of the central role of present giving.

When I asked about the extent of undeclared transfers, every person in the shipping industry — whether commercial or private — looked at me with the same expression. It clearly said I was asking about the obvious. One answered:

> Oh, 80 percent, 90 percent. You know, darn near all of it, in one way or another.

As one official said:

> There's a culture among crews of not asking questions.

An agent with the Los Angeles Port Authority leaned back in his chair, smiling. He had his own way of explaining the system:

> You want to know how it works so easily? Look at the flow. The other day we got a call. . . . *The man laughed so hard he had to wipe tears from his eyes.* A hotshot captain from a well-known ship had gone to town for din-

ner. He was in full uniform, but he didn't have his identity papers, and the guards at the port gates wouldn't let him through to get back to his ship. He shouted and pointed to his uniform and his captain's insignia and tried logic and shouted some more. It was all for naught. The guards wouldn't let him through without his pass or papers. So he called me.

But as he's standing there, held up at the gates, groups of prostitutes are wandering past him in and out of the gates freely, with no one stopping them or asking for passes or papers.

PHOTOGRAPH OF OPIUM. MUSEUM ON NARCOTIC DRUGS, MONGLA, MYANMAR.

CHAPTER 13

DRUGS

TWO BUSTS

On March 16, 2002, *The Herald* (South Africa) ran two brief articles on drug busts. Both were short pieces on the inside pages; neither warranted headline status. Both were about raids of illegal shipments coming into South African ports.

The first embodied the lore of drugs: shipping containers carrying many kilos of cocaine. Multi-million-dollar dreams and disruption. The newspaper didn't give a detailed picture of the ship, its crew, and the drug runners, but they didn't have to. Popular movies, incensed community leaders, and chain-bookstore publications have long painted a graphic picture of shadowy people in dark clothing and darker morals peddling the dangerous sweets of addiction. In our mind's eye, we immediately see grim factories in a barren countryside or decayed urban zone where criminal "elements" wearing dusty jeans and threadbare T-shirts work for overlord bosses in bad suits who are protected by guns, gangs, mercenaries, and payoffs.

The second drug bust involved shipping containers with twenty-two tons of illegal merchandise, which could also fetch millions of dollars in dreams and disruption. But the drugs aboard this ship weren't cocaine; they were pharmaceuticals, controlled antibiotics worth rand 211 million (approximately $30 million). The drugs had been packaged in Hong Kong and shipped to South Africa. A prominent businessman had purchased them for rand 500 ($70) (Neethling 2002: 4).

No media images and political rhetoric accompanied this bust. There are no ready-made ideas of what these smugglers look like, where they come from, or who their bosses are. Are these shady characters wearing dusty jeans, working for gangland bosses, or are they sophisticated executives in expensive suits? Who smuggles pharmaceuticals? Who profits? And what is their impact on society?

The United Nations estimates that the illegal narcotics business generates some $500 billion a year. People like urban sociologist Manuel Castells put it at closer to a trillion. No figures exist for the illicit pharmaceutical trade, though my data suggest the profits are immense. Narcotics is the focus of massive police, research, publishing, and governmental work. Pharmaceuticals smuggling is largely ignored. Why?

The day these two drug busts were reported in the paper, I happened to be at a dance in a South African coastal town halfway between the two ports. The townspeople I was with began discussing my research interests, and when sufficient trust had been gained, one of the group clapped another man on the back, turned to me, and said, "You're looking at the largest drug dealer in the area." The dealer smiled, and, after some obligatory small talk, explained that the whole business of pulling into port was a waste of time and security. Here, large cargo ships merely stopped in coastal waters and fishing boats went out, ostensibly to work, and met the ships to transfer drugs for dollars, he said. Or perhaps for diamonds. Fast, efficient, effective. I looked at the "largest drug dealer in the region" and thought about stereotypes, none of which he fit. He wasn't some marginal, shadowy character in dark stubble and leather, but a member of the community with investments in a string of legitimate business interests. The smuggler had an easy smile and a firm handshake and was dressed in Docker khakis and a brand-name polo shirt.

"Drugs" perhaps captures as well as any commodity the complexities and ironies that surround the globalization of the il/licit. The very word shows the conundrums: the word means everything and nothing, depending on context. If you say "drugs" at a hospital, it generally refers to pharmaceuticals. If you are talking about a drug bust, it means illegal narcotics. One undifferentiated word for two realms of activity so frequently seen as polar opposites. In practice, the only discernible difference is that illegal narcotics are luxury items taken for recreation, while pharmaceuticals, legal or illegal, are generally health necessities.

For me, illegal narcotics are only mildly interesting. Their impact on global economics and law enforcement is central to understanding unregulated markets. But they are predictable: from production through marketing to consumption, they are illegal. They aren't tied to life's necessities, but are luxury commodities, and as such affect the lives of a select group. In some important ways, the illegal narcotic industries are run like parallel-economy multinational enterprises.

Illicit pharmaceuticals, on the other hand, represent the very heart of perdurability. Virtually all of the earth's 6.7 billion citizens will become ill and require medications at some point in their lives. Their quest for health is not a luxury. The pharmaceutical industry has been called one of the most critical to the survival of societies, and one of the most corrupt.

The attention "drugs" receives in law enforcement, the media, and literature has little relationship to the reality of the impact of illegal drugs in people's lives. Walk into any law-enforcement institution and ask what most preoccupies their attention, and the topic almost always turns to illegal drugs. I have never heard illegal pharmaceuticals mentioned.

ON THE STREETS: RESEARCH THROUGH MALARIA

Some time after the 2002 drug busts in South Africa, I had the good fortune to interview several experts at the World Health Organization in Geneva, as well as Howard Marks, aka "Mr. Nice," one of the biggest and most successful late twentieth-century cannabis smugglers in the world. I present these conversations over this and the next chapter.

But the story actually begins earlier, back in Angola and the hometown of the war orphan. Southern Africa, with its transitional politics and need for hard currency, is one of the new hot transit spots for illegal narcotics. Given the limited health resources, the illicit pharmaceutical trade flourishes as well. The trades aren't reckoned in the millions of dollars, but in the billions. The stakes are high. Higher, with the recognition that illicit pharmaceuticals are addressing life-and-death issues such as high infant mortality rates (those in Angola, DR Congo, and Zimbabwe are among the world's highest), HIV/AIDS (Southern Africa has the highest rates of infection in the world), malaria, TB, and a host of urban ills such as coronary disease.

The contradictions of countries like Angola — where illicit pharmaceuticals are often people's only hope of obtaining needed medicines — have long prompted me to follow the story of "drugs." But I know from my own personal experience in Angola that even the legal clinical pharmaceuticals I encountered could be substandard or dangerous. A straightforward case of dysentery took two weeks to cure because the pharmacy-procured antibiotics I took were so substandard. The malaria drug I was given (I later found out) had been banned by the WHO for causing heart damage and then had been dumped illegally — and without warnings — by large pharmaceutical companies in needy locales like Angola. My luck finding decent pharmaceuticals was at least as good, if not better, buying from the unlicensed "street drug markets."

This prompted me to look into the availability of "drugs" in general. Basically, I found that illegal narcotics occupied people's thoughts very little. They are largely found in transit (from producing countries to consumer countries). Drugs in licensed dispensaries were affordable to the wealthy. Unlicensed street-market drugs were available and affordable to everyone. People said clinic drugs and street pharmaceuticals didn't differ too much in quality, only in availability and cost. In Mata'lo, the war-torn Angolan town described in chapter 4 where people were dying from lack of basic necessities, I found four pharmaceutical vendors with a range of drugs from name-brand antibiotics, through malaria drugs, to analgesics in a market still so poor that cooking oil was sold in one-ounce units carefully tied into tiny strips of plastic wrap and hung from trees like precious ornaments. The hospital, when it was open, had no medicines.

Street vendors of pharmaceuticals provide a service, one that they are often proud of. They frequently work in the same spot for years and accumulate a loyal clientele. Such businesspeople don't think of themselves as smugglers or as merchants of the illicit. I got to know some of them over the years I visited Angola. The more established worked off wooden tables set up in open markets, their wares neatly and carefully arranged, most in their original packets, according to function: antibiotics, analgesics, birth control pills, vitamins, and so on. The smaller "pharmacies" operated out of cardboard boxes right on the streets. Their inventories were smaller, but given a request, they could get almost anything.

One of the sellers — I'll call him "Lucas" — explained the system to me. He's a soft-spoken man of slight build, with an animated face. He radiates professionalism. He gives the impression of truly listening to what a person says, of being a person you can trust with your health-care woes.

I've built up my networks over years. We each have our favorite sources. There are a number of them. There is the container trade (we often go directly to containers, where container agents sell directly to vendors). Over time, we get to know what manufacturers are reliable, inexpensive, honest. Indian products tend to be a favorite. No one I know of pays duties and tariffs on drugs. They would be unaffordable if we did.

There is the military trade. The military orders large amounts of pharmaceuticals, which they are more likely to sell to the general population than for military use. Those selling do not spend any of their own money, and sell at a good price. It's low enough for people to afford. Pure profit for them, good products for us.

Some comes through the hospitals, through the backdoor.

And there are [counterfeit drug] factories that make a number of popular drugs—people here tend to think the best drugs come from the reputable ones in Southern Africa and in places like India. They can make a good copy of just about any major drug from any major drug company, like Pfizer, or a good generic.

LUCAS—A JOURNEY INTO THE BUSINESS ETHICS OF COUNTERFEITING

Pharmaceuticals travel well in containers, planes, trucks, cars, donkey carts, and shoulder bags. They are the quintessential "small-size, low-weight, high-value, high-profit, and highly taxed" commodity that according to customs people worldwide drives smuggling. As I discuss later, most governments, INGOs, and the United Nations see this trade as dangerous. There is no doubt that lack of regulation in an industry dealing with living and dying is serious. But the issue is far more complex.

Three general assumptions underpin official views of illegal drugs:

1. Street vendors and counterfeit factories are responsible for the majority of substandard drugs.

2. Legally produced pharmaceuticals are safe.

3. The war on drugs is, and should be, about illegal narcotics.

The first assumption: Lucas isn't a shadowy street figure who exploits human misery by selling substandard drugs to the desperate, only to disappear back into the shadows to avoid prosecution. Dressed in neat slacks and a button-down shirt, his pharmaceuticals carefully packaged, he has shown up at the same wooden table in the same spot in the central market day after day for years. His customers are neither stupid nor passive: if Lucas, and the others like him, sell bad drugs, their careers, and potentially even their lives, are at risk. Angolans often take it upon themselves to "discipline" thieves and cheats. I have seen such punishment meted out: it is swift and effective. But this is not the only reason Lucas avoids selling bad drugs. Like most any businessperson, he seeks the respect of his community.

I sell good drugs and people come back. What do you think will happen to me if I sell bad pharmaceuticals? People will say, "That Lucas is not to be trusted, his goods are bad," and they will not come back. If someone gets sick from my drugs, they will be angry with me, and that is worse. What do you think they will do to me? I have a family to keep, I can't afford to lose my income. Why would I risk that?

I have done this work for years. I am professional. I know every brand; I know which factories around the world produce the best drugs for the best prices. I know how to get them. I know which counterfeit factories make decent drugs. I know how to read the trademarks, no matter what the boxes say. I know what works, what doesn't, and why.

And I know without these drugs, many people wouldn't make it. It's my home, my community. I care.

Lucas explains that these sentiments can extend to counterfeit factories:

The best ones have well-trained personnel. They run good organizations, and if their products are good, they stay in business, become respected, and grow. When one of us learns of a good one, we try it, and if its reputation is deserved, we tell all our friends selling too. If the factory sells bad drugs, we stop buying. Then what does that factory do? What do the workers do? They have no job now, no way to put food on the table for their children. They can't just go out and start another factory; their reputations follow them. Of course, this isn't always true. But the tendency is to do good work.

Clearly, not all unlicensed pharmaceutical manufacturers and vendors produce safe, reliable, industry-standard drugs. But neither do all licensed manufacturers. This gets to the heart of the second assumption, that legally produced and sold drugs are of legal quality. The WHO, increasingly concerned with the problem of substandard drugs, has collected a number of studies and instituted international conferences on this topic.

The studies are generally conducted in what the WHO calls developing countries. In these studies, the WHO analyzes pharmaceuticals collected from retail sales markets. One set of results is not surprising: substandard drugs more often come from unlicensed factories. But another set of results is surprising: licensed manufacturers produce a substantial number of substandard drugs. Studies find that substandard drugs — with less of the active ingredients than required, with the wrong ingredients, with missing ingredients, or with no active ingredients at all — generally account for between 5 and 25 percent of drugs tested. I was told at WHO headquarters in Geneva that studies have not been done on counterfeit drug manufacturers — those who forge brand-name and trademark pharmaceuticals. The assumption is that such factories, by definition, would produce dangerous drugs with no or little active ingredients. WHO has not met the Lucases of the pharmaceutical world.

The fact that some 25 percent of all pharmaceuticals in places like Southeast Asia may be substandard or counterfeit throws the whole question of "the war on drugs" into a new light.

Throughout this research, I have been asking law-enforcement personnel, lawyers, human-rights advocates, and smugglers whether it's better to have smuggled pharmaceuticals than no pharmaceuticals, and if illegal pharmaceuticals are as illegal as illegal narcotics. Virtually all said there is a hierarchy of illegality, and smuggled pharmaceuticals are a lesser offense. Police say they aren't as likely to bust pharmaceutical smuggling as they are narcotics. In the words of a British Crown Agent expert responsible for developing the "zero-tolerance policy" for customs fraud in Angola: "We don't even try to stop or ask questions when crates of pharmaceuticals come in and are picked up and whisked away by the military for untaxed distribution." But in all these interviews, no one has ever mentioned the problem of substandard drugs produced by licensed manufacturers. Everyone seems to assume that pharmaceuticals by brand-name companies, whether sold legally or illicitly, meet industry standards.

If one assumes that licensed manufacturers produce quality pharmaceuticals, smuggling them to desperately needy populations can be seen as a humanitarian act rather than as a crime. But what happens to this equation when legally made substandard pharmaceuticals are dumped on unsuspecting populations?

FROM THE STREETS TO THE WORLD HEALTH ORGANIZATION

The question comes into strong relief with an observation by Eshetu Wondemagegnehu, who works at the World Health Organization headquarters in Geneva.[1] Upon introducing myself, I explained I was interested in why law enforcement and the media tended to focus almost exclusively on illegal narcotics, given the ubiquity of pharmaceutical smuggling. What was the WHO finding out about smuggled and counterfeit pharmaceuticals? I asked. Mr. Wondemagegnehu shook my hand and commented:

> I am surprised to hear you say this. I have just returned from Hong Kong and a large conference on pharmaceuticals, and we were all just saying this. That at the bottom line, taking illegal narcotics is something people choose to do. A relatively small percentage of people. It is a drug defined by choice.

But counterfeit pharmaceuticals—this is something people have to take, it is a matter of life and death. It is not a drug defined by choice, but by necessity. If you smuggle narcotics, you smuggle to people who elect to take them. If you provide substandard drugs to the world's ill, they have no choice.

Why do the police and the policies focus on illegal narcotics when the problems of substandard pharmaceuticals produce greater suffering, death, and disaster?

At the end of our conversation, Mr. Wondemagegnehu returned to the question he raised above: Why, in the "war on drugs," security forces focused their energies on illegal narcotics, while few beyond the WHO investigated illicit pharmaceuticals.

In my personal opinion—I can't speak for the WHO and the UN here— it's politics. Politics and simple economics. Look at Angola; the wealth is not equally distributed. Why do we find illegal outlets in developing countries? Because the legal is expensive, highly taxed, unattainable. This same gap exists in the USA. As long as the gap between what people have and can have continues to increase, the majority of people are going to be affected, not only in terms of having to access illegal pharmaceuticals, but in all aspects of their lives. Illegal pharmaceuticals? The problem can be solved: share the wealth. Truth is, most problems relate to politics.

Here at the WHO, dealing with the problems of illegal pharmaceuticals, we look at pharmaceuticals. We can't talk of politics; we can't talk of economics. We can only talk of pharmaceutical regulatory mechanisms.

I think sometimes we aren't giving the right advice. Perhaps we should be telling people to fight corruption, to advance freedom of speech, to advocate for a change of government in working to solve the problems of substandard and illegal pharmaceuticals.

I asked Wondemagegnehu my standard question: no matter how much we would wish for affordable and accessible legal pharmaceuticals, this does not yet exist. Until it does, does the WHO support smuggled pharmaceuticals to populations who otherwise would have no access to drugs?

That is a very difficult question. The truth is, technically it should not happen. I may not like it, but it will happen. What alternative do people have? The WHO isn't here to promote illegal importation. But it is very, very difficult to say if smuggling is good or bad when people are living in desperation.

These situations are very complex. It has to do with the authorities. It all boils down to politics, to the gap between rich and poor, between who has the right to speak and who does not. Those who run the politics also run the economics.

But I would like to point out to you that pharmaceuticals is just one aspect. Do you really want to focus just on this in terms of the health of people? It is a sensitive area, but ask why few people have access to adequate food and clean water, why we have starvation. Think politics.

I am not supporting illegal manufacturing nor making a moral argument here; I am assessing the risk, danger, and power in illicit economies. As I walk through the vulnerable populations of war-torn countries, transitional nations, and economic empires, I observe that illicit pharmaceuticals constitute a domain as large as that of illegal narcotics in terms of profit — larger in that it affects a significant part of any given population, not just a self-selected minority. Yet the domain of illegal narcotics is central in legal, media, and popular awareness, whereas pharmaceutical smuggling remains largely invisible and unrecognized.

Why?

PHOTOGRAPH OF OPIUM ADDICT DISPLAY. MUSEUM ON NARCOTIC DRUGS, MONGLA, MYANMAR.

CHAPTER 14

THE CULTURES OF CRIMINALS

Trust, *said Howard Marks,* is at the heart of criminal activity.[1]

Marks, a legendary figure in the annals of British crime, reckons that his cannabis smuggling in the 1980s ran to hundreds of tons.

"That's a lot of trust," I replied.

Marks was my last interview after a year and a half traveling several of the world's continents doing research for this book. I grew up on gangster movies, the *Godfather* books, and sensationalist media accounts of triad, mafia, cartel, and criminal gang violence. But in my research, I meet hundreds of people who make a living by bending the laws, and I know hundreds more who wander across the lines of legality with a vague sense of entitlement ("What, copying this CD is wrong?"). I have encountered very few acts of violence. Granted, I have read the accounts of Pablo Escobar. His penchant for "violence as business" is as bad as anything I have seen in war. Granted, I have chronicled shoot-outs like the one between gangsters and police over Patagonian Toothfish smuggling. But the people I have seen die due to the structural violence of inequality embedded in a world of unequal legal business institutions is far worse. Frankly, I have found this research on the world of the "outlaw" a much-needed respite from the raw world of violence I have encountered in my years of work in warzones.

Several years and thousands of field hours ago, I wrote this in one of my first theoretical explorations of "shadow powers":

One of the more interesting questions regarding these vast econo-political networks is how such massive amounts of goods and money, which follow such a complex set of exchange routes and political associations, flow as smoothly as they do. In plain words: Savimbi's gems get to Antwerp, Belgium, and then onto rings on our global fingers without a great deal more, and sometimes less, murder and mayhem than state-based transactions do. The billions that flow through the informal banks of Asia function quite a bit like state-supported banks in that their customers don't usually lose their money. In a nutshell, the system works. But *how* is another matter.

One of the answers to the question of how these vast international extra-state networks operate as coherently as they do is that people in these systems generally "trust" that the transaction will occur as predicted, and that they will remain safe (Gambetta, 1988). The fact that large-scale massacres, wars, and trails of dead bodies take place with far less regularity within these shadow networks than in and among states' wars attests to the fact that the systems do work. This is no mean feat when we consider we are talking of millions of people exchanging billions of dollars worth of goods and services. Ernest Gellner (1988:147) provides an interesting take:

> The Hobbesian problem arises from the assumption that anarchy, absence of enforcement, leads to distrust and social disintegration . . . but there is a certain amount of interesting empirical evidence which points the other way. The paradox is: it is precisely anarchy which engenders trust or, if you want to use another name, which engenders social cohesion.

(Nordstrom 2000: 45 – 47)

I find that these observations largely still stand. The worst excesses of violence I see in the extra-legal world involve businesses straddling the boundaries of in/formality and carving out new domains (such as the taxi trade in South Africa); the military; and the brutality of the powerful against the powerless, such as that against women, girls, and boys in the sex and labor industries.

Howard Marks is the researcher's dream informant. Social scientists and journalists swap tales about the "perfect" informant, that one person in a hundred who can see the bigger world, the philosophical world made alive in a way that allows us to see where it is we live out our lives. See it — and put it into words. Marks was one of the hardest interviews to get in my career. Preston King, a leading political scientist, had told me several years before that I needed to interview Marks if I was going to do a book on the extra-legal. Easier said than done. I'm not sure which is more difficult: smuggling, or getting an interview with a famous former smuggler. Through sheer serendipity — the basic tool of research — I got Marks's e-mail address from a friend of his I ran into at a yoga studio in

London. I e-mailed him in 2001, and he ignored me. Six months later, I tried again, with the same result. In 2002, road-weary after nearly twenty months of international research, I shot Marks a final e-mail: "Why don't you answer your e-mails?" I asked, explaining I was far too travel-battered to keep writing him. He wrote back that day: I could meet him at Gatwick Airport the next morning.

Marks allowed me several days of interviews, and given his wealth of information, I could have used several more. Once settled into conversation, I asked Marks about how business is done in what he calls the criminal world. He doesn't pretend to speak for all people or all contexts. He is under no illusion that the criminal world is free from violence and oppression. But for him, the culture of criminality is a rich universe of symbol, value, and action:

> You know, you can run a criminal organization without violence. Like I said, it's about trust. The criminal has to rely more on trust and a handshake than on the "contracts" of the straight world. So what evolves in the criminal world is stable and solid. In the criminal world, there is no recourse if you encounter problems—you can't take your complaints to a formal outside authority. There has to be decent systems of business trust to get the work done.
>
> You can say there is more trust in the criminal world than in the straight business world. Look: a contract is between two people who don't trust each other, otherwise they wouldn't write them in the first place. There are laws and courts and penalties to enforce these contracts. And this creates an environment where people trust less, take advantage more—for it's not their word, their work, that is on the line, but an adversarial competition backed up by abstract contracts. I would trust criminals any day over the legal, impersonal financial world.
>
> Look at the term *outlaw*. The first meaning of the word was precisely that: someone who dropped out, lived outside the law. It didn't necessarily mean to break the law. The word was first used with Hereward in the thirteenth century. Curiously, his name means "Howard." He was an outlaw, he moved outside the scope of the law. He had a Robin Hood–like connotation; he was a folk hero. Of course, then came the rise of highwaymen and crooks and the term evolved. But the original connotation of outlaw is important to remember: people who dropped out and went to live in the forest. But even today, people aren't ashamed of what they are doing; they don't view themselves as the enemy.

Marks speaks easily and gives a sense of gracious familiarity. A convicted drug smuggler, he is also a folk hero to many. I didn't realize the extent of this until I moved through his day. At meals, restaurant staff treated him with the respect they might accord a visiting dignitary.

People would come up to me and ask if it really was Howard Marks — could I get an autograph for them? Did I know he was their hero? I told Marks about meeting grandmothers in South Africa clutching his autobiography, *Mr. Nice,* and saying, "He could be my Jimmy."

The year before my interview with Marks, customs officer David Hesketh had told me the story of busting Marks for drugs several decades earlier. He and his mates had worked patiently for months putting together what appeared to be an airtight case. Marks was one of the world's biggest drug smugglers in those days. During the mid-1980s, he had forty-three aliases and eighty-nine phone lines, and he owned twenty-five companies trading throughout the world. After painstaking surveillance and data collection, Hesketh arrested Marks. The officer described the ensuing courtroom drama:

> Marks is really great looking. He has unbelievable charisma and charm. We would ask him about undeniable criminal acts, and he would smile and look at the people in the jury, give that boyish shrug, spin his tales, and the jury smiled and said, "Not guilty." By virtue of charm.

Hesketh laughed. He had more than a grudging respect for Marks — "even if we were on the opposite sides of the law." When Marks was arrested years later and sent to a prison in Indiana, Hesketh felt the curious camaraderie that often links cops and criminals, enemy soldiers, and players on opposing sports teams: "How dare the Americans? He's one of ours!"

Howard Marks laughed delightedly when I told him this story, and then continued:

> I find more violence in legal society than in the criminal world.
>
> Illegal markets are self-regulating, much more so than traditional legal business. For those of us who follow a nonviolent ethic, we just don't ever do business again with someone who screws you over. This ruins the person's career. Sure, some favor retribution, so they don't look wimpy for getting taken.
>
> "The horse head in the bed?" I asked.
>
> Yeah, you know, movies like *The Godfather* created this kind of violence, not the other way. People come out with these movies, and it creates an image. People ended up liking *The Godfather* and then taking on the stereotypes the film invented. This created a greater resort to violence.
>
> "You've been talking about times when someone intentionally screws someone over," I said. "What about times when there are misunderstandings, when both sides think they've done what they agreed to, but each has a different idea of what that is?"

This is the case more often than not. Especially when you're working across cultures and languages where both people are acting in good faith.

"How do people deal with this?"

Generally, people use an arbitrator. A bit like *The Godfather* thing: a respected senior whom both sides trust. The person who introduced the two is an obvious choice. Someone connected to both, yet impartial. It's not necessary for people to meet face to face for this mediation. And in the end, in the criminal world, most conflicts get successfully resolved.

In a legal business, things can be ground to a halt by injunctions and court battles to decide outcomes. This can take years. In crime, there is no way people can wait for this kind of shit. You have to get on with it. In the legal world, these battles just become another business: business for the lawyers, accountants, and so on.

I thought about the term *outlaw* in this context. I realized the disconnect between popular portrayals of criminals (dark, shadowy, amoral threats) from what I mostly saw (people raising families, enmeshed in friendships, and wed to social values like democracy and community good). This was certainly true for Howard Marks; it is also true for white-collar criminals. One of the first things Marks did when we met was proudly show me pictures of his children.

The mainstream view holds that criminals live outside all law, all society, in a world of anarchy. But of course, in leaving one social universe, a person merely enters another. All societies are grounded in norms, codes of conduct, rules of behavior, and ethics. These can differ significantly, but many share core values.

What Marks says below captures the "culture of criminality" that I see shaping the extra-state networks that in the twenty-first century span cultures, languages, criminal domains, and community norms globally.

The system works because, at the core of it all, people care about respect. You have said that WHO didn't believe that counterfeit pharmaceutical factories would or could put out decent drugs. But of course, such factories can and do put out good pharmaceuticals. It's no different from those who produce legally: Who is going to come back to do business with a person who puts out a lousy product? And then how does that person keep feeding their families if no one comes back? This is why arbitration works. People's livelihoods depend on doing good work and being recognized for it. This is why nonviolent means of dealing with someone who intentionally screws you over works: just don't deal with them again. This blow to their career is a big deal. The criminal world is self-regulating, much more so than traditional business with its contracts and pension schemes and company loyalty—and then the employee gets sacked.

> People care about their reputation. They want to be respected. They want return business. This is their form of old-age pension.

For Howard Marks, the code of ethics that governs criminals holds tremendous importance. He refers to it often in conversation. In stories, he often cites the trust he relied on, the loyalty that got him through tough negotiations, the camaraderie that gave him community and support.

I asked Marks to explain how this code of ethics works in the criminal world.

> Not snitching. Not ripping people off. Not much more than that, really. Stand by your connections. Being responsible for your people—don't lay blame on others. Like, if you send a kid to do your job, don't blame him for fucking up. Take responsibility.
>
> Loyalty, that's a big one. If I introduce you to someone else, and you think it won't work out because there is not enough money in it, and I ask for 10 percent for the introduction . . . you don't cut me out. It happens all the time in the straight world, but it's frowned upon in criminal ethics. It goes through to families. If you get caught and sent to prison, your family will be taken care of. It's not formal, like some institution or organization, but the code of looking after people is there.

Marks and I began comparing some of my recent experiences with "business" in Africa with what he was saying.

> The codes are the same around the world. I could go anywhere, to any country, and pretty much know the basic codes of conduct for doing business. But it's more than that. Crime is getting multicultural and multiethnic. Today, crime is a cross-cultural exchange. What we used to think of as separate "crime groups" are losing this idea of specific identities. We now see a global exchange of mafias. But the bottom line is still the same: the ethics are similar, shared, for everyone; for Europeans, for Russians, for everyone.

This last discussion captures what anthropology can offer the twenty-first century. Western societies, and along with them Western theories, often work with Enlightenment notions of culture. As colonial rule spread across the globe and the modern nation-states sought to solidify their control over competing forms of power — from kingdoms to dynasties —"culture" became a tool of politics. Renaissance mapmakers marked these conquests on static maps color-coded for state and ideology, and culture became a concept linking "state" (a political terrain) with "nation" (a cultural terrain). People no longer belonged to themselves alone — able, as the Mozambicans say, to "vote with their feet," to choose which political leader and location they preferred. Now people were born to an "identity" that came custom-packaged with religious, political, and social overtones, with what was deemed culture. Culture in modernist thought became so fixed that it took on quasi-biological overtones.

In fact, from premodern to postmodern times, what we call culture is no more and no less than a core existential informational system: fluid, flexible, and profoundly multifaceted. When Howard Marks does business with a person — whether from his hometown in Wales or a city in South Asia — each negotiates multiple cultural universes in constant states of flux, being defined as circumstance and necessity suggest. For example, as criminal organizations globalize, so too do norms of extralegal association, of money laundering, of resolving conflict.

Culture — habits of knowledge — also shapes how we are accustomed to thinking of crime. The definitions of legal society and criminal network have traditionally been oppositional. What is criminal is non-legal. Full stop. Yet what happens at the points of merger? What modes of thought and action hold sway here? What of legality bleeds into illegality? What of illegality enters mainstream society?

Marks reflected on laundering money and on the intersections of il/legality:

> Most criminals aren't that good at financial affairs and investing, so they tend to give large suitcases full of money to their accountants to handle. But the interface between the legal and illegal, like accountants and bad cops, is not bound by the same codes of criminal ethics I have been describing. Unless you have a situation like the Corsican ethnic code of ethics and solidarity, where Corsican cops and criminals share strong background codes of ethics. But on a larger scale, in general, this isn't the case.
>
> The world of laundering is nuts: you can't buy a pack of chewing gum with illicit money, but you can buy fabulous stolen artwork, and just about any other big-name things you want. But the point is not necessarily to make money. No legitimate business that I described in the book *Mr. Nice* made money. I didn't need money. I needed laundering. This way you can be something—be an expert, a professional, a businessperson—be legit. . . . So when you travel, for example, and people ask you what you do, you have a clean answer. There are tons of easy ways to clean money.

I asked Marks for some examples; he began with off-track betting. He explained that if you bet the same amount of money on every horse in the race, you'll get back 85 percent. Then he smiled and said, you just have to keep going down the list of high-turnover industries, from betting shops to copy centers. From copy centers, he went to garbage:

> The criminal world intersects with the legal world in all kinds of ways. You can take it all the way to garbage. Why is the mafia in garbage collection in New York? They run garbage collection better than drugs. And it runs effectively. The streets are clean of garbage, it's legal, and people don't go to prison for this work.

Marks then began to speak of society in general, and of the larger intersections of il/legality. Criminality, and its attendant practices, like laundering, pervade the business world as we know it.

> But the picture is much bigger than this. In truth, the USA's economy is fiddled by those with money. Unrecorded money. People expect big business to fiddle. Hey, only the poor pay taxes. Legal businesses—banking, stock exchange, diamond exchange, currency exchange rates—the whole thing is a fiddle. Its not like the economy was once straight and then got corrupted. It's always been this way. It's how it was set up.
>
> And, in the end, the big guys don't get caught.
>
> "How many businesses in the USA do you think cross the lines of legality?" I asked.
>
> One hundred percent, *said Marks.*

COPS AND ROBBERS. COLORADO, USA.

Trust

CHAPTER 15

THE CULTURES OF COPS

"How many of the legal enterprises in the West do you think cross the lines of legality in some way in the course of their business?" I asked.
        One hundred percent, *replied Richard Flynn, detective at Scotland Yard in London.*

JIMMY THE BUTCHER, A PARABLE OF CONSCIENCE AND CRIME

David Hesketh, the head of International Assistance, U.K. Customs, warmed to the topic of crime and morality. He is a man who is bored by simple black-and-white assessments. To talk of legality alone, he explained, doesn't begin to capture the fullness, the truly interesting aspects, of crime and law in the world. "Take Jimmy the Butcher," he said.

Jimmy the Butcher, Hesketh explained, was a heroin trafficker. He was a big, stocky man. The "butcher" part of his name might suggest a penchant for certain kinds of violence — but in fact Jimmy actually was a butcher, owning a meat shop in a bustling part of London.

Hesketh had been on covert surveillance, assigned to bust Jimmy. One day while he was watching Jimmy at his shop, a blind man came walking down the street. He was just about to crash into some scaffolding he didn't realize was there. The streets were full of people, and everyone just pushed past the blind man. Not one of those fine upstanding citizens took a moment to help the blind man, Hesketh said with a smile. But Jimmy did. He was engaged in animated conversation with several people at his shop, but when he saw the blind man about to run into the scaffolding, he excused himself, walked over to the man, and escorted him around the scaffolding — smiling, chatting with him, and steering him along a safe course.

For Hesketh, this was an existential statement on his work and the ironies of the world. He sat in his surveillance location and wondered at the curious definitions of good and bad: of those who proudly hold themselves up as law abiding and are willing to watch a blind man hurt himself; of the man who helps, and is a heroin trafficker. With a wry smile, Hesketh shrugged and added:

> Jimmy was always like that. He's a kind and helpful man and he's in jail for seven years for trafficking. I can muse all I want to about good and bad, but my job is to bust people who traffic, and Jimmy sold heroin.
>
> The point of the story is that I can't say what's morally right and wrong. Legal and illegal, yes, but morally? This is a far more complex matter. Jimmy was a really nice guy. What happens when stakeholders go to the government and say, "Give me access to info earlier than my competitor — give me preferential treatment — and I'll give you money; I'll make you look good. Or I'll go to the minister and have you kicked out"?

David Hesketh wasn't telling me this story because he was confused about the morality of his work or of sending Jimmy the Butcher to prison. He is clear about that. He works on the legal side of the law; he arrests people who cross the lines of legality. But I think Hesketh is tired of the platitudes that underlie much of the rhetoric about law in the media and popular culture today. I think he is frustrated with the simplistic dichotomies of morality that misrepresent reality rather than explain it. Network news, blockbuster movies, and popular culture routinely draw one-dimensional lines in the legal sand. But where, Hesketh prompts us to ask, does morality reside if the good-hearted man can sell heroin and the law abiding are willing to watch the innocent suffer needless injury? How does this translate into larger patterns of political representation and violence? Wherein resides crime, and how do societies protect themselves?

Hesketh isn't questioning legality — far from it. He wants to understand the font of societal morality.

> Some cocaine smugglers just aren't bad people. When I've arrested some of them they say, "Hey, I work eighteen hours a day and this is the only way I can feed my family." And I say, "Hey, it's illegal and I have to bust you."
>
> But at the end of the day, the whole system doesn't hold together totally. Who makes the rules? The dominant class. How does this compare with some poor family with three kids who gets chucked out of their flat. What are the morals? Where is the good and the bad? How do we balance the values of money with caring societies?

And where, Hesketh asks, is trust? People on both sides of the law seem profoundly concerned with trust. It was the first topic that Howard Marks mentioned. For Hesketh, trust is critical to the fabric of contemporary society, certainly to the worlds of trade and transaction he oversees in customs work. But trust is fragile and elusive. War plays hell with trust: Hesketh sees the same patterns of power and profiteering described in this book characterizing war in general, from the long-term impact of the world wars to the wars of the twenty-first century. He was speaking in the wake of the large corporate scandals in the USA, such as Enron, WorldCom, and the charges that Halliburton was profit(eer)ing from the USA war against Iraq.

> If you don't have those socioeconomic and political institutions you can trust, especially after war, how do you create them? How do you create trust?

SCOTLAND YARD HITS THE STREETS

These weren't the only conversations to begin with trust. Detective Richard Flynn welcomed me to Scotland Yard, handed me a cup of coffee, leaned forward in his chair, and began:

> One of the biggest dangers to the future is organized crime.

I thought of R. T. Naylor, professor of economics at McGill University, who writes extensively on crime. He critiques the widespread lament that organized crime is the greatest threat to society today — that the violence and the untaxed economies will undermine political and economic stability. I decided Naylor might amend his views upon hearing Detective Flynn.

People rely on systems and on trust, Flynn continued. Systems, he said, are interlinking institutions like banking and legal institutions and the contractual relations that support these; trust is grounded in the faith people have in social interactions. Trust puts a face, and face-to-face interactions, to the system. Without this, the system fails. At worst, it collapses altogether. By way of definition, consider what happens, Flynn rubbed his forehead in contemplation, if people lose all faith in their society's legal and financial systems.

> The bottom line in all this is that if you can't trust the system in late capitalist society, it's chaos.
> The capitalist system is terrified that people will lose trust in the system.

If they don't trust it, they will move to what they do trust, to bartering, to another system.

With these words, Flynn captured one of the most difficult theoretical ideas I have struggled to portray in my writings: the sheer fragility and transience of the power systems that seem so all-pervasive in our lives.

Ultimately, this is the lesson taught by the fall of kingly rule and the rise of the modern state in the 1600s, and by the traders who worked outside of monarchial law to set the foundations for state-based capitalist and judicial systems. Systems do collapse, and are replaced by others. The state is here only because people choose to believe in it — because they trust its systems. The relationship is a tenuous and evanescent one. This, then, is the threat of crime to modern society: not that it will overcome civilization with violence, but that it will undermine trust in, and thus the viability of, the system.

Shifting direction slightly as he elaborated, the detective added:

> Criminals use the same methods as legitimate businesses. For example, they can "buy" the expertise they need, from lawyers to MBAs. The more successful ones [criminals] have a social conscience. They build schools, health-care clinics, lending services at decent rates; they pay for the funerals of widows—and all this gives them some legitimacy. So people begin to "protect" criminals. Like in Northern Ireland. People buy into the community that gives these kinds of protective structures.

A shift of trust and legitimacy, and states collapse. It's a story told time and again throughout history, from the dynasties of China through the feudal empires of the middle ages to the fall of colonial expansionism and the proxy battles of the Cold War.

The difficulty in untangling all this is that the racketeer in forced child prostitution and the Nobel Peace Prize Laureate Daw Aung San Suu Kyi, who stands against oppressive rule in Burma, can both be painted with the label "criminal" in formal legal terms.

Flynn turned to speak of crime in general:

> In truth, society deserves the type of crime it gets. Looking at crime honestly raises uncomfortable questions: about the inequality in society, about who holds the power in society.
> It's all a result of late capitalist society. Market forces and consumerism give rise to the illicit system we have.
> There are legitimate opportunity structures, and illegal, illicit ones. Which

you have access to boils down to individual background. Who you know, the
money you have, the access you have to education.

Flynn went on to explain that in times of peace, legitimate opportunity structures are (or have been) relatively stable. But the legacies of war,
and more importantly today, the explosion in global capital, have made
traditional opportunity structures unstable. Informal economies pick up
where the legitimate economy doesn't deliver.

Herein, the detective said, lies the problem with police work today;
and it helps explain the new, and successful, era in criminality. In the past
criminal strongholds were fairly fixed, like gaming in the previous century. These were well-known operations, and the police could take action
against them. Now the police are working in markets they don't understand, using tactics they don't understand, and advanced technology they
don't understand.

In an increasingly complex world, the criminal thrives on being the
most advanced in financial, intelligence, and network knowledge and
access. This is the heart of understanding crime and its resilience, Flynn
explained. Extra-legal structures find the weaknesses and holes in legitimate structures and exploit them.

> The curious thing is that the vibrancy of the economy as a whole, its adapt-
> ability to pressures and change, often comes from the non-formal sector.
> Organizations, legitimate or illegitimate, tend to become "organized" over
> time. They settle into structures that socialize people into their ways of think-
> ing and doing business. They ossify. They met the needs of a society in the
> past, but as they become large, tradition bound, and ossified, they don't
> respond well to change and pressing new needs.

It's the lowest sector of "unorganized" crime that meets the new needs of
a society that legal systems can't, for whatever reason. Criminality is about
markets, Flynn stressed. It's about supply and demand. When there is
demand, and legitimate enterprises can't respond, illicit ones do.

These are fragile and weak markets — they break up easily on raids, and
they reconstitute in new forms and in new places to meet new needs. But
with ongoing success, they develop better structures, better markets, and
they become more resistant to raids and attacks by outside forces. They
gain power. But they become more resistant to change and adaptability
themselves. In fact, the top layers of criminal organizations are quite similar in the way they operate. It's only as one goes down the hierarchy that

criminal activities get more atomized, that you find different practices and different ways of doing business.

So it's at the very bottom that the vibrancy of the market emerges. The market as a whole. It's a bubbling up of frenetic activity looking for new markets. This keeps the whole system going. Here societies find need meeting creative solution. It's dynamism: constant activity, constant new solutions—it's where tomorrow's answers are forged today. Some fail, and these markets wither away; some are successful and move up the ladder to bigger and bigger commodities, services, organizations . . . until they are "eaten" by an already existing organization. And then they too become settled into "organized" market services and the new ideas are again coming from below them, from the bottom.

And of course, it's only those at the bottom that get caught. The guy selling cigarettes on the streets isn't the brains behind the system. The people who get caught are those with low self-esteem. As people work their way up the system, they become more and more divorced from the "illicitness" of the system. It's extremely hard to bust them. Those higher up are protected by layers and layers of laundering, organization, and seeming legitimacy.

Listening to this, I was reminded of the philosopher Alexander Düttmann's *Between Cultures,* and the problems and creativities that adhere to these realms of questionable recognition:

If one wished to understand the expression "between cultures" as an abbreviated or cryptic imperative, it would oddly prescribe the impossibility of catching up with something, of bringing it back, and would read: *Stay in the gap of an in-between, keep creating new connections and forging new contexts!* (Düttmann 2000: 77; italics in the original)

And why does the system work? What is it that drives small-scale informal structures to develop? It works, Detective Flynn says, because at the everyday level, average people are involved. People buy cigarettes cheaper on the streets. Doctors provide unrecorded services outside of clinic hours.

People simply are not averse to going to a Spiv.

When I looked confused at the word *Spiv,* Flynn explained that this is also called "Dad's Economy": a well-dressed person who gets you what you need on the informal market, nicely. He continued:

Listen, you have to understand, it's not about criminals forcing society, it's about everyday people making decisions and choices. People make decisions, and they make the system.

And how does a normal, "law-abiding" person engage in the illicit and keep their sense of integrity? Like [sociologist Erving] Goffman says, they downplay their sense of wrongdoing. It's a psychological defense: "Everyone does it, it's not really bad, I'm not involved in criminal activity . . ."

This keeps the entire system running.

Crim as a way for the formally disenfranchised to gain entitlement!

and they may realize that whats illegal is not necessarily immoral or unethical ...

see p. 150

Agency

TYPICAL DAY. PORT OF ROTTERDAM.

CHAPTER 16

THE WORLD-PORT

> For the police, the key to solving crime is transport. I can't overstate this point. From gangs to big illegal organizations, transport lies at their core: Whatever it is, whatever they are dealing in or doing, they have to get something from one point to another. They have to transport. Look at transport sites — ships, lorries, customs, containers — and you are looking at the heart of crime.
>
> TON HOUGEE, ROTTERDAM POLICE DEPARTMENT

THE "MAGIC" OF CONTAINERS

Arriving in Rotterdam from Africa, I was greeted by an orderly world. It is one of the world's largest and most successful ports; there is a good chance the cigarettes the war orphan was selling in Africa passed through Rotterdam.

Scrubbed streets lead to well-maintained berths with carefully stacked skyscrapers of containers loaded by technologically sophisticated machines onto sleek freighters. Clean buildings and even cleaner port authorities project an impression of "clean business." The system, like the ships, looks sleek and secure. A sense of comfort and security is transmitted; twenty-first-century commerce passes through these portals and sustains life as we know it.

There is little to prompt a person to question what illegal commodities might be snuggling amid the medicines, what dangerous substances might be traveling with sofas and chairs, what containers might be outfitted with air conditioning to keep illegally trafficked people alive for transoceanic voyages. There is little to suggest that in the very act of such order, the dis/ordering of laws is possible. But magicians know that it's visibility itself that allows for sleight-of-hand, the ability to disappear and conjure things in apparently thin air. The lowly container sitting so very visibly on docks and ships is indeed a paragon of in/visibility — and of revolutionary significance in twenty-first-century global criminality. In a world of advanced computer systems, ultramodern ships, and an elite command and communication system, the humble 20 × 8 × 8–foot metal box with swinging doors is the fulcrum of transformation in shipping.

Globalization is being debated both peacefully and violently throughout the world. The legal world dominates these debates. Yet hidden in the sheer volume of trade, in the economics of immediacy, in the logistics of transport, and in the contemporary revolutions in shipping lies the globalization of the illegal.

But in all of this, the humble container plays a startlingly important role in the success and globalization of unregulated trade: containers are effective, efficient, and safe — and they're hard to inspect. The pallets of yore were unwieldy, nonstandardized, and transparent. In the words of a shipping agent working for a company whose maritime genealogy goes back through centuries of Dutch seafaring:

> Now you see the most sophisticated smuggling systems imaginable, just because of the advent of containers. Today we see containers set up to smuggle people that are so technologically advanced it's hard to believe until you see it. Containers with full atmospheric controls to provide oxygen and eliminate carbon dioxide and all odors or gases that might alert monitoring systems; with toilets to eliminate waste without smell or filth; with food and water and noise-proof padding. They move people with an ease unimaginable just years back. Think how easy it is to move drugs, to underdeclare your goods, to move sanctioned commodities. Essentially, there is no catching this.

The simple efficiency of mass transport is summed up in the words of Damián Zaitch, an academic specializing in illegal drug research in the Netherlands:

> I just don't understand the focus on these drug "mules," the people who carry narcotics in themselves or their bags as they travel across borders. They carry a miniscule fraction of the total trade. For real quantities, you pop it into a container and ship it.

But what is the "it" that is popped into a container? Drugs, it would appear, are habit forming, even to law enforcement. This "habit" — a focus on one area of smuggling to the exclusion of others — creates an invisibility that hides the gamut of extra-legal activities. We need to start from scratch and ask, What is hidden? What constitutes danger?

Ton Hougee of the Rotterdam police echoes the sentiments of his colleagues in Scotland Yard and the British and South African customs services. He says that illegal narcotics are clearly dangerous, but they garner a disproportionate amount of police, customs, and security attention while representing a minority of all illegal activity. Smuggling cigarettes, he notes by way of example, and stealing from customs by not paying accurate taxes on commercial goods add up to considerable sums.

> We are used to talking about drugs. It's a habit, you might say. When we think of smuggling, we have a tradition of focusing on the high profile and the highly criminal.
>
> But perhaps this focus on drugs, this habit of fixing on drugs, drugs, drugs is old-fashioned. If you look at everything that is illegal, drugs are not always the greatest crime, nor the greatest part of crime.
>
> If you look at the actual volume of what is smuggled, you find market articles, copyright infractions for CDs, videos and DVDs, jeans, designer labels, watches, all these kinds of things counterfeited, smuggled, and sold across every port around.
>
> For the police, we have priorities in what we attend to. Where are the most complaints? This is what drives us. Drugs, they are the scourge of habit. Stolen cars, they are a real problem. Stolen cars link up with all kinds of activities from Eastern European and Russian gangs. CDs? That's just not in the same league. What is the real price for a CD? In raw economic terms, it's five cents of plastic and a chip. So a 20-euro copy comes out of Europe and a 10-euro one from Eastern Europe. Which will people buy?

WELCOME TO ROTTERDAM AND THE ILLUSION OF INSPECTION

Rotterdam is a window into the world of containers, into the successes and secrets of mass shipping. It is the world's largest port in terms of raw size, with the most freight passing through its gateways. Port facilities and strategic location make the Netherlands a global crossroads where the legal, the illicit, and the downright dangerous go hand in hand. People sometimes assume that Holland's liberal social values are implicated in this. For some, a legal sex and drug trade equates to an accepted smuggling ethos. Dutch tolerance, I have heard people suggest, is the culprit. A foray into the world of trade shows that liberal attitudes don't explain illicit trade. As we will see in exploring the Ports of Los Angeles and Long

Beach, Holland is no different from any major port in the world; global business practices are the answer.

Page one of the Port of Rotterdam's formal Municipal Port Management publication calls Rotterdam "the front and back door to the continent." Whether the irony of these words is apparent to the authors is unclear. Their words capture, perhaps unwittingly, the inability to regulate the unregulated.

In the Port of Rotterdam's success, size, and sophistication lies the secret of the extra-legal. It covers 26,000 acres — an area bigger than many cities. In 2005, over 30,000 seagoing vessels and 133,000 inland ships visited this port. They carried approximately 400 million metric tons of cargo throughput, and over 9 million containers. Serious about keeping its top position in the world of shipping, the port boasts that most of Europe is accessible within twenty-four hours.

On an average day, 81 seagoing and 364 inland vessels visit Rotterdam, carrying 1.095 million metric tons of cargo and 24,657 containers. Only the smallest percentage can be checked by police, security, or customs. Rotterdam has portable, state-of-the-art scanning machines. While this sounds like an ideal solution, it takes several hours to scan a single container. Each container must be off-loaded, transported to the scanner, monitored by the appropriate authorities, potentially unpacked if the scanner picks up anything, reloaded, and retransported. Large, 6,000-plus container ships are common here: consider inspecting a container at the bottom of the ship under tightly packed, towering stacks of multi-ton metal boxes that can only be moved one by one.

The economic pressure to move cargo is tremendous, as a representative of the local chamber of commerce explained:

> If we want to stay the number one port, we have to deliver. Businesses now plan to the day, and often to the hour, when they need critical supplies. The calculations are straightforward: The ship arrives, the cargo is off-loaded onto inland road, rail, or sea transport and it arrives at their door, usually within twenty-four hours. These are essential supplies; businesses need to ensure they arrive as planned. So what happens if we hold up these shipments for inspection?
>
> This isn't just a matter of disrupting people's businesses by holding essential cargo. It's also a matter of who pays for all this. Scans are expensive. The people needed to off-load, scan, monitor, and reload cargo are expensive. The port fees for the ship are expensive. Rebooking inland transport is expensive—assuming it's available at a later date. The potential slowdown to the business is expensive. Care for refrigeration items that can spoil is expensive. Who pays for all this?

> Of course, security is a top concern, but so is staying competitive. If we hold up crucial cargo, then the business just moves to a port in the next country. These are very difficult issues.

The world of shipping can't be calculated in national terms, nor can it be seen in discrete segments — ships versus rail versus road. These are articulated and fluid transnational transport systems — or, as the official Port of Rotterdam publication says, the "multimodal" realities of the twenty-first century. This very multimodality explains why the Netherlands is a formal trade empire and an informal trade crossroads.

The Port of Rotterdam marketing material promises

> transit hubs where goods can switch modes fast; from inland barge to train and truck, from truck to train, from short sea/feeder to rail. Everything is made possible. High shipment volumes mean waiting times are short, efficiency high, and costs moderate.

Rotterdam can reach 350 million people in a 1,300-kilometer radius within twenty-four hours, from southern Norway and Sweden to northern Italy, and from Ireland to Poland and Hungary. The port boasts the following:

- 10,000 haulers run 12,500 trucks a day from the Port of Rotterdam to Europe.
- Over 200 container shuttles weekly connect to the 230,000-kilometer European rail network.
- 27 container inland barge operators and 110 scheduled container services handle almost 25 percent of Rotterdam's containers along inland waterways. Their motto? "No traffic jams to hold up your cargo."
- A short sail links Rotterdam to over 200 European, Mediterranean, and North African ports.

Looking just at Europe: more than a billion tons of seaborne cargo alone moved through just ten of the major European Union ports in 2005. According to the Institute of Shipping Economics and Logistics (ISL), approximately 20 million containers moved through European ports in 2005. Expand this to worldwide proportions: in 2005 the ISL estimated the total world cargo trade at 8.7 billion metric tons. The total container traffic at the top fifty ports was approximately 200 million TEUs (Twenty-foot Equivalent Units).

Large numbers also hold true for the most exclusive trade routing: air cargo. In Europe, 26,000 commercially recognized flights take place each day. (By comparison, 48,000 flights are handled by air traffic control daily in the USA.) A Rotterdam chamber of commerce representative noted:

> What we've said holds doubly for air transport and cargo. Air transport is obviously more expensive, so the goods that are carried tend to be the more valuable. They are not only valuable in cost, but in importance—they are needed immediately. Perishables. Crucial industrial parts. Sophisticated electronic equipment. Essentials. You fly them in, get them onto transport, and get them to where they are going with no delay. Inspections are delay.

A TRADE EMPIRE LOOKS AT DEFINITIONS AND SOLUTIONS

Two-thirds of all trade moves outside of legal channels, according to David Hesketh. When all forms of illegality are considered, from the mundane to the outrageous, specialists from Scotland Yard to South Africa estimate that 90 percent to virtually all trade crosses some border of acceptable regulation. The unregulated — the illicit and the smuggled — is fundamental to the world of business, economics, and politics as we know them in the modern world. Crime, it seems, pays. Well.

Of course, national laws and international overseers determine what is legal at any given point in time. And as governing bodies change, so too do the rules of legality.

> You don't have smuggling, *says Hesketh,* if you don't have taxes and prohibitions.

Working internationally, Hesketh has struggled with answering the dilemmas of commerce and law from his home country (a long-established monarchy, colonial power, and dominant sea force) through small peaceful countries seeking development (as in the Caribbean), to war-torn countries hoping to rebuild a feasible infrastructure (like Afghanistan):

> Trade, not smuggling, is a tradition.
> Trade has always existed; it only becomes smuggling when restrictions are put on trade. It all boils down to two things: smuggling is trade for money, like all trade; and it falls under a set of laws seeking to control the legitimacy of trade. Taxing trade provides money for the powers that be, but it also restricts the power of the traders.
> Look at early U.K.: taxing trade was a way for kings to raise money for militaries and war, but it also was a way of controlling access across their

lands. Without this, it was trade, and not smuggling. But for many, the priorities of the king and the way the rulers put taxes to use did not represent their needs: as traders, they might find themselves more repressed, might be the targets or the casualties of war, with this tax money. A lot of what we are dealing with today was born in the industrial revolution, and you can see the same trends. Profit was made out of the expense of average people.

But who decided the rules? How did they get control? Who owns the land that incurs taxes? The answer is, people with money. So power and money equate to the ability to create and impose the rules.

Hesketh settled into his chair in his London office to reflect for a moment on how this system of power linked to larger social worlds. Rules, he explained, are often set by people with "old values." These are the people who occupy traditional authority structures, he said, who hold old English notions of upper and lower class. We all know these class-based systems, he said, sitting up to pantomime an authority figure and saying: "Don't answer back. Do as I say and not as I do." Turning serious, he concluded that these values are then protected by the power structure. He then turned to consider the larger picture:

> What are the morals of society in total? I'm not for criminal activity; I'm talking about the values of a caring society. The values that create conditions where people don't feel they have to cross into illegal activities.
>
> One answer I see, for example, follows from what you could call the Dubai example. Don't focus on smuggling per se, but make the best use of trade. Don't lower your values, but don't use old outdated dogmas.

Before he explained what he meant, Hesketh said, it was important to understand the reality of today's world. To look at goods through the idea of virtual warehousing. An old system of charging taxes for going across frontiers still operates. But in practice, goods move outside of the concept of borders and customs. Even certificates of origin are impossible now, Hesketh noted. What does this mean for customs and taxes? What are ports in a world of virtual warehouses? He cited the example of cannabis, saying it is just too hard to control — too much cannabis and too few officers. "So we raise the threshold and focus on cocaine and heroin, saying cannabis isn't that bad. We must turn a blind eye to the 'little bits,' but the little bits get bigger and bigger." On another front, he noted, customs goes to British Airways and DHL, for example, and asks them to open their records and offer full compliance and in exchange, customs will leave them alone. They agree, and customs reduces their staff, focusing instead on computerized risk assessment systems. But no one, he admits, is really looking at what is going on with British Airways and DHL. Hesketh rubbed his forehead, the enduring headache: more is put into containers, and increasingly fewer staff are available to open them. "And when a problem arises, when the little bits get out of hand, we have even fewer staff and less ability to deal with it."

> There is a better way. This takes us back to the Dubai example, and a focus on trade. Don't have the old traditional system of tariffs, levies, taxes, and duties along national regulatory lines. Instead, become a shareholder in all the companies doing business across your borders. Don't tax, just take a percentage of the profits. Tell businesses making a profit within your borders that the government will take 1 percent. This system recognizes of course that illegal commodities remain illegal, but if a greater incentive exists for legitimate profit, there will be less attraction to engage in illegal activities.
>
> Compare this to what we have now: in trying to make a map fit on a country where it just does not fit, we are making opportunities for corrupt people to continue to make substantial amounts of money. In trying to impose a system the majority of the world does not use, we have ended up with a world where two thirds of all trade goes outside of legal controls.

Alan Hall, a well-respected customs expert who has worked worldwide, told me that customs was getting hit hard for not controlling illicit activity. Some of this was warranted, he noted, and customs needed to revise its procedures. Like everyone I spoke with on this topic, from South Africa to Britain, he stressed that paying a customs officer $50 a week was just asking for corruption. Despite this, he concluded, customs is in essence a self-assessment system. It is the businesses themselves who must self-regulate.

> The largest perpetrators of fraud are the multinationals. Sure, we can focus on corrupt customs officials who take a kickback or a radio.
>
> But look at these people: they are poorly paid workers who are approached by a large company and given a huge incentive the first time to turn a blind eye. Then, the corporations say, "Hey, we have you now," and they then begin to pay the customs worker poorly as well. And the big businesses walk away scot-free.
>
> Where does the morality begin? Where do you go to stop this? How do you opt out of a destructive system?

The answer, it would appear, is in making visible the entire system of un/regulated trade and il/licit activity. The multinationals as well as the cartels; the respected corporations as well as the street criminals; the gov-

(what Nordstrom is doing in her book)

ernments breaking sanctions for arms and supplies as well as the organized crime rings.

Rather than denying the fact that regulation is well nigh impossible in a world with a symbolic handful of officials expected to cover an immense commercial universe, perhaps revising the dogmas, as David Hesketh suggests, or placing responsibility for ethics on businesses, as Alan Hall said, would prove more fruitful. If the citizenry points out that many of our beloved daily products are coming to us underdeclared; if they show that this represents a substantial profit for company shareholders but amounts to billions of tax dollars lost to the entire social good in health, education, and opportunity systems for a country, then companies might find ways to be more accountable to both the market and to a social ethos. If security specialists point out that inspection and regulation are impossible under the current system; if they show how to remove the incentives for corporate tax evasion, then the purely criminal and dangerous will become more visible and controllable.

DOWNTOWN SINGAPORE.

CHAPTER 17

THE INVESTMENT MACHINE
LAUNDERING, PART TWO

Offshore Survival Kit

The Complete Offshore Package for The International Man

1. Central American Citizenship — excellent visa-free travel opportunities *(click here)* & Driving Permit (retail: US$40,000).
2. Anonymous Panama Corporation with Nominee Directors (retail: US$999).
3. Asset Protection Offshore Trust (retail: US$150).
4. International Driving Permit — 5 years validity (retail: US$200).
5. Travel Agent ID Card — lifetime validity (retail: US$300).
6. Anonymized Visa Gold Credit Card with immediate US$170 credit line (retail: US$900).
7. Baltic Offshore Bank Account without banking reference (retail: US$250).
8. 2 Czech Anonymous Savings Accounts (retail: US$1,000).
9. Swiss Maildrop Service with street address, phone, fax and US$250 deposit, 3 years (retail: US$800).
10. Anonymized Mobile Phone with Card (GSM) and 1 year's basic fees paid in advance, plus US$300 connect charges deposit (retail: US$1,200).
11. The Offshore Manual & Directory (retail: US$147).
12. Multiple DHL air courier deliveries: US$250.

The above items do normally retail together for *US$46,146*. Our price: US$39,000.

Delivery Time: 3–4 weeks.

WWW.OFFSHORE-MANUAL.COM, ACCESSED FEBRUARY 3, 2005

In 2001, the South African rand suddenly went from 7 to 14 to the US dollar. That was a boon for people paid in dollars, but a severe blow to the majority of the population. Overnight, people found themselves unable to afford life's basic necessities. As most of these necessities — food, medicines, fuel, industrial equipment, technology — are purchased in the world's cosmopolitan centers with dollars or other strong global currencies, people with rands could only buy half of what they had been able to just days before.

It seemed logical to conclude that a group of people had made a run on the nation's monies by manipulating the financial markets, in all likelihood using unrecorded profits. At the time, I was tracking money laundering and was learning how stock and bond markets, business financing, industrial loans, currency values, interest rates, and international exchange are playgrounds for money launderers. And I had just read John McDowell and Gary Novis's paper on the kinds of power money laundering can generate:

Unchecked, money laundering can erode the integrity of a nation's financial institutions. Due to the high integration of capital markets, money laundering can also adversely affect currencies and interest rates. Ultimately, laundered money flows into global financial systems, where it can undermine national economies and currencies. (2001: 4)

And:

In some emerging market countries, these illicit proceeds may dwarf government budgets, resulting in a loss of control of economic policy by governments. Indeed, in some cases, the sheer magnitude of the accumulated asset base of laundered proceeds can be used to corner markets — or even small economies. (2001: 2)

Suggesting that extra-state as well as legal monies can be used to manipulate the financial health of an emergent national economy might seem excessive. Many in South Africa agreed — at first. But as the economic distress continued for the better part of a year and experts were called on to study the rand's precipitous crash, more began reporting that Machiavellian minds and secret flows of capital might well be at play. A year after the rand crashed, it regained its former health of 7 to the dollar, where it has since remained, largely unchanged.

Some things, though, were changed forever. A number of businesses were unable to weather the financial storms. Those with the resources were not only able to ride out the economic lows but also to acquire new holdings from those who'd had to sell. Many of the little fish were fished out, the successful big fish gained greater monopolies, and a handful of the elite used the economic downturn to acquire real political and financial control.

. . .

Estimates place money laundering at 10 percent of global GDP. That equals $5.9 trillion a year (Naím 2005).[1] Yet even these figures are conservative. Money-laundering estimates are generally based on high-profile, extra-legal commodities and services like narcotics, weapons, and trafficking. No estimate I know of factors in all extra-legal profit. Charles Goredema, a leading scholar on money laundering at South Africa's Institute for Security Studies in Cape Town, captured these problems well:

> There is no agreed-upon definition of what "money" we consider in money laundering. It certainly isn't all the money in the world that is laundered. Generally, the experts focus on the high-profile criminal profits: drugs, illegal arms, mafia enterprises, that sort of thing. But even here, experts don't agree. Do we include (unreliable) estimates on small-scale low-impact drugs, or stick with the large criminal networks? Consider unrecorded arms transfers by governments or only non-state actors? What about the sex industry?—something, curiously, many don't include.
>
> "What about white-collar crime?" I asked.
>
> Habits get started; camps get set up. Those who define laundering by focusing on the heavily criminal don't tend to even recognize white-collar profits. There are people who do try to calculate this, but it is not generally included in figures on yearly global laundering.
>
> "Do people ever try to figure in all the unrecorded trade in the basics: food, petrol, medicines; or the high-tech goods like computers, software, and industrial equipment?"
>
> Nope.
>
> "Do people at the expert meetings even talk about including these monies?"
>
> Almost never. Oh, once in a while. There are some innovative people trying to tackle this. But the question is still, "How do you do it?"

At the most conservative level, what is the impact of moving up to 5 trillion unrecorded dollars into the legal economy in ways that can't, by definition, be assessed?

The answer is that it yields invisible power: the ability to shape markets, politics, and the financial stability of countries and even continents outside regulation and the control of law.

. . .

When I was crafting this chapter in 2005, John Perkins's 2004 *Confessions of an Economic Hit Man* was among the top ten best-selling nonfiction books, according to the *New York Times*. Given its searing message about corporate abuses of power, I find the book's popularity interesting, even surprising. In the context of South Africa, and all the countries that have faced similar conditions, it's a telling story:

Economic hit men (EHMs) are highly paid professionals who cheat countries around the globe out of trillions of dollars. They funnel money from the World Bank, the U.S. Agency for International Development (USAID), and other foreign "aid" organizations into the coffers of huge corporations and the pockets of a few wealthy families who control the planet's natural resources. Their tools include fraudulent financial reports, rigged elections, payoffs, extortion, sex, and murder. They play a game as old as empire, but one that has taken on new and terrifying dimensions during this time of globalization.

I should know; I was an EHM. (ix)

Perkins continues,

Claudine told me that there were two primary objectives of my work. First, I was to justify huge international loans that would funnel money back to MAIN [the US Corporation Perkins worked for, with implicit support of the NSA] and other U.S. companies (such as Bechtel, Halliburton, Stone & Webster, and Brown & Root) through massive engineering and construction projects. Second, I would work to bankrupt the countries that received those loans (after they had paid MAIN and the other U.S. contractors, of course) so that they would be forever beholden to their creditors, and so they would present easy targets when we needed favors, including military bases, UN votes, or access to oil and other natural resources. (15)

If corporations regularly do this kind of work — and Perkins writes that such professionals are employed in nearly every major corporation in the world, from General Electric and General Motors to Nike, Monsanto, and Wal-Mart — then their business counterparts working extra-legally do the same. Profits aren't simply about money, they're about power, for legal corporations and criminal organizations alike. Both employ similar methods. Manipulation of national financial structures is central to the acquisition of power.

Both legal and criminal businesses must launder, as crime expert R. T. Naylor (2002: 137–38) writes:

If underground entrepreneurs — from stock market manipulators to cigarette smugglers — must launder money, so too must legitimate corporations, to disguise a bribe or kickback. Even government agencies have recourse to the apparatus to break an embargo or fund a coup in some rival state. . . . The offenses that generate serious money are committed by eminently respectable citizens who run big-name corporations by day and patronize the opera at night. Their take comes in corporate checks, stock options, and kickbacks deposited into offshore slush funds by foreign suppliers.

These aren't people who worry about getting audited for depositing $10,000 in a bank account.[2] In this world, that's pocket change. And the pockets often belong to respected businesspeople whose millions and billions banks actively seek.

Few millionaires or billionaires who need to launder money worry about being investigated: people who have achieved this kind of wealth have generally also achieved respectability and interconnected legal businesses that can easily absorb unrecorded funds. But should the need to avoid detection arise, solutions abound. Naylor (2002) writes about "insta-banks" — banks that can be purchased cheaply in cash-strapped countries. In the same vein, Peter Lilley (2001: 13) shows there are always advertisements in leading newspapers worldwide offering banks and banking licenses. In fact, he notes, today a person can buy an offshore bank over the Internet with a credit card. Banks can be purchased for as little as $25,000. Complete anonymity can be guaranteed by buying your bank with an anonymous credit card. Why worry about laundering when you can run your funds through your own bank and authorize the money's legitimacy yourself?

Naylor expands upon the options: not only are there insta-banks, he says, but also "insta-countries." The launderer can buy a country and route financial transactions through it. Instant laundering. There are islands, small territories, and other physical bits of geography for sale. But as Naylor (2002: 183) concludes, why worry about such old-fashioned notions in the postmodern era? Why settle for an insta-country with a fixed address when you can have a cyber-state, with no fixed address?

There are certainly people who find buying banks and countries profitable, even exhilarating. However, most launderers I have talked to don't find this necessary. The majority are competent businesspeople who are comfortable in today's globalized markets. They are at home overseeing complex interlocking networks of legal, offshore, shell, and unregistered business interests, all variously linked through an equally complex network of financial institutions that stretch across countries and continents. In a world where 50 percent of all corporate monies are moved within a corporation's holdings, laundering is so easy and invisible to legal assessment that it is virtually fail-safe. For the most part, most people who launder money don't see themselves as criminals. They are doing smart business. As Lilley (2001: 102) writes:

What is vital to realize is that these Offshore Financial Centres can be utilized together to create an almost impenetrable maze of International Business Companies, Trusts, anonymous bank accounts and offshore banks.

Once money enters the system anywhere — from a corporate account, an insta-bank, or an offshore fund — it can instantaneously, easily, and anonymously be transferred around the world, from account to account, stock purchase to loan, business investment to divestment, via computer and the Internet.

Professionals laugh at movie depictions where computers show the minutes and seconds it takes for money transfers to take place. Outside of Hollywood, scores of transfers take place across the globe in that time — any single one taking no more time than a single film frame. These amount to scores of transfers that can obfuscate the identity of the launderers so that no court of law can legally prosecute them: for what court has jurisdiction over multiple countries, holdings by different people and corporations, and anonymous offshore financial transactions? Today, money is washed squeaky clean in nanoseconds.

. . .

Offshore Companies:

It has been estimated that 65% of the world's hard currency is held in offshore banks and that around 40% of world trade in goods [is] transacted through offshore finance centres. Offshore companies and/or offshore trusts are not the illicit hideaways that many would have you believe. They can in fact provide you with enormous tax savings and asset protection in a legal manner if set up correctly. They can also afford the ultimate beneficial owner a certain amount of anonymity.

CONSTANTINOU & KYRIACOU ACCOUNTANTS, AUDITORS & BUSINESS CONSULTANTS
WWW.OFFSHORE-COMPANY.ORG, ACCESSED 3 FEBRUARY 2005

How easy is this?

The answer is, dangerously easy. In several hours on the Net one night I found all the information a person needs to set up a completely anonymous complex of untraceably interwoven businesses, banking accounts, communications systems, and financial transfers across the world's continents — making it almost impossible to track these linked businesses or to find any coherent legal structures to investigate them across all these countries and continents. The fact that part of these services includes the option to buy secondary citizenships and passports (in new names, if desired) ensures invisibility. The ability to buy diplomatic passports and all the attendant immunities, academic diplomas, and a title of nobility (from the Internet) adds status and an aura of legitimacy, however fraudulent.

Let me be clear here: in two hours, I found over a dozen companies from a list of hundreds that were of sufficient quality to begin comparison shopping. Should I need help picking my companies, a score of publications, from books on Amazon.com, through print journals, to online magazines are devoted to answering the investor's every question. Legal and financial advice is available from a host of lawyers and accountants, specialists and banking officials around the world who advertise on the Net.

A surprising number of these companies dedicated to setting up offshore services cite "Freedom" and "Democracy" (often with quotes by the USA's founding fathers) as the critical philosophy justifying offshore activities — not merely "wealth." Obtaining privacy, as they would have it, is a political right, not a criminal act; and it is presented as being eroded by today's government. Offshore is thus often presented, curiously, as patriotic.

Here is an average basic package (I have removed all names in this announcement):

Ultimate Asset Protector Package! Privacy, wealth and freedom will no longer be dreams, but reality for you! Contrary to popular belief, you don't ever have to go to the country where you incorporate or open a bank account. What does the package include?

- A [Country A] Offshore Foundation (reg. $1,295): Issuance of "bearer" share certificates, powers of attorney, no legal liability for nominee directors, and complete zero-tax status for non-profit business conducted OUT-SIDE of [Country A] enable you to keep your affairs 100% confidential and anonymized.

- A [Country B] Offshore Corporation (reg. $1,595): Issuance of "bearer" share certificates, nominee director, and complete zero-tax status for business conducted OUTSIDE of [Country B] enable you to conduct your business 100% confidential and anonymized.

- A Multi-Currency Bank Account Introduction with Global Debit ATM Card Availability (reg. $650) for the foundation: [Country C] is an EXCEL-

LENT choice when it comes to safe and secure offshore banking. Being not as "obvious" an offshore jurisdiction as maybe [Country D or Country E], foreign pressure and information sharing treaties are minimal at best! This country has a stable economy and excellent privacy laws.

- A [Country B] Based Corporate Bank Account Introduction (reg. $350) for [Country B] is an EXCELLENT choice when it comes to safe and secure off-shore banking. Foreign pressure and information sharing treaties are minimal at best! [Country B] has a stable economy and comprehensive privacy laws.

- [Country F] Post Personal Account Introduction (reg. $450) : Hold your personal funds with one of the safest, most established Financial Services Organizations in [Country F].

- 10 Hours Personalized Consulting (reg. $2,750+): FREE for a full year!

How much will this valuable package cost you? Considering all the numerous benefits you get, and the increasing worldwide demand, we could easily charge $5,000 or more. If you decide to take advantage of this unique offer right now, the Ultimate Asset Protector Package will be yours for only US $2,995!!! Click here to order your ULTIMATE ASSET PROTECTOR PACKAGE today.[3]

A smorgasbord of Web sites offer complementary services: Anonymous banking. Anonymous trust. Anonymous Internet banking. Anonymous ATM MasterCard. Anonymous Cirrus debit card with Internet access. And E-Gold, billed as the "ultimate worldwide anonymous Internet marketing currency." As one site advertised:

When a notorious bank robber was asked why he robbed banks, he reportedly replied —"Because that's where the money is!" International investors have discovered for themselves that owning a bank can be even more lucrative than a career in bank robbery. Because running one's own bank dramatically demonstrates the benefits of offshore financial operations, it is the first case study of what can be accomplished once the investor breaks free of domestic confines. Banking is not as exotic as it might seem at first glance. A bank is merely a company organised much like other companies. It is built upon trust and it flourishes, as all companies do, by keeping promises.[4]

The list continues: linked offshore companies around the world, from Euro 1,999 to 4,999. Merchant accounts. And of course: Citizenship. Second passport. Diplomatic passport. Press ID. Nobility titles.

Should you require another identity and/or name other than your own, official, legal, name change documents must be filed. Your name change will be recorded by the issuing country, but nowhere else. There is an additional fee for this procedure.

Question. What can I gain from second citizenship?

Answer. Many people see a very ominous trend developing in the "free countries of the world". Every year, more and more of our freedoms are being shaved away. Already, many Western Governments have removed their citizens right to obtain a second passport (and therefore to travel) if the hapless citizen is having any of a number of civil disputes with government, including tax disputes. Even if the citizen is completely in the right he cannot leave. This would have been inconceivable just ten, fifteen years ago. Unfortunately, things seem to be getting worse rather than better and many thoughtful observers are becoming quite concerned for the future of freedom.

For the moment our firm is holding open a window of opportunity that allows one to obtain what many forward thinking individuals now consider an essential element of insurance against further loss of freedoms. How long we will be able to keep this window open is uncertain at this time, but many feel that this is a very appropriate moment to obtain supplementary citizenship, against some future "rainy day".

Question. Is it possible for me to obtain documents under a different name?

Answer. Yes. The question often arises from Middle Eastern clients whose surname might subject them to terrorism. Therefore once we are satisfied that your record is free of criminal convictions, it is possible to apply under a different name, by using a deed-poll legalised name change procedure. We can legally change your name in the country from where your new passport will be issued. To do this we must file the documents necessary for a legal name change in the issuing country, which will then allow us to apply for the passport in the new name. The name change will only be recorded in the issuing country and nowhere else. The additional fee is US$7,500 but we must emphasise that although it is perfectly legal to carry out this task, we must first be satisfied that your intentions are proper.

Question. Are my affairs kept confidential?

Answer. We are professionals of many years standing. When you become our client your secrets and your privacy are absolutely safe. No one and no other government or any other authority will be notified that you have applied for, much less obtained, a second passport. It is a private affair.[5]

Services are included: Anonymized GSM Sony Ericsson P900 Triple Band world mobile phone with Swiss (and/or Czech, Hong Kong, Philippines, Singapore) number. Encryption. As one site explains:

Whenever you make a call from a mobile phone you are leaving an "electronic trail" readily available to government agencies from your local telephone operator upon request. Phone calls are even often automatically being scanned to monitor for "suspicious words" by various agencies' computer surveillance systems and then analyzed and the phone holder recorded in Big Brother's files of suspicious persons — guilty or not of any wrongdoing.[6]

Paperless office. Mail drops. Remailing. Anonymous Internet (sites and addresses). Internet storage with encryption.

Comprehensive identity, privacy and anonymity services for ultimate secure, private, anonymous Internet use. Anonymous untraceable e-mailing, surfing, publishing, dialup, and much more.[7]

To conclude, don't forget your Travel Agent ID Card:

Don't get us wrong. This item is for novelty purposes only.

Obviously, what you do with the card after we deliver it is totally up to you. Our responsibility ends when you have the card in hand. However, the possible uses for such an item are only limited by your imagination, intestinal fortitude and believability.[8]

Your diplomatic immunity:

Diplomatic Passports and Honorary Consulships

Through our contacts at governmental level we are now able to offer diplomatic passports and honorary consulships from only US$50,000![9]

And, of course, your new "you":

Identity theft was once a serious problem. Thousands of people around the world had their identification stolen and were forced to pay large debts created by others. Up until now, law enforcement agencies and the general public have viewed this situation as chaotic. But here at A New Identity, Inc., we feel differently. If someone really wants your identity, good! Let them have it. We can get an even better one for you. Why bother with credit card debt, car loans, and home mortgages when you can leave them all behind? All you need to do is complete our free evaluation form, tell us a little bit about yourself now, and who you would like to become in the future. We'll analyze your information, determine the best identity for you, and send you a confirmation profile of the new you. Your identity will come complete with all necessary proof of existence, and cross-referenced by local and federal authorities. Once you accept your new identity, you may begin to enjoy the new you.[10]

. . .

People can set up an international business company (an IBC, in the vernacular) in one country with a sister corporation in a second, a bank in a third, and a credit card from a fourth. They receive an anonymous cell phone with service from a fifth country and an Internet site from a sixth. A mail drop and remailing service is set up in a seventh country. All this can be done from the privacy of their living room with a computer and Internet access. All anonymous, listed only by a number — or by their dog's name. Package services include a second passport and full citizenship, if desired, in the country of choice — under their real name or a new one. All this is available for under $10,000, easily purchased with an untraceable anonymous credit card from any country of the buyer's choice.

What legal system is capable of tracking, much less prosecuting, anyone setting up this nameless international maze? What national and international laws exist to allow multinational investigations, information sharing, and legal action? The answer is, virtually none. Even if such laws did exist, no country on earth has even a fraction of the numbers of law enforcement personnel or technology needed to track these global networks.

Consider the fact that a person can buy five of the above packages for $50,000 — or fifty for $500,000 — creating an impenetrable maze of invisibly interlocking corporations, financial institutions, communications networks, and identities across dozens of countries.

. . .

The classic example of the arms merchant illuminates this kind of enterprise. Johan Peleman, the former director of the International Peace and Information Service, has been tracking these extra-state linkages in an effort to bring transparency to the world of business that supplies wars in Africa. In a conversation in Antwerp, Peleman described the typical networks he uncovers:

> Arms dealers broker a deal, almost always between different nations and generally different continents. They may act as middlemen, creating the bridge between arms producer and military purchaser. But as they accumulate wealth, reputation in the industry, and business connections, they may purchase their own weapons production enterprise.
>
> Such businesspeople can manipulate commercial transport systems, sending their commodities with established airlines or shipping companies. It is more profitable, in the long run, for established merchants to buy their own airplanes or ships and set up their own shipping company.
>
> Manipulating the borders of the illegal is, for many, simply good business practice. For example, arms dealers need export licenses and end-user certificates. End-user certificates are issued by the exporting government to certify that the military and/or political recipients will be end users of the weapons, and none will go to a third party. You can buy end-user certificates from willing government officials for $20,000 – $50,000. But another way to proceed is to send one legal shipment with the correct documentation, and

more illegal ones with copies of legal documents. The process is relatively straightforward and easy to manipulate, even with competent and honest government officials. An arms dealer takes documents to an official and says, "I have all the official documents, may I get an export license?" An official from an arms-producing country deals with several thousand requests a year. So the license committee will look at the request in a formal way, asking:

1. Is there an embargo in the country?
2. Is it on a blacklist?
3. Are the weapons banned?

And the arms dealer answers: "No, no, no . . ." Maybe they lie about the weapons, maybe not. The authorities grant the license, the plane leaves. The shipment goes on a legitimate plane; but perhaps the plane doesn't go where it is scheduled to go; or maybe it goes on to a second, unscheduled stop; or just unloads at the correct destination and freights the weapons to an undeclared third-party user. Few countries that sell weapons have embassies in countries purchasing arms, and no way of checking if the planes listed on the manifests arrived, or if the arms are in the depot.[11]

The more successful can land United Nations contracts. Johan Peleman has written about Victor Bout, who ran arms deals for years and has obtained a number of UN contracts. His case is classic: he bought and sold any number of companies, aircraft, and officials. His holdings and business registrations are a tangled web of changing company names, flags of convenience, and variously legal and extra-state associations. As Peleman notes, untangling such complex multinational business structures — even, for example, to try and prove who owns what — can prove impossible for law enforcement officials.

.   .   .

Manipulating multicountry and offshore business interests is easiest for the rich. Most of these people aren't the kingpins of criminal groups and drug cartels, but respected international businesspeople. Such people gain the success and stature they enjoy in large measure by recognizing, and using, the gray areas between legal and illegal, not by overt criminal acts.

In many contexts, the following are not strictly illegal:

– buying your own bank in a tax haven and moving funds gained internationally through this (i.e., avoiding taxes);

- making loans from these banks and businesses to yourself (i.e., laundering money);

- setting up layers of interpenetrating businesses variously registered and licensed in multiple countries of convenience and sets of ownership names (i.e., formally obfuscating ownership);

- moving profits intercontinentally among these companies as interbusiness finance without declaring them in any taxable form (i.e., avoiding taxes); and

- hiring the most respected accountants, lawyers, and financiers to manage these activities (i.e., hiding profits and ownership).

These actions fall in the cracks between sovereign national law and international controls. As Greg Rawlings, of Australian National University writes, this is the dignified world of high finance (2004a, 2004b). He notes, by way of example, the fact that some of the most respected banks in the United States move their monies offshore to tax haven banks over the weekends to enhance profits, moving them back when the workweek begins again.[12] These monies from the most esteemed financial institutions in the world comingle with less reputable profits in these offshore sites. Reports such as the following can be found in newspapers around the world:

The *Daily Telegraph* has learned details of a confidential Australian Federal Police intelligence report that says Russian organized crime is involved in heroin supply, complex fraud, murder, extortion, false passports, prostitution, Internet child pornography, and foreign acquisition and takeovers of genuine companies to launder monies. . . . Up to $60 million is understood to have been laundered in Australia by Russians using bogus offshore "banks" in Pacific nations such as Nauru, Tonga, and Vanuatu. (Miranda 2005: 2)

The repercussions of this business ethos are extensive. One of the most important is that unrecorded profits are used to build, influence, and demolish economic structures throughout the world in ways that aren't transparent. And because these classic high-wealth business practices rely on moving monies and commodities outside legal detection and accountability along the same pathways terrorist and extra-state organizations use, measures to control the latter are less likely to be implemented.

HUMAN CARGO: AUTHOR ON FREIGHTER.

CHAPTER 18

HUMAN CARGO

On a balmy late summer day in 2004, several thousand containers and I sailed across the Atlantic on a freighter. The ship's voyage originated in the USA, making several stops along the eastern seaboard before sailing across the Atlantic to call at several ports in Europe.[1] In the high-security, post-9/11 world, this seemed like the closest way to see the world as a commodity would. Or a smuggler.

Like the cargo, I went from public roads to private shipping with no inspection. Worse, I couldn't find anyone to provide an inspection, immigration clearance, or customs stamp, even if I had wanted to.

From the first day, it became obvious that security does not exist, in fact it cannot exist, in the world today. Nothing I have encountered since then has challenged this conclusion. Security may exist in policy — good words printed on a page. Security may exist in the hearts and minds of people — ideals to be cherished. Security may exist as an industry — complete with infrastructure and personnel. But it does not exist in practice.

PORT OF DEPARTURE

A sole guard booth at an entrance gate, where I stopped to give my name, was the only official protection encountered upon arriving to board the freighter, which I am calling the *"Henry Braithwaite."* The gate signaled a vague interest in security, at least a fleeting acknowledgment that post-9/11 ports should appear to be guarded. Even I, middle-aged academic, could easily have jumped the fence a few hundred feet down the road without being seen. Trained professionals seeking to enter the port unseen would scoff at the ease of entry. A friend, J'Jay — who fit virtually every criterion of profiling used by USA security forces today — gave me a ride to the port and was able to enter without inspection or identification.

Any symbolic gesture of security ended at that point. We drove unheeded across the port area, through stacks of containers, and around warehouses to the ship. The few people we encountered paid no attention to us. It would have been child's play to take anything out of the car and put it into a container, a warehouse, a truck, or onto a ship; or to load anything from a container or warehouse into the car. Nor was this an isolated occurrence. The *Henry Braithwaite*'s sailing was delayed, and I wound up entering and leaving the port area several more times in identical fashion. I was curious what an immigration stamp from this port of exit would look like, so I searched for a government agent or office. But no one was there to provide it.

If looks matter in this era of profiling, I didn't fit the stereotype of a university professor; nor an official with right of access. I was dressed in scruffy jeans and a T-shirt and carried a worn duffle bag acquired on the streets of Africa for a couple of dollars.

Both the cargo and I boarded the ship easily: no one held either of us up. I was asked to show my passport; but neither I nor my bag was given even a cursory inspection. My friend was allowed free access to the ship without showing any identification at all. It would have been easy to carry any item of reasonable size to Europe undetected. Anything larger could have been slipped into a container.

During the time the ship was delayed, I twice explored the entire port area on foot, once in the afternoon, and once at midnight. Without any authorization, I meandered undisturbed around the towering stacks of containers, poking in a few that were open. Virtually none had security seals on them. It became apparent that security seals are ridiculously easy to break and copy. I was free to explore every warehouse building front to back: none were closed or locked. Nothing barred me from walking down the waterfront to look into other ships, and — perhaps the best — clamber over the large mobile loading machines that looked like strange metallic beasts lumbering through a Steven Spielberg movie. I was never stopped or questioned, nor, at night, did I encounter a single person. Had I been a criminal, I wouldn't have had to avoid security — there was none to avoid.

ATLANTIC SEAPORT, USA

When we sailed into port on our last stop before leaving the USA, the routine was identical. A long line of trucks wound slowly across the port compound, stopping for a moment to unload their cargo onto a loading crane, to be swung carefully onto the ship. A man stood nearby marking off container numbers as they arrived. In two full days and thousands of containers, I didn't see a *single* container stopped, removed from the line, opened, or inspected. Nor did I see any such inspections for any cargo on the other ships in the port. I walked the length and breadth of the port again, generally getting in the way, and looked for any indication of a customs representative, inspections of any kind, or anyone in a uniform. None were to be found. No one interrupted the line of cargo trucks that reached from the ship, out across the port and the nation's highways, into stores and businesses and ultimately, people's homes. No one interrupted me, until I finally went to the water's edge by the freighter to relax and watch the sunset. That was the only time I was approached in my entire trip. A man in jeans drove up in an unmarked truck and asked who the hell I was. "No one," I said, "just cargo off the freighter." "Well," he said, "why don't you get on the freighter like the rest of the cargo?"

Once fully loaded, the *Henry Braithwaite* pulled away from the dock to begin its ten-day voyage to Europe. In the age of terrorism, no country is to allow a person into their sovereign nation without having legally exited another sovereign nation — a fact conveyed in an official immigration exit stamp in a passport. My passport had none, so technically, I shouldn't have been able to enter any European country without investigation. But this wasn't a problem: there were no officials to check my passport in the European ports, either.

AT SEA, THE NORTH ATLANTIC

I was given free run of the *Henry Braithwaite*. It was a researcher's dream. I went from the bridge to the bowels of the ship, where giant shafts turned heavy propellers in puddles of dirty, oil-stained water. I learned how to read the symbols on the containers to see which carried toxic or dangerous substances like corrosives and explosives. The crew showed me the engine rooms, workrooms, crawl spaces, and emergency response systems. I clambered over and around the large machinery that runs the ship. I made late-night runs on the refrigerator. The first night I went to the galley for a snack, I found several of the officers sitting there eating and talking before starting the midnight watch. The officers of the ship were from Europe and Eastern Europe, the Philippines, and various points in between. None were from the USA. They asked me what I was doing, and I explained my research on illegal trade flows and security. Every man present burst into laughter. They said:

> God, that's a great topic; we can't figure out the USA at all. There is all this table pounding about terrorism and security, and absolutely none exists.
>
> We talk about this all the time: we could blow up just about anything anywhere here and no one is even around to see it. It's even worse than that: did you notice when we left port . . .

The men went on to describe the vulnerabilities of the USA fleet, visible to all sailing by, and the ways in which it would be easy to launch a crippling attack using the simplest of means and technology — a ship. An earlier version of this chapter had the full quote, and one of the editors e-mailed me expressing concern that someone might read this and try to enact it — it was so simple and destructive. I countered that everyone who sails these waters apparently knows this, and shouldn't we improve security rather than hiding vulnerabilities? Yet I prefer this book not be the font of any injurious ideas, so I pick up the thread of their conversation when the officers returned to a more general level:

> If all of us can see that untrained sailors can inflict such damage, well, if trained professionals wanted to, it would be a cinch. We can't figure out why the USA cries security and leaves themselves open and vulnerable to public shipping. It's a joke: if some old freighter could cripple USA security, imagine.
>
> As far as smuggling? Who even notices? We take on containers, we offload them, no one looks. Inspections . . . *They snorted in laughter.*

On a freighter, containers are inescapable: they create the scenery, shape the horizon, and define the work. I spent several weeks looking at, talking about, walking on, and pondering containers. The heart and soul of global survival travels in these twenty- or forty-foot metal boxes. A TEU is made to carry up to thirty tons, and customs officials I interviewed explained that cranes had scales on them to check the weight to see if it matched the manifest. Crane operators, however, told me only the newest cranes had scales; and even if they did, what operator knew what the manifest said, or would hold up a container for being ten tons overweight? "Only if the container pushes up against the maximum weight the crane can carry," one crane operator told me, "do we begin to notice, and complain that this is dangerous. Like, at fifty-five tons we begin to worry."

Each container has an identity: a company ownership mark and an individual number. They're painted on by stencil. Technically, each container can be tracked according to this "foolproof" system. I noticed that a number of containers had one set of numbers painted out and others restenciled over. A can of spray paint, some construction paper, and a pair of scissors is all it takes to change the container's identity. Some containers also have repainted areas where the metal has been cut open, resealed, and painted over. Given that containers are easily accessible through large doors, why, one wonders, would holes be cut in the sides? At first, it might appear the answer is locked doors with "tamper-proof" seals. But, the doors don't lock, and those seals themselves tell a story of the illusion of security.

When I first heard about tamper-proof seals on containers, I envisioned the twenty-first-century equivalent of a medieval wax seal imprinted with the king's signet ring — something impossible to open or reproduce without detection. As I walked about the containers, I looked for the seals, and my eyes scanned the metal boxes for something large and imposing. I saw large decals painted on the sides of containers declaring "Bureau Veritas 1828" with an impressive crest showing a man standing on the scales of justice and holding a torch in one hand and an orb in the other — but these were merely symbolic declarations of security and served no functional purpose of sealing containers. I certainly couldn't find the king's ring.

The first time I saw the so-called tamper-proof seals, I laughed. They were simple bands of plastic, fashioned much like a hospital bracelet, with a one-way closure that must be cut to be opened, and each was stamped with a number. They are threaded through the eyeholes of one of the door levers, one per container. A simple device from an office supply company could make these by the carload lot. If smugglers are sophisticated enough to move billions of dollars of cargo across international borders and launder money through the world's most professional financial institutions, they can easily churn out plastic bands stamped with any number desired.

A large percentage of the containers had no seals at all. It would be hard to hold someone accountable for their containers not having a security seal — the bands are easily cut with a pair of household scissors or a chunk of metal. How well could this hold up in a journey moving a 67,200-pound container by crane from a truck through a maze of other containers and into the hold of a ship?

"Ports were never built, never meant, to be secure," I remembered a Long Beach longshoreman saying. It would have been ridiculously easy to drop something in a container load of innocent Barbie dolls or industrial cable. And this in a post-9/11 USA with, arguably, the best security available.

During the voyage, I talked with the crew of the *Henry Braithwaite* at length about how they perceived containers and their work. The following is part of a conversation with several deckhands. All my discussions with various crew reflected these same sentiments.

> "What's in the containers?" I asked.
> Who knows?
> "Do you ever care to know?"
> We work for nine to twelve months before we get off the ship for a vacation home. Every day we see containers, every port we load and unload containers. We travel with hundreds of thousands of them in a year. Many of us have worked ships for years. No, we mostly don't care what's in the containers. Caring about what's in them doesn't help us do our job one bit. When we see containers, what we see is our job.
> "What about dangerous items?"
> They're run of the ship. We've always got something hazardous on board. We take precautions.
> "How about if people don't declare dangerous cargo?" I asked.
> It happens. That's a risk we live with. People die because of this, we've all heard the stories.
> "And still you don't care about what's in the containers?"
> You can't, really—we don't have any ability, any authorization, to inspect or control anyway. We move cargo. A container is just a thing. A one-time thing. Shipping, movement, is where it's at.
> "Could people, gangs, get together and sign on to crew a ship and use it to smuggle—people who have networks, like partners in shipping, freight, and transport that get the items to and from the ship?"
> Sure. That goes on. Everyone knows about ships like this.

Everyone who works ships also knows that human cargo is illegally transported in containers. Amid the several thousand containers being loaded onto a ship in any given port — virtually none of which are actually inspected — containers with living people inside pass through with frightening ease. Like all accommodation and travel, there are grades of service. The impoverished, the trafficked, and the kidnapped may find themselves in a cold, dark container with little more than a blanket, a jug of water, and some bread. At the high end, there are containers outfitted with air-conditioning, toilets, sleeping bunks, lighting systems, and healthy food. As military and security forces, militia, and home guard units patrol the borders of their countries to stop unregistered people from entering, unchecked containers move from country to country by the hundreds of thousands, unloading their cargo and passengers with a remarkable, and invisible, efficiency.

DOCKSIDE, EUROPE

The cargo and I entered and left the ship's first stop in Europe as easily and as invisibly as in the USA. It wasn't customs, or immigration, or security that anticipated our arrival, worried about it, prepared for it. It was trade. Commerce. As the Yoruba say, there is a god of the marketplace, Eshu: he is a trickster; all mouth and balls (Hecht and Simone 1994).

I remembered the words of the chamber of commerce official I had interviewed in the Netherlands, realizing just how universal these words are:

> If we want to stay the number one port, we have to deliver. So what happens if we hold up these shipments for inspection?

Antwerp, for example, would love it if Rotterdam began to hold up cargo for inspections, disrupting business and profit. Port authorities are not oblivious to these truths. They can hear Eshu, the trickster deity of the markets, laughing.

As the freighter was sailing across the Atlantic, trucks, trains, cars, and airplanes were moving across Europe — all to meet up at the nodal juncture where not only land and sea, but sovereign state and international statelessness meet. *Port,* to carry; and *portal,* entry. In the same ballet seen in all major ports, as the ship docked, the crane swung beside the ship, and the first in the line of trucks waiting for their payload moved underneath the cranes. From an eagle's point of view, it looks like a long line of ants converging to carry off pieces of the day's kill. One truck, one container. No inspections halted this steady progress.[2]

When I went ashore, I couldn't even find a person to tell me how to get out of the port and into town. No customs, no immigration, no one to even ignore me. Walking around stacks of containers, I finally found a longshoreman who pointed me toward an exit. There I found a small ramshackle office where a man and a woman, apparently married, worked while their two kids, probably eight and ten, played with the stacks of paper and items on their desk, towering nearly as high as the containers outside. They took pity on me and called a cab. When it arrived, I simply left. In a world where the media and security services talk about "border security" and the difficulty of crossing borders undetected, I could not pass through immigration even if I'd tried. There is no record of me entering or leaving the country.

The same held true when I docked at my last port of call. I simply left the *Henry Braithwaite* and caught a ride into town with a man doing business at the port. When I passed through immigration at the airport when leaving the country, no immigration officers noticed that I lacked an entry stamp into the country — a red flag that can signal the threat of illegal entry. I was waved through with a smile.

According to my passport, I never made this trip.

HOME

"SECURED" PORT OFFLOADING AREA. SOUTH SEAS.

CHAPTER 19

POST-TERROR
CREATING (THE ILLUSION OF) SECURITY

> It's the end of the world here at the ports. For a long time, no one — not the journalists, not the politicians, not the policy makers — came here to see what it was really like. There are dragons here, like in the sailing days of the Middle Ages, and no one comes to look over the edge of the world.

ART WONG, PORT AUTHORITY, LONG BEACH

> End of the world? No. It's the beginning of the world.

DAVID ARIAN, PRESIDENT, ILWU LOCAL 13, LOS ANGELES

If you want to believe in security, don't visit the ports. A journey to these borderlands shows that security is an illusion. The notion of security is the magician's trick: smoke and mirrors, with a good dose of mis/direction.

But if you want to join the small in-group of people who "get it" — a phrase those who see the reality of global supply chains and the illusion of security frequently use — walk the frontlines where water meets land; where the anarchy of the sea washes up against sovereignty. "Getting it," Captain Neffenger of the U.S. Coast Guard at Los Angeles and Long Beach explains, refers to people who can see the bigger truths. The global ones. Either you have it, or you don't, he explained: you can see it, but you can't even find a good word to define it. If you don't get it, you buy the illusion of security. Finding people who get it, as we will see below, can be a headache for the captain: he was the commanding officer of the Coast Guard for the entire Los Angeles/Long Beach area when I spoke to him in 2004.

The Ports of Los Angeles and Long Beach are the end and the beginning of the world. The ports lie side by side, creating one large area divided only by an arbitrary governmental line designating two different townships — and I do mean town-*ship*. Together, the two dwarf Rotterdam, standing as the world's third-largest port system after Hong Kong and Singapore.

In 2005 over 14 million containers passed through Los Angeles/Long Beach. In total, $250 billion of legal trade passed through these ports. In longhand, that's $250,000,000,000. Forty-two percent of all the containerized cargo enters the USA through these conjoined ports. The lifeblood of American industry, food, and energy flows through Los Angeles/Long Beach.

These numbers numb the mind, and in doing so, they blunt our understanding of world trade and global security. As person after person said at the port, "No one seems to be adding two and two."

"When is the last time you saw a container being scanned by mobile X-ray or inspected by customs?" I asked the crane operator who moves the containers on and off the ships.

I can't remember the last time.

"If it takes five or six hours to do the most basic inspection opening a container, how many can you realistically do?" I asked the customs officer.

You do the math.

"What happens if you hold up transportation—ships, trains, trucks—to inspect cargo?" I asked Los Angeles Port Authority officials.

You can essentially shut down industries by delaying critical products, both in the USA and abroad. If you shut down critical industries, you can shut down countries.

"What happens if a bomb placed in a container goes off and closes the port?" I asked the Coast Guard.

You could disrupt business and service throughout the USA.[1]

"How would you smuggle something into the USA?" I asked the longshoreman.[2]

Check out China.

The majority of shipping now comes through China. It is now emerging as the world's new manufacturing giant. Hundreds of companies and countries move goods through China, thousands of products are manufactured there, millions of containers move through there. And they check so very few.

I just got back from China: they have three gamma-ray machines; with these, seventy to eighty containers maximum a day can be scanned. They have one nonmobile scanner.

> There simply are no controls.
> Smuggling? You want to talk smuggling? Or terrorism?
> An endless river of Barbie dolls, even counterfeit Barbie dolls, flows in from China to the Wal-Marts of the USA. Containers upon containers upon containers of Barbies wash up on our shores. Who inspects these? Who could?
> Drop a bomb in a container of Barbies and smuggle it in that way.

"Drop a bomb in a container of Barbies." That phrase became an icon of smuggling for me. While we look for containers coming from politically suspect ports and questionable companies, our greatest vulnerability comes from dangerous items swimming across our shores in a vast uncharted ocean of Barbie dolls. Probably counterfeit ones. Barbies made of products coming from around the globe, transshipping from port to port, country to country in ways that make "country of origin" stamped on any bill of lading or shipped product meaningless.

THE ILLUSION

Security has a formal voice. It is here, in public declarations that we can and do protect our shores and citizenry, that a country comes to believe security is indeed possible. The script, always positive, runs as follows:

> Of course we can't open every container, but we have put in place sophisticated means of inspection based on risk assessment and management. With this in place, with the advent of the kind of technology we have at our fingertips, we have what can be considered 100 percent coverage of all containers.

I have heard these reassuring words, presented like a mantra, from port authorities, customs agents, and security officers throughout the USA. This security is seen to rest on the following:

- Up to 6 percent of incoming containers are inspected.

- Preshipment inspection adds a second layer of security.

- Tamper-proof container seals are used.

- Customs officials from the USA work at several dozen of the world's largest ports to check cargo and vessels bound for the USA.

- Most importantly, a computerized risk assessment matrix oversees all containers coming into the USA. Corporations and shipping lines with a proven track record of legal integrity and safety are given a low-risk assessment.[3] Customs then focuses on "aberra-

tions": cargo from unknown companies or "trouble-spot" locations, cargo that follows erratic shipping routes (canceled from one
port, rerouted to another, carrying poor documentation, etc.), or
any other "red flag" activities. A large risk analysis matrix for
global cargo is continuously expanded. The data is fed in, the risk
assessment is generated, and cargo with a clean bill of health is
allowed to continue at will while containers with a high-risk value
are tagged for inspection.

As I listened to these explanations, I found myself lulled into a sense
of secure well-being. As these people spoke, I found I *believed* in security;
I trusted that the borders of the USA were secure; I knew all those Barbies
were coming in free of weapons of mass destruction.

In all the research I have done on several continents, this was the first
time, in post-9/11 USA, that I found myself swept along on a set of convictions that security really did work. These same words were uttered by
professionals from Cape Town to Rotterdam, but with an ironic smile of
recognition that there was a large gap between the rhetoric and the reality
of security and smuggling. But here in the USA, it felt different. I found I
had to consciously work to remember the myriad data I had collected firsthand on the ease and fluidity of the extra-legal, of the way people breaking
the law explained how little these "security measures" mattered to them.

In this context, it seemed too disturbing to remember the rejoinders
to the security points listed above:

- It is impossible to check 6 percent of the cargo coming through the
  Los Angeles/Long Beach ports. That would be 1,973 containers
  every day.

- Preshipment inspections are generally seen as a joke in the world
  of commerce. Large-scale operations can little afford the time (or
  goodwill) to open all a client's goods, and preshipment authoriza-
  tions often rest on paperwork, declarations by the client, and in the
  best of conditions, a cursory glance.

- Tamper-proof technology is child's play. Everyone in shipping rec-
  ognizes that when an advance is made in security, an advance is
  made in getting around it.

- A USA customs agent in a place like Rotterdam isn't a local. In the
  vast flow of tens of thousands of containers daily, one or two people can't possibly stop, open, inspect, or control the flow of commodities and vessels.

– The risk assessment matrix is based on allowing respected corporations relative freedom from inspections. Yet every interview from Africa through Europe to the USA on smuggling said the most commonly smuggled items and routes pass through "clean" corporations.

RESEARCHING AN ILLUSION

In exploring the world of ports in Los Angeles, I often drove and walked for hours without direction, taking the routes, byways, and back roads that defined "the end of the world." Leaving the main thoroughfares, I would try to make my way to water — the routes from land transport to sea lanes. It is the anthropologist's lot to be cursed with curiosity: how do things move, who moves them, and how? But sometimes, I was simply curious how far I could go from public roadways to the private universe of shipping — from land to sea. What, and where, is security? How far, as an undefined person — possibly a shipping agent or a terrorist — could I get across the so-called protected zones of the USA borders? I often made it to the water and to ships, and back, without being stopped. Even those berths with wire fences and closed gates guarded by security personnel asking for identification were surprisingly easy to enter: I had mastered such enclosures at the rail yards in my hometown by the age of ten.

Once, driving toward a large industrial loading and berth area, I got caught in what seemed an infinite line of trucks, each carrying one container to be loaded on an outgoing vessel. They coursed nose to tail from the main roadway through the berth gates, across the long expanse of port compound to a spot beside the ship, where the crane operator removed their payload and swung it onto the ship. An empty truck is an anomaly in commerce: it is a red mark in the company financial ledger; so the trucks snaked back out in a long line to collect a payload of incoming cargo to carry out across the industrial landscapes of America. It was like being caught in rush-hour traffic on a congested interstate, with one difference: the truckers never stopped. This was efficiency at its best; flow uninterrupted. Remember that a typical large ship carries six thousand or more TEUs. Each container must be carried to the crane to be loaded, one by one, on the ship. Each truck can carry one container. That equates to lines of thousands of trucks. Per ship. In a port with dozens of ships a day. In a world where holding a ship in port more than a day disrupts a long chain of commerce spanning across countries.

And it is here, caught in one of these lines, that one can best see why inspections are rare: hold up one line of trucks, one train, one ship, and a global supply chain feels the ripples. So much so that in a line of trucks, no one stopped a lone female in a rental car to find out why she was here, or why she drove all the way to the shoreline past all security checks and got out to walk freely amid the bustle and cargo of the "secured" wharf.

Questions are impediments — they hold up the flow. Checkpoints, barriers, and authorization points are merely bigger questions: bigger impediments to the whole point of ports.

When I asked a group of longshoremen about security, they scoffed:

> Security?
> Just add two and two. We have a couple dozen ships in here every day. We run five to six shifts; each with a turnaround of fifty-five hundred containers. That's five thousand gateways [entries and exits] a day.
> In all this, there's no staging area. This is the largest and most sophisticated port in the USA, and we don't have a staging area for trains, trucks, and cargo entering and exiting.
> We let all truckers into the terminals . . .

The longshoreman paused for effect:

> No supervisor.
> No oversight.
> The truckers have access to all parts of the terminal. We have four to five hundred truckers per terminal. Add it up.

David Arian, president of ILWU Local 13, a Los Angeles longshoremen's union, voiced the same concerns:[4]

> Security?
> You can put any spin on it you want to.
> But do the math.
> President Bush talks about his commitment to security — and the ports are the way all international people and goods enter the USA.
> This government has spent $43 million in three years on port security here in the USA.
> They've spent $5.4 billion a month on Iraq.

I spent more than a week prowling the Los Angeles/Long Beach roadways and docks. Each time I wandered unimpeded through inspection sheds, terminals, staging grounds, stacks of containers, and docks, I thought about how dangerously easy it would be for me, for anyone, to pop open containers and take or add something, pass something onto a ship, exchange something with someone else in the area, smuggle, plant a bomb. If I were bent on destruction I could shut down the port, and in doing so disrupt the supply chain across the entire country.

"No one really gets the true role of shipping in our lives," said Art Wong, of Long Beach Port Authority. He's right; most of us take it for granted, little recognizing that the world's economy rests on shipping. Stop the flow, and the world economy is crippled.

GETTING IT: THE GLOBAL SUPPLY CHAIN

A cup of coffee in his hand, Manny Aschemeyer turned to me and said: "I don't get why people don't get it." Aschemeyer needed the coffee: it was seven in the evening when he granted me an interview, and he had worked since the early hours of the day. Captain Manny Aschemeyer is the executive director of Marine Exchange of Southern California, which oversees the radar surveillance of all ships entering and leaving the Los Angeles/Long Beach port areas. They log all shipping information and supervise routing.

An imposing man with a jovial laugh, Aschemeyer looks like a captain; I wouldn't have been surprised if he had a wooden leg and a parrot on his shoulder. After I spent days of pleading, begging, and cajoling for interviews with the typical cast of characters at the port, this man stood out by granting quick, easy, and gracious access to me. This is often a truism in the curious world of research: those with the least time and the most responsibilities often extend the greatest hospitality.

I asked Aschemeyer about security, and his answer was a window on what people in positions of responsibility see as critical:

> Here in the USA, we go to Wal-Mart, to JCPenney, to Home Depot, and it's magic: the stores are filled with everything we need, and more. Everything is just there—it *is* magic.
> We don't think about it.
> But sometimes I go to places like Wal-Mart and just walk the aisles, turning over merchandise and looking where it comes from. Most everything says Made in China, Made in Korea, Made in Anywhere But Here.
> Most consumer goods are outsourced today, they come in from overseas.[5]
> Think pipelines—flows of goods—made up of fleets of ships. There are no parts, no necessities, at hand's reach; you have to start down the production line at the factory to get anything.

Stop a ship, and you send ripples throughout the entire USA; 62 percent of all containerized cargo from the Pacific Rim and 42 percent of containerized cargo of the world is coming into Los Angeles/Long Beach. Sneeze here, it sends ripples through the whole country. We aren't a manufacturing country anymore. The bulk of consumer goods, even food, is imported now. But we are doing this for, and at, a price.

Let something disrupt shipping and the country would be in a panic.

In an effort to bring order to chaos, every ship entering the harbors of Los Angeles/Long Beach has to check in with the Marine Exchange, which operates like the sea equivalent of air traffic control. But in fact, "every ship" does not mean every ship. Aschemeyer scoffed at the word *security*:

> Ports were never designed to be secure. Indeed, as nodal points of trade, they function best when truly open. And then the word comes out to make the ports secure. OK, how? A craft less than 130 feet long doesn't have to check in with Marine Exchange. Within a hundred-mile range of these two ports there are 250,000 registered recreational crafts. And how many unregistered ones, *the captain mused*—perhaps twice as many? Boats, *he noted,* are probably the most unregulated industry, especially those designated "recreational." You can buy a sixty-foot yacht and take off without any tests, license, or registration—something impossible for a car, train, or aircraft.

GETTING IT: PANDORA'S BOX

"How do you balance the need for security against the need to keep the commodities flowing to meet a country's basic needs?" I asked.

The almighty dollar, Van Dijk responded.

Marcel Van Dijk, Eric Caris, and Sheila Gonzales of the Los Angeles Port Authority explained: "Most of the shipping is done by reputable companies, and these companies have little incentive to lie, cheat, steal, or smuggle." The bottom line for nearly everyone, Caris said, is that in today's environment we are more concerned with explosives, not with misrepresenting data. A company like Nike isn't likely to bring in explosives.[6]

The large corporations of the world do not applaud security efforts if their vessel and its cargo are stopped—if the pipeline of global commodity flow is interrupted. Instead, as I was told numerous times: lobbying groups, from department stores to oil companies, go to Washington. One minute there's a problem, the next minute there's no problem: no more interruptions.

Most of the professionals I spoke with in Los Angeles, from port authority staff to security specialists, told me that security generally involved "looking for terrorists," stressing that

- the vast majority of traffic was by reputable companies with commendable security; and
- risk assessment covered 100 percent of the world's trade by sophisticated computer matrices.

However, they also said that

- the most common goods moving illegally were common corporate commodities;
- dollars more than intelligence defined the international balance of security (checking cargo) and uninterrupted trade (not checking cargo);
- any security system and computer matrix could be hacked; and
- it was almost impossible to monitor the flows of trade so vast that illegal weapons (valued at some half a trillion dollars a year) constituted a miniscule amount of trade and profit.

I asked everyone I interviewed in Los Angeles, government and shipping officials alike, if in the course of their work they discussed issues like who really smuggled; what the commonly smuggled commodities really are; what ethical and legal issues apply (how do we balance smuggled clothing from a respected corporation against weapons?); who is engaged in the illegal, how, and why (how do legal as well as illegal enterprises use transshipping, doctored bills of lading and manifests, and misdeclarations?); and how the balance of security and trade flow is really determined. Almost everyone said the same thing: "We hardly ever discuss these issues."

During a tour of the Port of Los Angeles, Sheila Gonzales and I pondered these issues as we passed hundreds of ships and millions of containers. Sheila is one of the people who "gets it." She sees the global supply chain in all the matrices of power that define it. She gets the ironies of believing in security while seeing the stockpiles of StairMasters and running shoes, industrial parts and electronics that are busted by customs.

People don't want to look at the big picture, because they are opening Pandora's box.

What happens is that they open the box and see all kinds of trails: Who's linked in? What are the linkages? There are always bigger boys out there.

There's the problem now of ILWU Local 13 [the longshoremen's union] saying security isn't adequate because supposedly empty containers leaving the country aren't always empty, and one exploded recently. Well, who is putting cargo in these empties, and how? Is it the small fry marginal breaking the law, or is it a valued big name in the industry?

If you even ask this question, if you even consider that it might be the latter, this leads to Pandora's box. How far does the trail go?

So it remains an unspoken topic. People see these things, but they don't have an answer—if we bring it up without having a solution, well, we feel we have egg on our face. Like a sore on your arm; you just hope it doesn't get any bigger.

So it's like there are two levels of knowledge: the first is the face people want out there: "Sure, there's security, sure, we trust the reputable corporations, sure, the empties are empty . . ."

And then there's what is really going on.

We feel we have to put a fresh face on for the public. Because a sense of security, even if it's a false sense of security . . . well: It's OK, you're OK . . . even if the gash, the sore on your arm, is five feet long, you're OK.

Gonzales was careful to end on a more positive note, saying that officials at the Port Authority did want to change this. One of the most important ways, she explained, is educating the general public about the realities of trade and shipping. One solution the Port Authority is talking about is developing ways of teaching this in the local schools.

GETTING IT: CAPTAIN NEFFENGER'S STORY AND SECURITY

You can't build a big wall around ships, berths, the port, Los Angeles, the USA. . . . It wouldn't work anyway. You have to fundamentally change the concept of security.

Superiors don't walk the frontlines. And then they say, "We've got it all locked down, all is fine." We just laugh and say: "You know we don't have it all locked down, why are you saying this?" They kind of know, and kind of live in the public eye and don't really know.

So, I look for people on my staff who "get it." There's no good word to describe this, so we use the term "get it." It's something you can see, work with, depend on, but you can't teach it.

And I make sure to link into the larger community here of people who get it — and these tend to be the people who live and work on the tough life-and-death stuff: fire, earthquake, riots, security, and so on . . . These are the people I will work with if a disaster occurs, and we prepare for this. These people come to the table, and say, "If you 'get it,' you're welcome to come to the table. If not, we'll take care of it."

Captain Peter Neffenger "got it." He saw the realities of the global supply chain in a way that I had encountered only with Manny Aschemeyer, David Arian, and Sheila Gonzales.

> If you want to understand security, if you want to improve security, you have to understand the global supply chain.
>
> These are all parts in an intricate maritime system that you must think of in toto, globally: when you are making a decision of any kind, you have to think in terms of not only this port, but all the ports interconnected globally.

With Neffenger's words, I got an insight into the real meaning of security. It isn't forged in the abstract proclamations of policy directives by people who don't walk the frontlines. It isn't initiated in the table banging of politicians who may not know what a container looks like, but who know voting behaviors. It isn't drafted by experts and specialists who come up with the "solution" in comfortable offices far from "the end and the beginning of the world." Security is forged on the frontlines, with people like Captain Neffenger, who constantly navigate the fine line between balancing security with the necessities of trade: between the smooth functioning of the US economy and the proverbial bomb in the Barbies.

> We live in a dynamic world and we must be dynamic in dealing with it.
>
> The media, the experts, the politicians all think that you put "something" into place and we'll be safe. Work done, end of story.
>
> Oops, 9/11 shows that such a static, unchanging model of security doesn't work. We need to adapt. Any system put into place can be defeated because all people, all systems, good and bad, adapt.
>
> This is a race with no finish line. The key is to stay ahead. The global war on terror implies no winning—because the world is moving: we put something into place, they work to surmount it, we work to figure out how they'll try, and block them . . . the cycle is unending.
>
> We become more secure by staying dynamic, by adapting and learning. Most people don't really like this, because it is really hard: can't we just come up with The Answer, Put It into Place, be done with this, and walk away, with everything now Safe. Staying ahead is a forever; continuously adapting to a constantly changing environment.

These aren't the stories we hear about in the media and in sound bites on policy. In talking to people like Manny Aschemeyer, Sheila Gonzales, and Peter Neffenger, I was struck by the incongruities between the realities of work these people do and the national rhetoric on security in policy and political discussions. Do these public figures really believe what they say? I always asked. Many answered that the general public preferred feeling safe to worrying about irresolvable facts; and that politicians, while neither ignorant nor ill-intended, play to a public who want to believe in the illusions of a safe world and nation-based trade. Perhaps, some noted, it might serve their business interests as well.

Those who get it know how misleading it is to say that smuggled Barbies aren't dangerous in a world where we are looking for explosives and toxins. While they know that opening and inspecting over thirty thousand containers a day is impossible, they also know that the seemingly innocuous indiscretions aren't as innocuous as people are wont to believe, as Captain Neffenger explained:

> Smuggling is smuggling: If something moves illegally, it's the same problem, whether it's drugs or counterfeit products we use in daily life.
>
> You can identify lots of problems if you study all smuggling. If you figure out smuggling for the more common, less dangerous, goods as well as the more harmful ones, you can begin to get a much better handle on how the more dangerous stuff is moved. You have to look at the whole picture.
>
> Levi's, Nikes . . . there's the biggest threat: You have a smuggling route, and you can put anything into it to move it. You move counterfeit Levi's, you can put weapons into this supply line and move them. A route is a route is a route.
>
> You have to stop and think like a terrorist to be prepared to stop a terrorist.
>
> Logically, a person who wanted to move dangerous things would watch the trade system in total, and look what gets caught moving through — what gets caught, how, when, and where. And look at what gets through: the simple everyday commodities smuggled in the vast flow of trade. This, then, would probably seem a good way to move dangerous things.

The beginning and end of the world are the loci of both security's definition and achievement. The politicians and policy makers, the think tanks and bureaucrats, may give the illusion of defining and controlling security, but it is the people who "get it," who belly up to the table and create systems of response, who are the real — and unseen — font of security. It is here that the very notions of safety are crafted; here security is given shape and form, here the responses to any disaster will emerge. As Neffenger noted:

You have to consider reality.

Radical words.

But how will the responses to any disaster emerge?

THE GLOBAL GAMBLE. MYANMAR–CHINA BORDER.

CHAPTER 20

CONCLUSION

You want to know who most commonly breaks the law? Who is the prototypical smuggler? It's a nice, educated, well-dressed mid-level corporate manager selling respectable commodities. He loves his family, his job, and his country. He sits in a mid-level office getting a shipment ready, and he thinks: "I want to look good to my superiors. I want to succeed. I want to get that raise for my family." And he knows if he cooks the customs forms a bit to avoid tariffs, inspections, and delays, he increases sales, profits, and efficiency for his company. He'll be successful, people will like him, he'll be promoted.

ALAN HALL, CUSTOMS SPECIALIST

You want to know who we most commonly catch breaking the law? The big-name corporations whose products we all buy every day. We bust them and they just call their "friends" in DC. We then get a call telling us to drop the case. We have no choice, the call comes from people too powerful for us to fight. This is the post-9/11 world we have to work in.

U.S. CUSTOMS OFFICIAL WHO ASKED TO REMAIN ANONYMOUS

Does the war orphan Okidi herald the emergence of new political formations? New economic (dis)orders? Does he represent one point in a vast sweep of relationships that are reconfiguring the world as we know it?

Is his story — linked through the altruistic and the robber barons, the transnational organizations and the allure of global markets — merely that of capital meeting the technology of this emergent century? A story that has been revised and updated each century without changing the basic premise? Or are the very conceptual and societal organizations that ground our world changing before our eyes into something as yet . . . undiscovered?

In a world defined by states, this question sounds ridiculous. Those that govern are the motors of change; those who are *seen* hold sway. Not the invisible, the marginal, the unnamed. Not war orphans.

Yet one of the most interesting findings of this research is that the war orphan can see the logic of this question, for he is capable of grasping the patterns of the entire spectrum of the extra-legal networks that move from the centers of cosmopolitan production across the various il/legalities of trade to bring a packet of cigarettes to his hand. Not many economists travel to the center of Angola to interview street children. If they did, they would find that Okidi knows anyone wanting to buy cigarettes — or tomatoes, weapons systems, and satellite communications gear — needs hard currency, and he knows the resources (from diamonds through oil to trafficked humans) that will procure this. It's clear to him that this system works because it is not a one-way exchange; it emerges from mutual necessity.

Like a house of cards, take out a simple card from the bottom — the proverbial war orphan, the person standing at the critical intersection of supply and demand — and the entire construction falls.

And of course, the parable of power is that in rebuilding a new house of cards, what was formerly on the bottom can reemerge on top.

Talk to Okidi, the shopkeeper, the truckers, the Gov'nor, and the multinational corporations walking both sides of the law, and you can see, in their descriptions of "business as usual," the complicated networks that describe the universe of the extra-legal and the power it wields in defining the twenty-first century. No illusions are allowed, for honesty is critical to business success: there are Gov'nors in every country; they control non-legal empires while holding respected legal offices. Reputable multinational corporations most commonly violate the laws controlling trade. Honest officials burn the midnight oil for little pay and less recognition, trying to forge solutions. For they know that the "legitimate" corporations fudging customs forms don't want their shipments of Barbies stopped; to protect against the terrorist "bomb in the Barbies," as the longshoreman said, is up to the deeply committed.

All these people know that economics is a dance of the il/legal: a pas de deux.

But talk to many formal economic and political analysts, and you find that these complex extra-state realities fade into incomprehensibility: isolated tales of crime removed from global understanding, shot through with myth, assumption, and emotionalism.

This is not surprising: the sciences have taken shape and definition within the confines of the state.[1] These confines are both tangible (research and teaching institutions, granting agencies and publishing concerns) and intangible (epistemology and the subtle ideologies that shape our academic worldview in the most Bourdieuian sense). Research knowledge, as Foucault long ago demonstrated, was born in the womb of the state, delivered by the midwife called modernity. Delivered with this is the idea that if the state reigns, it reigns supreme; if it falls, it will be replaced by something else (anarchy, to most theorists). One place, one power. Any other competing set of economic and political associations is by definition marginal.[2]

For most of the (hundreds of) people I spoke with for this research, the state is "somewhat" important. They look out on a world of state bodies and extra-state networks — variously disparate and intersecting as need dictates. Legality is a fluid concept.

The vast majority of those who participate in the extra-legal do not think of themselves as criminals, as smugglers, as "really" breaking the law. In their perspective, states, being only "somewhat" important, are only somewhat noticed, somewhat respected. Vast extra-state economic networks are equally, and sometimes more, important. Multiple nodes of power. Multiple constructs of privilege. Each balancing the hegemony of the other in global realities. Yet in academic circles, the state is visible, and the extra-state less so. Why?

Modernists have a long tradition of taking "place" very seriously and assuming its centrality in shaping identity. The state is about the static. The defined and bounded. It has borders that are set and inhabitants that have sovereign identities that are equally set.

How can analyses of *flow* emerge from these confines? Movement is unseen in a world focused on place. Yet it is a critical research site. Flow carries a set of cultural realities shaped by the people creating it; it *is* (rather than merely being composed of) political, economic, philosophical, and poetic forces.

If analysts cannot see the full compendium of economic, political, and social forces defining the emergent twenty-first century, yet the war orphan and the Gov'nor can, then who has power?

The question is not merely one of focus and scope — of studying process; it is also one of trying to grasp the "emergent" — what is just coming to be. How do we study what has not yet "become"? The state as we know it may be an Enlightenment project — in the process of giving way to new forms of power as yet undefined. The networks of the extra-state may well be windows on understanding new paradigms of power and authority. Yet that means being prepared to see what lies on the horizon of our tomorrows, to see what is as yet unseeable.

For this reason, many changes arrive unheralded — surprising researchers who attempt to read the future from the dusty pages of the past. The last decade has seen governments topple and people lose their life to poverty when economic crashes have blindsided nations.

It is knowledge, not weapons and laws, which will even this playing field. If we cannot perceive the true magnitude and dynamic character of both the legal and the extra-legal, we are impotent to respond. People can see only what they have the conceptual tools to see. That makes the unseen a powerful tool of both hegemony and resistance: seeing *is* power.

What we do not see often becomes not only invisible, but also inevitable. Before people could conceive of pathogens invisible to the human eye, we could not develop vaccinations or antibiotics. Death from infection was inevitable. In the same way, if we cannot see the fonts of power and the integral patterns defining the legal and illegal, we will see dangerous hegemonies and the lethal clash of il/legalities as inevitable, an inescapable fact of the human condition. What innovative solutions emerge from this?

The academy and its disciplines may have taken shape and definition in, and from, the state; but the twenty-first century has broken the fragile borders of the state and spilled across the earth's terrains and world's human populations in new ways — both positive and destructive. While concerned citizens debate the pros and cons of (legal) globalization, the people who populate the pages of this book are creating it — often in their own image.

GLOBAL OUTREACH. AFRICA.

NOTES

1. Translated by author.

2. "Call for Action" 2002: 7.

3. The term *extra-legal* refers to all activities that fall outside legality as it is formally defined and used in law and law enforcement. This includes illegal, illicit, and informal, as well as undeclared, unregistered, and unregulated, actions. For example, informal transactions — say, trading food for services — are not technically illegal in themselves, but they violate the letter of the law because they are not accountable to systems of declaration and taxation. They are clearly different from illegal transactions such as narcotics and trafficking, the province of cartels; or corruption, the province of elites. All are extra-legal.

Extra-state refers to all activities that take place outside of formal state ruling systems. In this book, those of most interest constitute economic and/or political forces. Like extra-legal activities, these are diverse: rebel groups are extra-state players quite different from mafias and cartels, and both of these differ significantly from extra-state activities performed by state actors (corruption). Yet as a whole, these can be an invisible part of the way states function, and they can also challenge the supremacy of the state as the twenty-first-century form of governance and community. Extra-legal networks often grow in economic sophistication and political authority so that they constitute serious extra-state forces.

4. I use the slash in this fashion in a number of related contexts, always with the intention of referring to both embedded terms together: extra/state, extra/legal, non/formal. Extra/state is something that is both extra-state and state at the same time, such as corruption that depends on holding a formal political office or laundering the profits from illicit activities into the formal economy. The slash is also a reminder that legality and illegality, state and extra-state, take their definitions in relation to one another.

5. The ethics and information advances of the twenty-first century ensure that researchers in all fields will be held far more accountable for what they

put in the public sphere. The days are happily gone when we could quote our informants, publish photos, give eyewitness accounts, or speculate about other people without worrying if we would create harm by our actions. When "author" meant "author-ity," we had the power to tell "other people's" information knowing they were powerless to retaliate. The mistakes of academics, journalists, and public officials have at times been lethal to those we profess to help. Conveniently, we never told our own stories. The challenge is not to stop research, but to create it in a way we are proud of. If we can author texts, we can author our disciplines. This book, then, joins others in exploring new genres of research and writing that are more responsive, and responsible, to the world in which we find ourselves, especially when that world is in any way dangerous.

There are excellent books on illegality, by way of example. In the academic vein consider Andreas 2000; Andreas and Biersteker 2003; Bayart, Ellis, and Hibou 1999; Cilliers and Dietrich 2000; Findlay 1999; Fiorentini and Peltzman 1995; Hodges 2001, 2003; MacGaffey and Bazenguissa-Ganga 2000; Naím 2005; Naylor 2005; Plissart and De Boeck 2006; Reno 1998; Riedel 2005; Roitman 2004; Slapper and Tombs 1999; van Schendel and Abraham 2005; Woodiwiss and Bewley-Taylor 2005. For journalist approaches see for example Brzezinski 2002; Lilley 2001; Robinson 2000. On the institutional level: Global Witness 1999, 2005b, 2006; Jost and Sandhu 2000; and, at the broader level, the United Nations Office on Drugs and Crime (www.unodc.org/unodc/index .html) and the U.S. Department of State Bureau for International Narcotics and Law Enforcement Affairs Publications (www.state.gov/p/inl). And in terms of fictionalized accounts: Breytenbach 2001; Neto 2001. One of the creative works I most appreciate is *O Roque: Romance de um Mercado* (The Roque: Novel of a Market), written by Hendrik Neto, an Angolan government minister who relates his own explorations of the vast sprawling unregulated market in Luanda and its impact on the country. It is simultaneously well-written literature and a treatise on contemporary economics at the borders of il/legality.

6. This experiment with creating a genre of creative academic nonfiction was graciously funded by the John Simon Guggenheim Memorial Foundation (2004–2005).

3. COCONUTS AND CIGARETTES

1. A similar pattern exists with stolen vehicles in the Southern African region. Peter Gastrow, of South Africa's Institute for Security Studies, conducted a study of organized crime in the fourteen-country Southern African Development Community (SADC), which represents the southern half of the continent. Because of political turmoil, rapid political and economic changes, emergent markets, and limited security budgets, this region has experienced a growth spurt in organized crime in recent years. Southern Africa has become an increasingly desirable and lucrative transit node for international drugs, money

laundering, counterfeiting (money, goods, pharmaceuticals), and racketeering as well as for the more traditional illicit trade in precious resources (from gold and gems, through endangered flora and fauna, to human trafficking). Experts from the SADC region were asked which crimes constituted the greatest threat. Vehicle theft came in as number one, ahead of robbery, drug-related offenses, gold and precious gems trade, illegal arms trade, government corruption, fraud and bank fraud, poaching, and forgery.

This answer held true for both indigenous and transnational crime. Echoing Detective Flynn's views on the threats posed by cigarette smuggling, Gastrow writes:

> The reason why this form of criminal activity is regarded as such a threat is not only because the theft of motor vehicles is widespread, but because this crime is closely intertwined with the trafficking of drugs, firearms, diamonds, and other illegally obtained goods. Stolen vehicles constitute a ready currency in exchange for a wide range of illicit goods. (Gastrow 2001a: 58)

Police estimate that around 50 percent of stolen or hijacked vehicles are smuggled across South Africa's borders into the rest of the Southern African region and beyond. There is a decent chance that the Mercedes truck that Kadonga offered for sale on the frontlines of a war thousands of kilometers and a number of borders away (chap. 2) came from here. There is an equally good chance that the truck was paid for with the proceeds from unregistered diamonds. Complementary flows.

Diamonds, like all precious and luxury resources, rest on a continuum that connects (status-) hungry consumers with (physically) hungry miners. From the moment of extraction to the consumption of the polished product, diamonds are one of the commodities most capable of blurring legal boundaries. For the miner, the gem represents freedom from oppressive poverty, while the wealthy, as one successful businessman told me,

> just pop a really good gem into their shirt pocket, board their plane, walk across customs without declaring it, and voila, they have the start-up costs for a new business, tuition at an exclusive school for their children, a significant offshore deposit, or the money to buy anything from weapons to state-of-the-art computer systems to take back to their country to sell for a strapping profit.

2. This brings up a final consideration regarding the difficulties of terminology and research. How do we speak of the impact of all economic activities that take place outside formal state channels? To date, no such word has been accepted into common usage. Without a term — a way — to define the parameters of study, comprehensive research is impossible: How do we assess the impact of all of these unregulated dollars (or yen, or euros, or gold) on regional economic stability, indices of development, stock market valuations and interest rates, currency conversion and speculation, trade flows? How do we gauge the ability of the extra-legal to affect the political process? One conclusion is clear: in this invisibility lies immense profiteering.

4. THE GOV'NOR'S RED TRACTORS

1. There are remarkable support systems in difficult situations. Thanks to the kind generosity of the UN representative and security officer who allowed me to travel with them, and the gutsy Irish INGO Concern that housed me, I was able to make the trip.

2. A huge secondary industry forms around humanitarian work: jobs are created; communities formed; and aid is used, misused, black-marketed, and bartered for power and privilege. A humanitarian lorry carrying invaluable seeds to IDP camps also carries beer, arms, pirated videos and VCRs, diamonds, and people — it carries hopes for a better tomorrow for the hungry and the means to extend a businessperson's empire. Humanitarian organizations do not wish for these complexities, nor, indeed, do they necessarily even know about them. Lorries are driven by local drivers who are beholden to local authorities, power mongers, and warlords. There are limits to any organization's ability to control its resources.

5. MILITARY TAKEOVERS

1. The complementarity is extensive: political and military elites are often friends as well as colleagues, working together, partying together, marrying into each other's families.

2. These mining operations are international in the truest sense of the word. A bare thumbnail sketch of the cast of characters that populate mining areas demonstrates both the transnational nature of a local grid of enterprises and the ways these facilitate actions that challenge simple notions of legality. Local citizens, along with soldiers, are "requisitioned" for work. This may be a boon to the local populace, who typically need any chance of income they can get. But it can also amount to little better than forced labor. Civilians work side by side with soldiers, who have been told their contribution to national security now involves digging for diamonds. Foreigners seeking their fortune secretly cross the borders into this country. Most work as grunt laborers, while a very few — friends of the military and political elite — gain concessions (legal rights to work a designated area).

All these people are first and foremost members of their own communities. They know each other regardless of which military they are affiliated with. For them, this is like a foreign war. No matter where they stand along political divides, they do business with each other. As they always have. This willingness to set aside political differences makes possible the very doing of business upon which all industry ultimately depends. It holds true, for example, with scuba divers, mining technicians, and concessionaires coming in from South Africa or Asia or Ireland to work, respectively, the deeper river areas, the more technically difficult mines, and the untapped districts. For more information on the intersections between (extra-state) resources and power in Angola, see Global Witness 1998, 1999.

3. Conversation, Antwerp, 2002. Dietrich continued,

This is not, per se, a war over resources. It facilitates the looting of resources. All these guys (the government and military) want the rebels around. The military's take is, "Gee, we have to close the roads and airports, and only our planes and vehicles can get through (with the only supplies available to desperate populations willing to pay). It's a matter of national security, we don't have to provide community services as we need everything the state has to fight this war. How could anyone find fault with this?" So is the government military really cutting off the rebels in these attacks? Or are they cutting off the rebels' external support structures but keeping them functioning internally with their networks?

And it isn't just about controlling the diamond trade, for example, it's about controlling the whole closed economy that supports and sustains the nation: soap, petrol, food, and so on.

This is "organized scarcity." In war, the controlling factions don't like it that average people grow crops—it means people are self-sufficient. They can't control the delivery of essentials.

For a more complete discussion see Cilliers and Dietrich 2000.

4. Conversation, Antwerp, 2002.

5. Though an enterprise like logging will create personal wealth for select military commanders, the further entanglements make simple public/private military/commerce distinctions difficult at best. Global Witness, a nongovernmental organization dedicated to economic integrity, has done groundbreaking work on the relationships of government/military logging, political conflict, and profiteering. They report that in 1995, the royal court in Cambodia secretly awarded thirty-two forest concessions covering 6,464,021 hectares — 35 percent of Cambodia's total land area. All but two of the companies receiving these awards had no experience in running forest concessions: they were investors taking advantage of political instability and connections to people in power. Global Witness points out that the companies have failed to make promised investments, thus denying the government significant revenues, but have themselves reaped considerable wealth while decimating the forests. Today, the concessions granted in secret in 1994 and 1995 are now treated as "legal" — though, as one Global Witness investigator told me: "Trying to find out what is legal, in order to determine what is illegal, isn't easy. I spent a lot of time at the Ministry of Forests in Cambodia just trying to find out what the laws were regarding the timber industry, and the officials were very reluctant to tell me even that." These associations obscure easy distinctions between national and international business, as many of these concessionaires represent transnational interests. They also blur the lines of commerce, profit, and security. Global Witness, extending its investigations of illicit timber enterprises to Liberia, found that at least seven out of twenty-five logging companies recorded in the Forest Development Authority's annual reports had direct links with arms suppliers. The links spread further still: Global Witness found evidence supporting the conclusion that Italian, Corsican, and Russian syndicates had ties with the timber industry in West and Central Africa. See Global Witness 2001a, 2001b.

7. ROBBER BARONS

1. In similar fashion, the extraction of resources does little to develop the country: most hard goods and soft technical labor are imported, most infra-structural development moves straight into international markets, and only the unskilled, demanding labor is left to locals.

2. This isn't restricted to the top levels of authority: in fact, the durability of this system rests in the fact that it permeates every level of society. Police require payments to avoid prosecution, civil servants sell permits, doctors and teachers require fees for free care, troops "liberate" goods from people, and guards take "honest money" to turn a blind eye.

3. The ambassador explained the regional specifics of war and regional "business":

> This isn't solely a national decision. Look at Namibia. The rebel forces here set up a series of trade and social relationships with the more peaceful society there. People (and soldiers) traded, they married, and they gained a stability. High-end goods moved, but so did basic goods, cattle, family members. The government of this country, for its part, had developed similar relationships across the border: moving minerals, timber, ivory, you name it. Equanimity in time of war. But then the government decided to break the trade routes of the rebel forces—in part because the war in Congo had re-erupted and Angola was sending troops, making new alliances, and scooping up loot and resource wealth in payment. Human rights abuses shot through the roof, all the trade and social relationships were disrupted—and the economies of three countries immediately changed. Zambia, where stable wartime trade and social relationships have developed over time, decided not to let Angola launch attacks from their borders, after watching the disruption this caused in Namibia. It felt that "peaceful war" was more stable than assaults intended to end the war.

4. She explained:

> All, and I do not use this word lightly, official economy is effectively controlled by the elite. It's hard for anyone else to get in. But there is a lot more to this: of the entire population, a maximum of 17 percent are in any way benefited from the present governing structure and formal economy. And I mean in any way— down to the poor street vendors who are selling small items on the streets imported by the elites and moving through middlemen—people who have any stake in the present economy. The rest are completely outside the formal system.

10. THE WASHING MACHINE

1. Research into laundering has developed largely around classical organized crime in cosmopolitan settings. Interest in the topic focuses mostly on the movement of direct gains — currency from drugs, gambling, the sex industry, and the like — into legitimate banks and businesses. Financial institutions, in the interests of curtailing laundering, are asked to verify the legitimacy of clients, of earnings, of international transfers, and of foreign financial establishments from

whom they receive monies. National revenue-monitoring and tax-collection systems are watchdogs for commercial enterprises where income and outflow do not match legitimate patterns. This type of research gives the impression that laundering is relatively straightforward, that people try to move large chunks of illicit money directly into legally recognized bank accounts and businesses. While this is certainly a part of the story, it is dangerously incomplete. Truck Stop and its sister city, Kalunga, with its illicit border crossings, offer a snapshot of the deep layers of complexity that can surround laundering.

12. PORTS

1. www.Marisec.org/shippingfacts, accessed 25 January 2005.

13. DRUGS

1. Wondemagegnehu works in the Office of Essential Drugs and Medicines Policy/Quality Assurance and Safety: Medicines, World Health Organization, Geneva.

14. THE CULTURE OF CRIMINALS

1. My goal in this chapter and the next, on the culture of cops, is to present the worldviews of people representing both sides of the law without direct editorialization. This is intended as classical contemporary anthropology: illuminating different cultural realities and inviting the reader to step in for a moment both analytically and experientially.

17. THE INVESTMENT MACHINE

1. Lilley (2001) and McDowell and Novis (2001), reporting older and more conservative figures of money laundering, estimate the annual amount at between 2 and 5 percent of the world's GDP. That is equivalent to between $1 and $3 trillion. To put this in perspective: Lilley (2001: 28) writes that the lower estimate of $1.5 trillion represents 17 percent of the United States' GDP — and eight times Switzerland's GDP of $191 billion.

The CIA places world GDP for 2005 at $59 trillion. http://www.cia.gov/cia/publications/factbook/rankorder/2001rank.html.

2. One of the more common tactics used by law enforcement officials in fighting money laundering is to monitor unrecognized bank deposits of more than $10,000.

3. http://www.offshore-companies.co.uk, accessed 3 February 2005.

4. "How to Operate Your Own Merchant Bank," www.offshore-manual.com, accessed 3 February 2005.

5. http://www.privacyworld.com, accessed 3 February 2005.

6. http:// offshore-manual.com, accessed 3 February 2005.

7. http:// offshore-manual.com, accessed 3 February 2005.

8. http:// offshore-manual.com, accessed 3 February 2005.

9. http://offshore-manual.com, accessed 3 February 2005. The ad continues:

Privileges of Accredited Diplomatic Appointments & Passports as an Honorary Consul Include:

1. You will enjoy the privileges and immunities granted by the Vienna Conventions of *Consular* and *Diplomatic* Relations.

2. Your home and office will be officially designated as a consulate and therefore are inviolable.

3. You may display "CC" (Corps Consulaire) plates on your car so that your status is known to the forces of control who may not detain you in any way.

4. When traveling, you may use the diplomatic channel at airports and will not be subject to time delaying and annoying customs checks.

5. You may purchase drinks, cigarettes and other supplies for your consulate duty free.

6. You will be exempt from all forms of tax on any of your income in the host country derived from outside of that country.

7. Doors which may have been previously closed will remarkably open once you have received your diplomatic status.

8. Top restaurants, hotels and clubs which may be "fully booked" will suddenly take your reservation.

9. You will receive free upgrades from many airlines to First/Business class at the check-in desks.

10. You will automatically receive numerous invitations to Royal/Diplomatic and Society parties and events.

11. You will meet top-ranking government officials and heads of state.

12. You will boost your business success as well as your social status and prestige.

Validity: 5 years (renewable for life thereafter!). Delivery Time: 4–6 weeks. What we need from you to proceed: Pre-paid Consultancy Fee (click on the below 'Add to Cart' button): US$1,000. Your Curriculum Vitae. Proof of Verifiable Funds in the Amount of Minimum: US$100,000 (e.g. bank statement).

10. www.anewidentity.com, accessed 3 February 2005.

11. Conversation, August 2004, Antwerp.

12. The post-9/11 Patriot Act in the United States banned the practice of using offshore banks — against the wishes of conservative republicans and powerful business interests. Rawlings, in following the intricacies of power and profit in tax sheltering, is curious to see how this particular section of the Patriot Act will be renegotiated over time.

18. HUMAN CARGO

1. I have purposely avoided identifying the cities I visited on this trip. My intention is not to point a finger at any specific shipping company or port location. What I have documented here is not the exception to a rule of security, but the norm of ports, and trade, today. Virtually all shipping functions like this.

2. In this several-week, multiport journey, only one port had inspectors looking at containers. Curiously, they looked *only* into the empty containers — clipping off the plastic security seals, opening the doors, and looking inside as the container was off-loaded at shipside. They wore jeans and T-shirts with no insignia. Not a single container with cargo was opened or inspected.

19. POST-TERROR

1. He continued: "If 42 percent of the cargo for the USA comes through these two ports, and if most commodities today have crossed international borders in some way, it's not hard to figure out how much of the USA would be without critical supplies if we were suddenly forced to close the port."

2. One of the editors wrote a note in the margins of the book manuscript asking if this really was a longshoreman speaking, or if I had written the wrong reference. The stereotypes surrounding trade, criminality, and the "end of the world" are well developed no matter what side of the law one is on. To round out the image: longshoremen (and "men" are still normative) have unions that conduct research, forge policy, have global associations, and value political and economic acumen.

3. Working with customs, these companies have agreed to oversee preshipment inspections, cargo verification, and tamper-proof transport systems.

4. Conversation, July 2004, Los Angeles.

5. Aschemeyer voiced his concern about this: "We live in a global economy, but few in the general public here in the USA think or care about it — and that's too bad, as these are the people who are most vulnerable."

6. In the midst of discussions on risk assessment, bombs on freighter hulls, and clandestine rerouting of shipments, Marcel Van Dijk offered a new view on all the discussions of security I had heard:

> There are two kinds of damage. There's terrorist damage; and here virtually all the attention today focuses on the Muslim countries.
>
> But there's also economic damage.
>
> Look at the textile industry, for example. It's now dying in the USA. The best cotton is grown in the USA; it is high value. But in this global economy that seeks to maximize profits, it is shipped to India to be spun. Then it may stay there, or go elsewhere in the Asian region to be sewn into panels—like the front panels and back panels of shirts and pants—but these aren't sewn together into a single shirt. That's because the corporations have written laws in the USA that say if these clothing panels are shipped to this country and sewn together here, then

the corporations can legally put in labels that say "Made in the USA." There are no quotas for textiles, but there are for clothing ... The textile industry will die in the USA.

20. CONCLUSION

1. Scholars, for the most part, are enmeshed in the world of the state. They work in institutions that are state recognized, they receive legal wages with formal taxes taken out, they live in officially authorized housing, and buy lawful commodities. They do not tend to travel with six passports, run illegal commodities and laundering scams, do research with powerful people running extra-legal industries, buy hot vehicles, deal drugs, or act as kingpins (or even littlepins) of successful criminal organizations. If they did, research on the state and its power might be different.

Academics' embeddedness in the state, however laudable, means that the state is, quite literally, the paramount site of power and privilege; and in turn, academics privilege the state. It becomes the focus, the definitive point, of research. Academics are as invested in the state as it is in them. A "state" is a conceptual category and not an objective entity — it exists only by virtue of the fact that people believe in the laws, geographical designations, and imagined communities that designate the flow and flux of humanity and space into discrete parts. A state is an abstract notion that is given substance in being recognized as substantive. A state needs academics to theorize it into being.

From the vantage point of a state-centered perspective, anything outside the state is seen as less substantive, less powerful, less dynamic. The state is posited as controlling non-state forces, and as the latter do not appear to dominate politics and economics, it would seem the state is successful, and therefore paramount.

2. In fact, multiple competing regimes of power exist, variously hindering and assisting one another. The vast network of extra-state alliances represents not merely an "outlaw" offshoot of the state, but a competing set of organized systems of accumulation, control, and action. These may at times benefit state structures and authorities; they may at times out-compete them. Should these extra-state networks become more adept at controlling resource extraction, capital accumulation, and a justification of violence than the state, they will supplant the latter in primary authority; if they prove less adept, they will wither and be supplanted by new and emergent forms of political and economic relations.

REFERENCES

Andreas, Peter. *Border Games: Policing the U.S.-Mexico Divide.* Ithaca, NY: Cornell University Press, 2000.

Andreas, Peter, and Thomas Biersteker, eds. *The Rebordering of North America: Integration and Exclusion in a New Security Context.* New York: Routledge, 2003.

Bayart, Jean François, Stephen Ellis, and Béatrice Hibou. *The Criminalization of the State in Africa.* Bloomington: Indiana University Press, 1999.

Breytenbach, Jay. *The Plunderers.* Johannesburg, South Africa: Covos Day Books, 2001.

Brzezinski, Matthew. *Casino Moscow: A Tale of Greed and Adventure on Capitalism's Wildest Frontier.* New York: Touchstone, 2002.

Castells, Manuel. *End of Millennium.* London: Blackwell, 1998.

Cilliers, Jakkie, and Christian Dietrich, eds. *Angola's War Economy.* Pretoria, South Africa: Institute for Security Studies, 2000.

Cookson, Rich. "Tobacco Firm: We Want Smugglers to Buy Our Fags." *The Big Issue* (London), 19–25 February 2001, 5.

Düttmann, Alexander. *Between Cultures: Tensions in the Struggle for Recognition.* London: Verso, 2000.

Findlay, Mark. *The Globalisation of Crime.* Cambridge: Cambridge University Press, 1999.

Fiorentini, Gianluca, and Sam Peltzman, eds. *The Economics of Organized Crime.* Cambridge: Cambridge University Press, 1995.

Friman, H. Richard, and Peter Andreas. *The Illicit Global Economy and State Power.* Lanham, MD: Rowman & Littlefield, 1999.

Gastrow, Peter. *Theft from South African Mines and Refineries: The Illicit Market for Gold and Platinum.* Pretoria, South Africa: Institute for Security Studies Monograph Series No. 54, 2001a.

———. *Organized Crime in the SADC Region*. Pretoria, South Africa: Institute for Security Studies Monograph Series No. 60, 2001b.

Global Witness. *Digging in Corruption*. London: Global Witness, 2006.

———. *Annual Report 2004*. London: Global Witness, 2005a.

———. *An Architecture of Instability*. London: Global Witness, 2005b.

———. *The Credibility Gap and the Need to Bridge It: Increasing the Pace of Forestry Reform*. London: Global Witness, 2001a.

———. *Taylor-Made: The Pivotal Role of Liberia's Forests and Flag of Convenience in Regional Conflict*. London: Global Witness, 2001b.

———. *A Crude Awakening*. London: Global Witness, 1999.

———. *A Rough Trade: The Role of Companies and Governments in the Angolan Conflict*. London: Global Witness, 1998.

Hecht, David, and Maliqalim Simone. *Invisible Governance: The Art of African Micropolitics*. Brooklyn: Autonomedia, 1994.

Hodges, Tony. *Angola from Afro-Stalinism to Petro-Diamond Capitalism*. Bloomington: Indiana University Press, 2001.

———. *Angola: The Anatomy of an Oil State*. Bloomington: Indiana University Press, 2003.

"How to Operate Your Own Merchant Bank." CarltonPress. http://www.offshore-manual.com (3 February 2005).

Jost, Patrick, and Harjit Singh Sandhu. *The Hawala Alternative Remittance System and Its Role in Money Laundering*. Lyon: Interpol General Secretariat, 2000.

Langewiesche, William. *The Outlaw Sea*. New York: North Point Press, 2004.

Lilley, Peter. *Dirty Dealing: The Untold Truth about Global Money Laundering*. London: Kogan Page, 2001.

MacGaffey, Janet, and Rémy Bazenguissa-Ganga. *Congo-Paris: Transnational Traders on the Margins of the Law*. Bloomington: Indiana University Press, 2000.

McDowell, John, and Gary Novis. "The Consequences of Money Laundering and Financial Crime." In "The Fight against Money Laundering." Special issue, *Economic Perspectives* 6, no. 2 (May 2001). http://usinfo.state.gov/journals/ites/0501/ijee/toc.htm.

Miranda, Charles. "From Russia with Hate." *The Daily Telegraph* (Australia), 11 April 2005, 2.

Naím, Moisés. *Illicit*. New York: Doubleday, 2005.

Naylor, R. T. *Wages of Crime: Black Markets, Illegal Finance, and the Underworld Economy*. Ithaca, NY: Cornell University Press, 2005.

Neethling, Trevor. "Top Businessman a Suspect in R211m PE Medicines Bust." *The Herald* (South Africa), 16 March 2002, 4.

Neto, Hendrik Vaal. *O Roque: Romance de um Mercado*. Luanda, Angola: Fundação Eshivo, 2001.

Nordstrom, Carolyn. "Extrastate Globalization of the Illicit." In *Why America's Top Pundits Are Wrong*. Catherine Besteman and Hugh Gusterson, eds. Berkeley: University of California Press, 2005, 138–53.

———. "Prestidigitation: Wars, Profits, and the Creation of Risk." *Bulletin of the Royal Institute for Inter-Faith Studies* 6, no. 1 (Spring/Summer 2004a), 97–112.

——. *Shadows of War: Violence, Power, and International Profiteering in the Twenty-First Century.* Berkeley: University of California Press, 2004b.

——. "IT and the Illicit." In *Bombs and Bandwidth: The Emerging Relationship between Information Technology and Security.* Robert Latham, ed. New York: The New Press, 2003a, 235–50.

——. "Public Bad, Public Good(s) and Private Realities." In *Political Transition: Politics and Cultures.* Paul Gready, ed. London: Pluto Press, 2003b, 212–24.

——. "Out of the Shadows." In *Intervention and Transnationalism in Africa: Global-Local Networks of Power.* T. Callaghy, R. Kassimir, R. Latham, eds. Cambridge: Cambridge University Press, 2002, 216–39.

——. "Shadows and Sovereigns." *Theory, Culture and Society* 17 (August 2000): 35–54.

O'Brien, Tim. *The Things They Carried.* Boston: Houghton Mifflin/Seymour Lawrence, 1990.

O'Kane, Maggie. "The Soldiers Are Out of Control: They Are Feasting on a Dying City." *The Guardian Weekly,* 5 September 1993.

Perkins, John. *Confessions of an Economic Hit Man.* San Francisco: Berrett-Koehler, 2004.

Plissart, Marie Françoise, and Filip De Boeck. *Kinshasa: Tales of the Invisible City.* New York: Distributed Art Publishers, 2006.

Rawlings, Greg. "Laws, Liquidity, and Eurobonds: The Making of the Vanuatu Tax Haven." *The Journal of Pacific History* 39 (2004a): 325–41.

——. "Globalization and the Continuing Appeal of Offshore Finance." Paper presented at the Oceanic Conference on International Studies, Australian National University, Canberra, Australia, 14–16 July 2004b.

Reno, William. *Warlord Politics and African States.* Boulder, CO: Lynne Rienner, 1998.

Riedel, Philip, ed. *Handbook of Transnational Crime and Justice.* Thousand Oaks, CA: Sage, 2005.

Robinson, Jeffrey. *The Merger: The Conglomeration of International Organized Crime.* Woodstock, NY: The Overlook Press, 2000.

Roitman, Janet. *Fiscal Disobedience: An Anthropology of Economic Regulation in Central Africa.* Princeton: Princeton University Press, 2004.

Slapper, Gary, and Steve Tombs. *Corporate Crime.* Essex, U.K.: Pearson Education, 1999.

Stiglitz, Joseph. *The Guardian* (London), 4 July 2002.

van Schendel, Willem, and Itty Abraham, eds. *Illicit Flows and Criminal Things: States, Borders, and the Other Side of Globalization.* Bloomington: Indiana University Press, 2005.

Weekend Argus. "Call for Action to Combat Growing Menace of Bogus Drugs." *Weekend Argus* (Cape Town), 6 April 2002, 7.

Woodiwiss, Michael. *Gangster Capitalism: The United States and the Globalization of Organized Crime.* New York: Carroll and Graf, 2005.

Woodiwiss, Michael, and David Bewley-Taylor. *The Global Fix: The Construction of a Global Enforcement Regime.* Amsterdam: Transnational Institute, 2005.

INDEX

abalone poaching, 106
Africa, Southern: major industries of, 13;
money laundering in, 98–99, 100–101;
narcotics trade in, 131; organized crime
in, 212–13n1. *See also* Angola; South
Africa; *specific country*
AIDS, 76, 131
air cargo, 34, 162
airlines, 34, 85
Alfredo, Augusto, 111–12, 113
American Vacation (trucker), 77–79, 80
amputees, female: informal economies of,
49–51, 54; INGO support of, 48; land
mines and, 47–48
anarchy, and social cohesion, 140
Angola: airline rights in, 34; corruption
in, 58; economy stolen in, 29–33; education in, 60, 72; extra-legal economy
in, 15, 100; fish smuggling in, 106–7;
food deprivation in, 85; infant mortality
rates in, 131; informal import earnings
in, 54; non-formal economy in, 108;
ownership of, 37–44, 59; pharmaceutical smuggling in, 135; regional war/
business relations and, 216n3; resources
and power in, 214n2 (Ch. 5); South
African stolen cars in, 90–91; substandard drugs dumped in, 131–32; U.S.
relations with, 77
Angola, Civil War (1975-2002): economic
impact of, 12; end of, and profiteering,
66–67; military violence during, 27–28;

organized scarcity during, 215n3; transit
routes during, 41; war orphans follow-
ing, 3–4
*Angola from Afro-Stalinism to Petro-
Diamond Capitalism* (Hodges), 57
anthropology, xvii, 144–45, 217n1 (Ch. 14)
Antwerp (Netherlands), 187
Arian, David, 191, 196
arms trade, 9, 177–78, 199
Artful Dodger, The (smuggling ship),
122–24
Aschemeyer, Manny, 197–98, 219n5
Asia, Southeast, illegal pharmaceuticals in,
135
Aung San Suu Kyi, 152
Australia, money laundering in, 179

backhands, 124
banks: currency speculation and, 86–87;
fear of, 94; money laundering and,
100–101, 171, 216–17n1; offshore, 172–
76, 218n12; U.S., offshore exchanges by,
179; women's, 49–51, 52–54
Bechtel, 170
beer: border post commerce and, 73–74;
as troop payment, 90, 94
Between Cultures (Düttmann), 154
blood diamonds, 91
Boots — The Philosopher (trucker), 77, 80
border posts: camaraderie at, 79, 80; commerce at, 84–86; currency speculation
at, 86–88; dollars as currency at, 72–73,

Text:	Galliard and Akzidenz Grotesk Light
Display:	Akzidenz Grotesk Condensed
Compositor:	BookMatters, Berkeley
Indexer:	Kevin B. Millham
Printer and binder:	Thomson-Shore, Inc.

CALIFORNIA SERIES IN PUBLIC ANTHROPOLOGY